NELLIE

NELLIE
Letters from Africa

with a memoir by
ELSPETH HUXLEY

Weidenfeld and Nicolson
London

For Nellie's descendants: Charles,
Josceline, Hugh and Alexander –
not forgetting Frederica without
whom the last three would
not have existed

Weidenfeld and Nicolson
91 Clapham High Street
London SW4

ISBN 0 297 77706 8

Printed in Great Britain by
Butler & Tanner Ltd, Frome and London

Contents

Kenya
before Independence

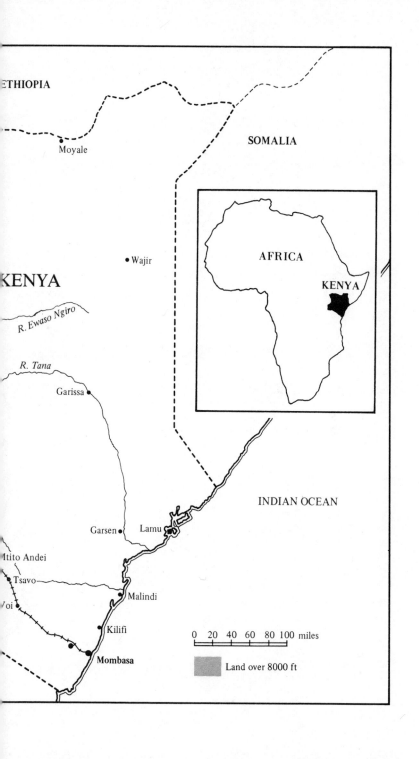

Foreword

If the title had not been pre-empted, this book might have been called *A Woman of No Importance*. Nellie's stage was small – a former British colony in Africa – and on it she never played a commanding role nor became a public figure. She was a countrywoman, her heart always in the land; a farmer and henwife; a dedicated gardener and ardent dog-lover; a generous hostess and experimental cook; an invincible optimist; and an active participator in the lives of the African families who shared her farm and her fortunes. With her husband Jos she emigrated to the East Africa Protectorate, as it was then called, before the First World War and in the heyday of the British Empire, then assumed to be if not eternal, very nearly so, and the bearer of the torch of civilization into the dark places of the earth. She left two years after that once remote Protectorate, the haunt of rugged pioneers, primitive tribes, missionaries and big game, had become the thriving independent Republic of Kenya. So she saw, within much less than her full span of years, the rise and fall of one corner of that Empire, and the birth, in Africa, of a new age.

The greater part of this record consists of extracts from Nellie's letters preserved in a more or less unbroken sequence from 1933 until her death in 1977. The earlier part of her life (which began in 1885) is covered by a memoir derived partly from recollections written down by her at my request, and partly from tape recordings. The aim of the selection of letters has been to illustrate day-to-day life on a Kenyan farm, and to reveal, at least in part, the character of a courageous, amusing and observant individual whose zest for life withstood many batterings. Comments on political and world events, pungent as these often were, have little interest once those events are over and done with, and so have for the most part been omitted. This selection from a correspondence spanning more than forty years reflects the minutiae of life, the small beer, not the 'Big Bow-Wow' at which Sir Walter Scott professed himself to be adept.

ix

Foreword

In his own modest estimation, Sir Walter lacked the touch 'which renders ordinary commonplace things and characters interesting'. This touch, I believe, vigorously as she would have denied it, was a gift that had been given to Nellie.

PART I

Memoir
1885–1933

Chapter 1

Nellie was born in Berkhamsted in Hertfordshire, a place with which her family had no connection whatever. Her elder brother Gillie, embarking at the age of seven on the story of his life, observed: 'I was born at Saighton Grange, Chester, on 22nd August 1881. Both my parents were away at the time.' Nellie's mother was doubtless at Berkhamsted for the event, but did not stay there long; her family was going through a peripatetic stage, renting houses for short periods pending the demise of Nellie's grandmother, the Marchioness of Westminster. This did not occur until 1891 when the old lady was in her ninety-fifth year. Meanwhile she had been firmly in occupation of Motcombe House in Dorset which, together with about ten thousand acres, was to pass on her death to her youngest son, Nellie's father. So, while his mother was still at Motcombe, he and his family could not settle anywhere for long, in case the summons came. At intervals the whole family, with horses, dogs, numerous servants and ample possessions, moved on, like a cavalcade of wealthy gipsies, waiting for the Angel of Death to alight.

Nellie was the sixth and youngest child of Lord Richard de Aquila Grosvenor, a younger brother of the first Duke of Westminster, and the year of her birth, 1885, marked a turning-point in her father's career. He had been born in the same year as Queen Victoria. His youth had been adventurous; he had lived for a while with the Mormons in Salt Lake City, also with the Sioux Indians somewhere near the embryonic Chicago, and been present at the sacking of the Summer Palace in Peking in 1860. Returning home to settle down, he went, as tradition decreed, into politics, and as a Liberal represented Flintshire, part of the Grosvenor bailiwick centred in Cheshire, for twenty-five years. After a spell (1872–4) as Vice-Chamberlain of the Royal household – Princess Alexandra called him 'Dick the Devil' – he became Liberal Chief Whip in Gladstone's administration of 1880–5. Then came the Irish crisis, when Gladstone split the Liberal Party over the issue of Home Rule.

Dick the Devil had married as his second wife (his first had died in childbirth) a lady from the Anglo-Irish ascendancy, Eleanor Hamilton-Stubber, who naturally took the poorest possible view of Mr Gladstone and refused to allow him to set foot in the house or to meet him on any social occasion. Whether by reason of domestic pressure, or of his own convictions, or a mixture of the two, her husband parted company with Gladstone over Home Rule and thus ended his political career. The year after Nellie's birth he resigned his seat in Parliament and devoted himself to the affairs of the London and North-Western Railway, of which he was a director, pending the day when Motcombe with its broad acres would be his. On resignation he received a peerage, choosing as his title Baron Stalbridge, after part of the Motcombe estate.

For the first seven years of Nellie's life the family was in temporary occupation of various stately homes whose owners were abroad, possibly governing some portion of the Empire: first Wilbury in Wiltshire, then Knoyle House (since demolished) also in Wiltshire, then Middleton Park in Oxfordshire, whose broad staircase, Nellie recalled, was excellent for tobogganing down on tea-trays. Ninety oil-lamps had to be lit each evening, and a man was employed for the sole purpose of cleaning them daily. (Eaton, the Grosvenor family seat in Cheshire, went one better; until some time in the Second World War, two men were employed to draw ale, given free to anyone who came to the door.) Dick Stalbridge's family now numbered six: his first wife's daughter Elsie; the twins, Hughie and Blanchie, born in 1881 to his second wife, followed by Gilbert, Richard Eustace, known as Ray or Chucks, and finally Nellie.

Every year, in May, there took place a migration to the family house in Upper Brook Street in London. A retinue set forth of servants, carriages, grooms and horses, and several ponies for the children's daily ride in Rotten Row. Dogs, however, stayed behind, so there were no indoor animals.

My sister and I were not ones to stand for an animal shortage in our lives, so we took in a big way to mice. Upper Brook Street, as we called it, not No. 12, as if the whole street belonged to us (no doubt we thought it did) was large enough to house the family and goodness knows how many – probably ten or eleven – servants, yet had a whole array of attics above the family's ornate rooms; and in these we had our very secret horde of exhibition mice.

We had a great ally, a very knowledgeable ally, in the second footman. Mice-keeping was very popular and profitable among the lower income groups in London, and was principally located in the East End. So on glorious occasions we used to sally forth with our knowledgeable footman and a variety of mouse-cages to seek our fortunes at the Monster Championship Mouse Show at the People's Palace in Whitechapel. I remember feeling slightly surprised that our ally, the knowledgeable footman, appeared in a gent's lounge suit – I supposed he always wore livery. Livery in our family was dark blue with an orange collar.

We might invest as much as half-a-crown for a mouse of a new line, or for a stud mouse, or even for a pair of Japanese waltzers. Sometimes mice used to escape in the attic, and what a hullaballoo that would mean. I really believe my parents had no inkling of our secret mouse-lives until we left Upper Brook Street for good and moved to Motcombe. Soon after settling in there my poor father, going up the noble oak staircase to bed, candle in hand, was confronted by a large and very tame orange mouse, who had avoided our final mouse-sale and travelled to Motcombe in a mattress. The mouse project made a handsome profit. A pair of really good mice might have a family of five or six almost once a fortnight, and although the parents might have cost as much as 15s there would be a steady sale for the progeny when a few weeks old at 9d a head.'

*   *   *

At last the long-awaited event took place; the Marchioness of West-minster died, and the Stalbridge family could take over the Mot-combe and Gillingham estates, which had been bought by Nellie's grandfather between 1824 and 1826. The old manor house, dating back to medieval times, had been reconstructed by a Mr Whittaker at the beginning of the nineteenth century. It was a well pro-portioned, handsome, unpretentious dwelling, cheerful and com-fortable, with plenty of room for everybody and the usual array of stables, greenhouses and outbuildings of all kinds. The children loved it.

First of all there was the great excitement, and indeed fun, of going into mourning. Deep, deep mourning for the unloved Marchioness. New clothes all round, even unto the lowest ranks of housemaid and kitchen staff, who were issued with dress-lengths, one apiece, of stiff, white cotton material, thickly patterned with black, which they had to stitch up themselves. I don't know what they wore when the one and only dress went to be washed.

'The unloved Marchioness' – why unloved? In her youth Lady Elizabeth Grosvenor, as she then was, had been gay, attractive, fond of fun and devoted to her husband, who kept changing his name in the confusing fashion of the aristocracy: Belgrave to begin with, then Earl Grosvenor, and finally Marquess of Westminster.* His wife took the advent of her thirteen children, nine of them daughters, in her stride; preferred simple country pursuits to ostentation and grandeur; adored animals; was far from unintelligent; and was in short an amiable was well as a praiseworthy character. But in old age she became imperious and difficult. Also there was a lawsuit concerning the inheritance which split the family down the middle, leaving the Marchioness and her youngest, favourite daughter Theodora on one side, and everyone else on the other.

In 1891, the old lady was laid to rest in Motcombe churchyard. Born in the reign of George III, she had become an institution in the village, seemingly immortal, and greatly revered. It was she who had started, and continued to support, the village school. A former pupil remembered how she would award the annual prizes, a small, upright figure clothed in black and always with a sprig of jasmine in her corsage. When she alighted from her carriage, a footman would cup his hand to receive her foot, lest it should be soiled by a puddle.

The move from Middleton in Oxfordshire to Motcombe in Dorset was a stirring event. A special train was chartered to convey the cavalcade from Bicester, on the London and North-Western line, to Semley, on the London and South-Western. 'Specials' could be hired for £1 a mile.

I can't remember how many coaches this train had, but it seemed to be a great, long snake. Next to the locomotive came some furniture vans, then third-class carriages for the under-servants, then second-class compartments for those of higher rank. In the middle came the saloon coach and restaurant car, where the family were ensconced in comfort. Then more vans and trucks and carriages, and finally lots of horse-boxes.

The 'snake' wound its way along; there had to be a lot of shunting, very intricate and exciting, as ordinary traffic had to be avoided and, in some cases, suspended. Finally Semley was reached. Then came the unloading and unbox-

* The story of this pair and their family is related in *Lady Elizabeth and the Grosvenors* by Gervas Huxley, Oxford University Press, 1965.

ing of the horses. I remember well the din and clatter of the last horse-box and the appearance therefrom of our minute and favourite pony, a 12-hand chestnut mare, Shottie or Shotover, born in the same year as the chestnut mare of that name won the Derby for my uncle Westminster.

We children loved Motcombe from the start. The house was Georgian, welcoming and rambling, and, best of all, practically adjoined the stables. These had twelve excellent loose-boxes, some six stalls, a large yard, wash-houses galore with rooms over them for the strappers; harness-rooms and so on, and the stud groom's cottage. There were lovely brick-walled gardens, and the whole property embraced some 10,000 acres, including the town of Shaftesbury, which was our market town.

My mother was an idle woman, very Irish; she took no part in all the packing and arrangements, everything was done for her. I don't think she was actually an invalid, although she got diabetes later, but she had a sort of nervous breakdown in the Boer War because Hughie and Gillie were taking part; she lost so much weight she almost faded away.

*   *   *

For the children, life at Motcombe was almost idyllic. No doubt it was far from idyllic for the governesses who came and went. Gillie, who shared them with his sisters until he went to school, wrote in his autobiography composed at the age of seven: 'We have a governess. We do not like her. She whistles for us. We are not dogs that we should be whistled for.' So he ignored the whistles and went off into the woods. 'There were lovely woods round Motcombe – Duncliffe, Kingsettle. Lot Pitman, the gamekeeper, was Gillie's idol: so loved an idol that he had Lot's suit exactly copied, down to the poacher's pockets, leather-capped elbows and strong whipcord.'

Winter was for fox-hunting. The actual chase began and ended with long hacks, ten or twelve miles perhaps, through muddy lanes and squelching woods, to reach the meet and then to come home in dusk and darkness to a hot bath and an enormous late tea. No horse-boxes then, no cars or lorries, no tarmac and, most important of all, no barbed wire. The South and West Wilts was not a 'smart' hunt attracting City gents and high-flyers from the Shires, but it was good honest sport of which the farmers were the main supporters; every farmer had a horse or two, of varying shape and size, and their children went out on shaggy ponies that pulled the dog-cart when not pursuing the fox.

'Horse-trading was a by-product of the hunt that provided endless interest and opportunities for the exercise of wits. There were dealers with whom you had to walk very warily. "Never ask a man his religion, how he voted or how much he paid for a horse", was one of my father's maxims.'

However, there was seldom much secrecy about the vote.

The labourers voted whichever way the farmers didn't, and the farmers voted with the landlords. Most of these, of course, were Tories. Owing to my father's well-known politics, Motcombe was at first a Liberal stronghold, but I think lapsed into Tory-ism as time went on. Also there were a few, very few, wicked Radicals. One such was Mr Inkpen who kept the Royal Oak, and another Mr Gatehouse the tailor who came in a dog-cart to fit us out with badly cut tweeds. His political views were shattered by my father, who once happened to be at the gate on Mr Gatehouse's arrival and held it open for him. 'Fancy having a lord hold a gate open for you', he almost gasped as he climbed out. It was said that he voted Tory ever after.

In the summer there was yachting. Stalbridge had an old 100-ton schooner, based on Cowes, with an all-Irish crew.

We five children were sewn up in hammocks in the saloon at night but let loose very early in the morning to mess about the decks and interfere as much as possible with the work of the crew. The skipper was a stage Irishman with a larger-than-life brogue, and thought to be permanently tight. Every morning, we children were seized by the seat of our pants and thrown overboard by the crew to learn to swim. Swim, I suppose, we did, somehow or other, but this aquatic treatment damped my ardour in both senses and I have never been an enthusiastic sea-bather since.

Another summer diversion was provided by Army manœuvres on Salisbury Plain.

All the hunting fraternity turned out in their carriages, and we children on our ponies. I well remember the finale, it must have been in the late nineties. The Red Army and the Blue Army advanced to within about a hundred yards of each other, somewhere near Tisbury, blazing away. Lord Roberts and his staff in glorious array were grouped together on horseback on an eminence. The Royal Horse Artillery limbered up and galloped into action, a stirring sight. Our ponies were going round and round like tops. Then suddenly an umpire called out 'All is over! The Reds have won!' Everyone stopped. My parents drove away in the landau, we cantered off on our ponies to an enormous so-called breakfast at Fonthill. My aunt Ockie [Lady Octavia, widow of Sir Michael Shaw-Stewart] lived there.

That part of Dorset was fairly well supplied with large country houses still occupied by their families; the Troyte-Bullocks at Zeals, the Portmans at Bryanston, the Hoares at Stourhead, the Wyndhams at Clouds.

There came a night when Clouds burnt to the ground.

I remember well watching from a window over the stairs the glorious progress of several local fire-engines, one of which lived in our coach-house. How much more glamorous they were than their stealthy later counterparts! Enormous galloping horses striking sparks from the cobbles of the stable yard at the start, engines all red and gold, bell tolling, and brave helmeted men hanging on at all angles. The excitement was sadly shattered by the arrival in *our* nursery of a batch of small Wyndham children snatched, I thought unnecessarily, from their burning nursery. We were told to welcome them: we did not. One, later to become the brilliant Edwardian socialite Cynthia Asquith, made a bee-line for *my* rocking-horse. I hit her, and disliked her ever afterwards.

* * *

One winter, news came from London that Stalbridge had been taken seriously ill with typhoid while staying at his club.

No woman had ever been allowed within the portals of Brooks's before, but in my mother went, and stayed until he recovered. Typhoid was known to be caused by 'drains', and suspicion fell upon the drains of Motcombe, which were found to come to rest under the kitchen floor. So my parents decided to build a new house and abandon the old one. Thus the project of a mansion was born.

How unnecessary it all seems now! Surely a new drainage system could have been installed? However, the building was a source of great delight to us children. The mansion was Elizabethan in design, with a large forecourt. The front door opened into a hall with a wide oak staircase, and beyond that an enormous drawing-room, then my mother's boudoir and my father's business-room. The dining-room was on the west side, also a large library. There was a wing for the girls of the family, three of us including my half-sister Elsie, with a school-room and governess's room. On the other side, parallel in design, was the bachelors' wing, but either the money ran out or there were no bachelors; it was never finished.

9

The architects, supposed to be the best of their kind, were Ernest George and Peto. Mr George was a nice, tidy man who often appeared at lunch with great quantities of delicious crackly blue papers under his arm – the Plans. Sometimes he brought with him a dark-haired girl who, we were told, was going to become the first qualified woman architect in England.* My parents were rather dubious about this. Was a 'career woman' respectable? Such an invasion of male preserves might be considered 'fast' – like waltzing in reverse and eating savouries at dinner.

The new drawing-room had a ceiling moulded and plastered by Italian workmen, who lay on their backs on planks suspended just below it. We tried to take a hand in this but it was beyond us. We were quite at home, however, with the foundations. Our favourite spot was a corner where they were seven feet deep and we could jump down into thick, sticky, grey-blue clay, well over our ankles. The mansion took two years to build, had, I believe, sixty rooms and a million bricks, and cost about £60,000.

The kitchen, with its vast range of ovens, was at the farthest end of a long, long passage that led eventually to the dining-room. In between was a pantry where a footman slept, his bed being pushed back into the wall in daytime. My parents' bedroom, and those for the principal guests, were on the first floor, and above that was another whole floor of bedrooms, maids' workrooms and so on. One room was made into an aviary for my mother's canaries. We used to let them loose on the roof and climb all over it – we knew every inch – to catch them and return them to their cages. My mother took a poor view of this, but we never lost a single canary.

Some seventy years later, Nellie re-visited Motcombe. It had become a boys' preparatory school, and the headmaster showed us round. The boudoir, in Nellie's day painted white with elegant furniture, had become a large school-room full of desks. There my grandmother had reclined on a sofa surrounded by her dogs and canaries, looking at seedsmen's catalogues – gardening was her passion – and perhaps that fascinating volume, the annual catalogue of the Army & Navy Stores. Every morning the cook, Alice Wigmore, would present herself with menu for the day, written in French. After glancing through it, and perhaps a little desultory discussion, my grandmother initialled it, and the cook withdrew.

Why, Nellie reflected, had her parents, of all people, embarked on such a vast project? Her mother hated entertaining and almost

* She did. She was Ethel Mary Charles, who was articled to Sir Ernest George and Peto in 1892 and qualified ARIBA in 1898, the first woman to do so. She died in 1962, aged ninety-one. Her sister Bessie became the second fully qualified woman architect.

never did so. Because of her father's involvement with the London and North-Western Railway, he was away a good deal, and in his home liked peace and quiet, riding about the estate, talking to tenants and inspecting plantations. 'Ten rooms would have been ample for them, let alone sixty.'

On to this peaceful scene in deepest Dorset, disaster fell. My grandfather was by then about fifty. Some thirty years before, when up at Trinity College, Cambridge, in order to oblige a fellow under-graduate, he had backed a bill for £100,000 – a large sum, one would think, for even the most spendthrift undergraduate, equivalent to at least a million pounds in latter-day currency. The undergraduate undertook to tear up the bill once his debts had been settled. Time passed, my grandfather reared his brood, improved his estates, pursued his career, acquired his peerage, and the spendthrift under-graduate (as family legend has it) became Lord Sudeley; then the blow fell. Lord Sudeley had not torn up the bill. He had gone bank-rupt, and the bill was suddenly presented. After such a lapse of time, my grandfather can scarcely have been legally obliged to meet it; but it was a debt of honour, and as such must be paid.

Even for a rich landowner, £100,000 in cash, all at once, could not be easily found. But found it was, by various means, including a life assurance policy said to have been, at that time, the largest ever taken out, and requiring an annual premium of £10,000, which exceeded the annual rent-roll of the Motcombe and Gillingham estates. The family was left with not much more than the £4,000 a year its head received as chairman of the London and North-Western Railway.

Economies became the order of the day.

The first step was to convert the footmen into parlour-maids, a practically unknown step in those days and one that carried with it an aura of shame and failure. Numbers were not affected, only sex and appearance. The economy achieved was in uniforms, and much lower wages. Black cashmere for dresses, frilly aprons and caps instead of cloth for trousers and livery coats, and no need for extra shoes and working clothes. An irritating economy, so far as I was concerned, was that my sister and I were told that we could no longer invite girl-friends to stay, because our parents couldn't afford to pay for the coals for a fire in the girl-friends' maids' bedrooms. To go away without one's maid was, of course, unthinkable.

11

Much worse was the reduction in the horse population.

We had a pair of large greys, Seagull and Starlight, for the heavy carriages – the landau, barouche and the luggage cart. Then a pair of bays for the lighter victoria, single brougham and dog-cart, and more lightweights for pony-carts. The stud groom had to go, a great sadness, and one or two of the strappers. The ratio was one groom to two horses. The hunters were reduced in numbers but by no means eliminated.

Economies also took place in our education. Hughie and Gillie had left Eton but Chucks, as a major economy, was sent to a cheaper prep school and then to Haileybury.

*   *   *

The major change that occurred in Nellie's education was not wholly due to the economy drive.

My sister Blanchie was now out of the school-room and prone to get engaged to various young men. She was supposed to be a 'bad influence' on me, and I must say I did enjoy galloping off for miles taking love-letters for her, or notes asking whether the young man of the moment really loved her as she wasn't quite sure. One of them gave me a silver cigarette-case. Time went on, the economies didn't work, Blanchie continued to be a bad influence and, in the summer of 1899, I was, to my horror, packed off to the Cheltenham Ladies' College, to the house of Miss Eales.

This was an altogether alien world to Nellie and at first she hated it.

I had, thank goodness, a room to myself, and soon made friends with a dashing girl called Sylvia Hunt. We found that we could get out of my bedroom window on to a wall, and creep along, drop off and take a walk around. No harm ever came our way, and the walks were pointless but fun. Once we had a perfectly innocent conversation with two youths over the wall, and were overheard, and I was summoned to the presence of the headmistress, the great Miss Beale. She told me that if my uncle hadn't been a duke, I should have been expelled. This incident blew sky-high all my illusions about the great Miss Beale. After that I thought her a bogus you-know-what.

As a punishment, Sylvia and I were forbidden to accompany a house 'outing' the following week, and segregated with a governess. This suited us perfectly; we took the governess to a place where we knew there was a racing stable, disengaged ourselves from her and spent a most enjoyable afternoon fraternizing with the head lad and seeing all the horses.

Miss Eales, like her boss, was a dreadful snob, and by virtue of my exalted rank (the only Hon. in the house) I was made a member of the College hockey team and captain of the house hockey and cricket teams. I would much rather have tried to learn tennis. Having got the competitive spirit rather badly at that age, I began to like bits of school life. I was just over two and a half years at the College and always did well at my books. I was moved into a class that sat for University entrance exams and became top of it; those who passed the exams well enough could go on to the University. I hankered for this at times, but my parents said no, I must go home to be the daughter of the house. So I went back to Motcombe a cynical and disillusioned brat.

In 1978, the bursar of the College was good enough to look up the records, and found that in the Oxford University Honours examinations offered for senior candidates by the Oxford Delegacy in 1901, Nellie came first in English History, third in Shakespeare, ninth in French and eleventh in German, and satisfied the examiners in three other subjects. This qualified her for the grand title of 'Associate in Arts'. (Girls had been first admitted as candidates in 1867, following a bold experiment by the Cambridge authorities 'which had come to the conclusion that allowing girls to enter had no ill effect on the examinations'.) She also got an Intermediate degree with an Honourable Mention from the Société Nationale des Professeurs de Français, and a Distinction in Harmony in an examination set by the Royal College of Music. So hers was a brief but distinguished scholastic career, and she would have had no difficulty in getting into one of the women's colleges at Oxford or Cambridge. This was, for her, a turning-point of destiny. She had to go home to be the daughter of the house.

Chapter 2

The time had now arrived for Nellie to 'come out'. Had it not been for her family's financial disaster, they would have taken a house in London for the Season, given dances, and launched their youngest daughter in fitting style. As it was, her aunt Katie Westminster, widow of her ducal uncle, came to the rescue and either took her to balls or provided the obligatory chaperon and carriage, while another titled relative, 'Cuckoo' Shaftesbury, presented her at Court.

'Cuckoo', Countess of Shaftesbury, was a lady-in-waiting to the newly crowned Queen Alexandra, and so had 'the entrée', which meant that she and her protégé could short-circuit the queue of débutantes and proceed with a minimum of delay into the royal presence. Nellie dressed up in the customary white gown with a long train, and three ostrich feathers in her hair. 'After your curtsey, when you moved off, a handsome young Guards officer whisked up your train on the point of his sword and you caught it over your arm and made off towards a lovely champagne supper.'

Aunt Katie Westminster had a house in Grosvenor Square. Grosvenor House itself had passed to the heir, known as Bend 'Or, after one of his race-horses. Nellie remarked disparagingly that she remembered the ducal residence as 'rather a dingy house, apart from the garden and Gainsborough's *Blue Boy* – quite a mean entrance, though I suppose it was grand enough when you got inside.' The parties held inside were also grand enough, but crowded and stuffy, and sometimes Nellie found them boring. Her cousin Mary Grosvenor, about the same age, agreed. 'Let's get out of this', she said on one occasion. 'Come into the garden and see a rabbit having its family.' Tucking up their ball-gowns, out they went to watch the lying-in of the rabbit.

All those big London houses destined to become hotels or to destruction were then in full flower: Londonderry House, Dorchester, Derby, Stafford House, with its dark staircase and the wonderfully beautiful Duchess of Sutherland, a-sparkle with superb jewels, 'receiving'. Lord Lansdowne, still in occupation of his House, was one of my father's oldest friends, and Minister for War. This came in useful for my brother Chucks, who desperately wanted to get into the Gunners, but had chopped off half a finger while investigating a bacon-slicing machine in Shaftesbury. This was held to disqualify him absolutely for the Gunners. Lord Lansdowne was his godfather, so a special exemption was obtained.

Once Nellie was 'out', suitors were to be expected. She was not perhaps a beauty in the classical style, but with her dark hair, fresh, creamy complexion and lovely eyes – deep blue, large and full of life and expression – she created a vivid impression, enhanced by her liveliness and wit. She held her own in any company, and could have a wicked gleam in the eye. No wonder suitors came. 'One was, or became, Admiral Meade. He proposed marriage, but I didn't really understand what he was saying – he mumbled, I suppose.' She was only eighteen at the time. Had she listened more carefully, and accepted him, she would in time have become mistress of Uppark in Sussex.

*   *   *

In 1891, Nellie's father had become chairman of the London and North-Western Railway, and so remained for twenty years. The affairs of the Premier Line of Great Britain, as it was generally called, were complex and far-flung and demanded considerable financial ability, as well as tact and judgement, from its head. He succeeded one of the great British railwaymen of all time, Sir Richard Moon, who held the chairmanship for thirty years and built up the company from a humble position. It began in 1846 with the amalgamation of three lines, and gobbled up no less than forty-five others to become the biggest joint-stock corporation in the world. It was said that no railway director had done so much riding on engine footplates as had Stalbridge, during the early years of his directorship. He did not only ride on footplates, he learnt to drive those thundering, hissing, imperial locomotives, and often did so – a schoolboy's dream come true. They were painted black, and had resplendent names – *Titan, Tamerlane, Dreadnought, Thunderer, Raven.*

15

During his regime occurred those historic races between the LNWR and the Great Northern line to capture the record for the run between London and Edinburgh, and later that between London and Aberdeen.* In 1885, honours were even, but in a renewed outburst of the competitive spirit in 1895, the Great Northern knocked ten minutes off the time of the run to Aberdeen. The LNWR responded, the Great Northern answered back and brought its 8 pm from King's Cross into Aberdeen at 7 am. After that, rivalry ran wild, until finally, on the morning of 23 August 1895, the LNWR's express reached Aberdeen at 4.32 am, having taken 512 minutes to make the run of 541 miles. The interests of the passengers seem to have been overlooked; it is most unlikely that anyone really wanted to arrive in Aberdeen at 4.32 am, or even at 6.25 am, at which the time of arrival was standardized. The chairman, always a moderate, was not in favour of this frenetic competition, but deferred to the enthusiasm of his staff. The company had, at Crewe, one of the greatest engineering works in the kingdom, 'a stud of three thousand roaring black locomotives', and a staff of internationally respected designers. The work-force, smartly uniformed when amongst passengers – guards took off their caps respectfully when passing through the restaurant car – and grimy, resolute and apparently oblivious of hours of duty when on the footplate, were dedicated men.

The law forbade the company to raise its fares, but maintenance and running costs nearly doubled during Stalbridge's regime; nevertheless business continued to expand, and dividends – actually dividends, not subsidies – never fell below five and a half per cent, and rose to over seven per cent. Today, it all seems like an economic miracle. In 1922, just ten years after Stalbridge's death, under the Grouping scheme the LNWR as such, together with the miracle, came to an end. It was to live on as part of the LMS until 1948.

Her father's job had some delightful repercussions for Nellie. On his watch-chain he carried a golden medallion which entitled him, together with his family, to free travel on any British line, and on several Continental ones as well. On the strength of this he took

* For the stretch north of Edinburgh, the two giants had as associates the Caledonian and the North British Railways respectively. The racing trains ran, as it were, neck and neck, one on the eastern, one on the western, route, and the signalman at Aberdeen accepted whichever was the first to reach the goal.

Nellie to Pau, Biarritz, Homberg and Marienbad; once, when she was still a child, the whole family with a retinue of servants went to Hyères, but this ended unfortunately; the children developed ringworm, a vulgar disease, caught generally from cattle, and had to be hustled out of the hotel by night before the management found out.

The golden medallion called forth impressive welcomes from station-masters in frock-coats and top-hats, and there was a directors' special coach for long journeys. In it was fitted a speedometer whose needle never registered above 60 mph, considered by the chairman to be the most suitable speed. As the chairman's wife disliked travel, Nellie often took her place, and launched two of the company's ships that plied between Holyhead and Dublin.*

The Directors' coach was attached to the Scottish Express, a very regal affair. The head chef from the Euston Hotel cooked luscious meals as we sped towards the Greenock shipyards. On arrival we were met by a crowd of people. There was terrific tension as one swung the champagne bottle against the bows of the vessel. Would she slide slowly and majestically past one's head as she left the stocks? It was considered terribly unlucky if the bottle didn't break – fortunately my efforts were successful. There was an enormous sigh of relief all round when the great ship began to move. Once she was safely in the water, we all went to a champagne luncheon, and I was presented with an attractive brooch.

Another exciting train journey, when I was much younger, was an expedition to the 1899 Derby. Not just a special coach this time but a whole special train, supplied by the host railway, the London Chatham and Dover (known as the London Smash 'em and Turn 'em Over), for the benefit of all the other boards of directors. The train went right up to Tattenham Corner and we had a marvellous view. It was Flying Fox's year, my uncle's fourth and last win, and a most dramatic race. Flying Fox was racing neck and neck with the second favourite at Tattenham Corner when the rival horse broke a leg, and Flying Fox went on to win easily. The Prince of Wales came aboard our train to congratulate my father on his brother's win; six months later, uncle Westminster was dead.

*   *   *

* These ships would have been two of the trio *Anglia*, *Hibernia* and *Scotia*, the first two built in 1900 and the latter in 1902. They were two-funnel, twin-screw vessels of 1862 gross tonnage, carrying passengers overnight to Dublin. Two of the three, *Anglia* and *Hibernia*, converted respectively into a hospital ship and an armoured cruiser, were sunk by enemy action in 1915. For this information I am indebted to the National Railway Museum at York.

'I often wished, and still do, that I had known my father better', Nellie wrote later in her life. He was a shy man. There is a story that when his eldest daughter became engaged to a naval officer, he summoned the young man to an interview and met him on Salisbury station. Naturally Aubrey was nervous, and expected to be invited to Motcombe, but the two walked up and down the platform in silence until the next train back to London came in. His prospective father-in-law opened the door of the carriage, shook him by the hand and said 'Goodbye', and that was the end of the interview.

Nellie inherited some of this shyness – reticence might be a better word. Ideas, opinions, shrewd *aperçus* – these she would toss into the conversational air like jugglers' balls, but she seldom revealed her deeper feelings, and liked to hatch her plans in secret. Once, when she was about to embark upon a journey, her father said: 'I wonder, Nellie, how you can ever bring yourself to buy a railway ticket.' She fell into the trap, and asked why. 'Because you have to tell the booking clerk where you want to go.'

Dick Stalbridge was known as a 'good' landlord. Every Saturday his agent put before him a list of suggestions concerning rent reductions, cottage repairs and so on. These were almost always approved. Cottages and farm buildings were kept in good trim and were advanced in design for their day, and farm tenancies were handed on from father to son. (They were annual tenancies, in those days, with no compulsion on the landlord to renew them.) At Christmas, each cottager received two rabbits shot by Lot Pitman and an assortment of garments provided by the Dorset Ladies' Work Guild. Each member of this body pledged herself to provide two garments, generally crocheted shawls, knitted comforters or flannelette nightshirts, which were assembled at Motcombe, and Nellie and Blanchie distributed them in a dog-cart. 'Our attitude towards "do-gooding" in the village was atrocious. By and large, towards anything that bored us we exercised all our ingenuity, which was considerable, to avoid. Nevertheless we were all quite convinced that we were much loved in the village.' As, oddly enough, they very likely were.

Church on Sunday morning was obligatory.

The only way of escape was to take a large dose of Epsom salts on Saturday night, and explain the situation to my father on Sunday morning. We recovered in time to accompany him on his Sunday afternoon walk, which was generally to the nearest farm, Arthur Hiscock's, and got no further than the model pig-styes. On weekdays we might well go to the Hiscocks' on our own, to be given a glass of home-made cider – brewed in old brandy casks – so sometimes we spent an hour or so asleep under the kitchen table before going home.

One of the Motcombe cottages had as its tenant Mr G. H. Prideaux, who had started his career as a porter at Semley station. Born with an inventive mind, he conducted in his kitchen experiments on the evaporation of milk to leave a residue of powder. His was one of those basic, simple ideas that can burgeon into great industries. Milk consists mainly of water; remove the water and you are left with concentrated, and easily transportable, essence of milk. Mr Prideaux had three daughters who, in their old age, retained a mental picture of two faces close together, one bearded and one clean-shaven, peering into saucers to see how things were getting on. They got on very well. Stalbridge helped to finance the first developments and in time a small factory, which grew into a large factory, blossomed in the village. The Prideaux family grew rich, and when the new Motcombe House was built, Mr Prideaux bought the old one, pulled it down and re-erected most of it, brick by brick, in the village, where it still stands. Eventually his dried-milk factory was bought by the firm of Cow and Gate.

What of the neighbours round about?

Most of them were considered 'not quite quite' by my parents, so were never invited to anything. One family brewed beer and built a mansion – how dared they? There was a family called Best who lived not far off but on the 'wrong', i.e. non-hunting, side of Shaftesbury. Father Best was a retired Colonel, Mrs Best every inch the Colonel's lady, and my mother liked her very much. They were, and no wonder, very hard up; they had four sons, the first in the Army, the second in the Navy, the third in the ICS and the fourth I forget, I expect the Church. And six daughters, no less – one became matron of St Thomas's. When Colonel Best suddenly became Lord Wynford, Lady W. at once drove over to see my mother in their shabby wagonette with a coachman in an ill-fitting livery, and they had already had coronets put on to the blinkers of the carriage horses.

Wagonette, landau, barouche, victoria, post-chaise, phaeton, britschka – the variety of vehicles to be found in the coach-houses of big country houses was bewildering. The Motcombe children travelled sometimes in

a tea-cart with a pair of spanking cobs. Often owner-driven, it held two in front, and a small seat behind was big enough for two children and the Tiger, a boy of fourteen or so who was training to be a groom. He wore a splendid livery, a replica of the coachman's, and travelled with his arms akimbo. I well remember an expedition to a charity fête at Ranston; Blanchie and I were dressed in Dolly Varden costumes to be sellers at a stall. It was a blazing hot day, everything was smothered in dust, and I never stopped being sick, both in the tea-cart and at the fête, which ended with a gigantic tea in a very hot tent.

*　　*　　*

There came an occasion when Motcombe House, for the first time in its life, was full of guests and bustle, the village *en fête*. Carriages rolled into the forecourt, billets were found for grooms and valets, there was music and dancing, a tenants' ball, the village street was gay with scarlet uniforms, gold-braided jackets and jingling spurs: all to celebrate sister Blanchie's marriage to a handsome young captain in the Seventh Hussars.

By the time Nellie's turn came to marry, Motcombe House had been abandoned: not sold, but left empty, the furniture in dust-sheets, the stables bare. The family's economies had not sufficed. For Nellie, and even more so for her mother, the move was traumatic. All three boys were abroad in the army, and so were less affected. The married Blanchie was living in Cheshire. But Nellie lost her much-loved home for ever; and for her mother the gardening catalogues, if they still came, must have mocked her urban solitude.

Nellie and her mother were translated to a London house 'on the wrong side of the Park', and therefore unfashionable, cheap and, by Grosvenor standards, small, cramped and dowdy. The family's departure from Motcombe in 1905 was a very different affair from their arrival thirteen years before. No special train, no cavalcade of horses, dogs, servants and possessions, but an 'aura of shame and failure'. Gone from Nellie's life were Motcombe's woods and fields, the fox-hunting and rabbiting, the walled gardens and the lake where everyone skated in winter. Gone were Lot Pitman the gamekeeper,

Jim Wigmore the cowman who once saved Nellie's life by driving off an infuriated freshly calved cow, and all those friendly and familiar farmers and villagers.

Nellie, aged twenty at the time of the move, was by then engaged to be married. She had met Josceline Grant, her senior by eleven years, in Dorset, where he had been staying with his stepmother who had a house not far from Motcombe. Both his parents were dead. His background and outlook were different from those of any of the young men she had hitherto met. He did not hunt, and was not at heart a country-lover, nor yet a townsman either; his heart was in the Highlands of Scotland, where his clan had dwelt for centuries among the heathery braes and glens of Inverness. Like so many Scots, he was a wanderer. After the Boer War, in which he had served in The Royal Scots, he had stayed on in southern Africa 'looking round', and in Rhodesia had fallen in with an Irish peer who had convinced him that a fortune was to be made from a potential diamond mine in Portuguese East Africa (now Mozambique).

Ethnically speaking there are, it has been said, two kinds of Scot: those of a predominantly Celtic strain, whose homeland lies on the western coast and in the Hebrides, whither they were driven by the second kind, marauding Norsemen who descended in fleets of long-ships on the eastern coast to slaughter, plunder and eventually settle down. Jos was an eastern Scot: sandy-haired, wide cheek-boned, blue-eyed, well set up, in those days slim and strong. But something had gone wrong with the stereotype, or perhaps the genes had changed their natures in the last thousand years. Nordic as Jos might be in looks, anyone less Viking-like in temperament it would be hard to imagine. He was a gentle, humorous, dreamy, impractical and most unaggressive man, with a faith in human nature sometimes carried to the length of gullibility. Like Nellie he was shy and, at heart, diffident. There was something very lovable about him, and Nellie fell in love.

*   *   *

Motor cars were all the rage by then, and Jos delighted in a large chain-driven Mercedes in which he had taken part in a Paris to Madrid race. (It overturned.) In this vehicle he came to do his courting, and taught Nellie to drive. Naturally this was exciting; motor cars were exotic objects in Dorset lanes, and very few women could drive them. Swathed in dustcoats, their wide hats anchored down by scarves tied under the chin, they left control of the machines to the gentlemen. The machines frequently broke down and then, as the music-hall song had it, 'you have to get out, get out and get under, get under the automobile'.

A large part of Jos's fortune had been invested in the diamond mine. No replies came to cables sent to the Irish peer, so he had to go back to Portuguese East Africa. 'When the time drew near for his departure, he braved the situation and popped the question on a stile in a field behind Motcombe post office. I said yes, or words to that effect, and when I told my mother she burst into tears, so it wasn't as happy a time as it should have been.'

Why the tears, I asked Nellie? Jos, after all, was socially respectable enough. If it came to ancient lineage, the Vikings got to Britain well before the Normans, from whom the Grosvenors could trace descent. (Grosvenor: *gros veneur*: head gamekeeper.) His clan was suitably headed by an ennobled chief. In the disaster of the '45 his forebears, like most of their compatriots, had been driven from their glens – his branch of the clan had a beautiful little one of their own, Glen Shewglie, an offshoot of Glen Urquhart – to death or exile. Jos could boast a most romantic ancestor, Alexander the Swordsman, who had worn long, fair hair, and who with two strokes of the claymore had slain a mounted Hanoverian trooper. Alexander's son had been born on the eve of Culloden and thirty clansmen had gathered round the cradle and sworn fealty to Prince Charles Edward, after whom the infant had been named. The Swordsman had been wounded in the battle, escaped, gone into hiding for several years and finally, driven by want to enlist in the king's army, perished of fever at the siege of Havana in 1762.

Alexander's son Charles grew in poverty to manhood, and in 1767 found his way to India where he prospered as a merchant and rose to become chairman of the East India Company. He represented Inverness in Parliament from 1802–18. (Raeburn painted his portrait.) Jos claimed that Sir Charles's eldest son, who became Lord Glenelg, was mainly responsible for the Boers' Great Trek in 1832; as Secretary of State for the Colonies he had insisted on the abolition of slavery at the Cape, so the Boers had trekked north to get away from the interfering British with their sentimental ideas. Sir Charles's other son, Jos's grandfather Sir Robert, after making a comfortable fortune, became Governor of Bombay. Jos's father, another Sir Charles, joined the Indian Civil Service, rose to become Foreign Secretary to the Indian Government, and retired in sufficient affluence to live in a large flat near Marble Arch, assemble a collection of porcelain and leave fifty thousand pounds to each of his three sons when he died in 1903.

This was the undoing of Jos. Instead of taking up a serious career – he had been intended for the Diplomatic Service – he gallivanted about the world, bought motor cars and got involved in the African diamond mine. This did eventually produce diamonds (three to be exact, according to Nellie), which were set into her engagement ring. So, to my question as to why her mother's tears, she replied: 'Because he had no fixed address' – no land, no property, no place in the country, no profession, no settled career. To Nellie he could offer no position in the world and no established home, only insecurity. And so, despite his charm and his integrity, he fell short of her parents' hopes for their youngest child.

*   *   *

When Jos returned from Africa, about a year later, they were married from her parents' home at No. 22 Sussex Square. Nellie was twenty-one. They departed for a honeymoon at Bagshot, in Surrey, in a house lent by Jos's aunt, in a 6 hp Panhard that had replaced the Mercedes and was just as unpredictable; when going uphill its driver had to lower the 'sprag', a device that prevented the motorcar from running backwards. Bagshot seems a dull place for a honeymoon, which could scarcely have been a romantic one; Jos was so much taken up with financial affairs that he went every day to the City, deserting his bride. He still had no fixed address, and after the honeymoon they shared a flat in Knightsbridge with Jos's younger brother Robin, a gay and handsome officer in the Rifle Brigade. Later they went to Scotland, where Jos was in his element wearing the kilt, slaying grouse and teaching Nellie to dance reels. They stayed in several castles which Nellie found to be draughty and cold.

Shooting parties to which they were invited in England were apt to go to the other extreme – too much comfort, if anything, and certainly too much food.

My first of such parties was at Bryanston, the new and hideous abode of the Portman family. You went down to breakfast in a cloth gown, and ate a very hearty meal. Then you returned to your bedroom to change into tweeds – ankle-length skirts of course – to go out with the guns. Before long a massive picnic lunch appeared, spread out by footmen in a barn or perhaps a keeper's cottage. Then the men continued shooting, the females returned to base and at about five o'clock appeared downstairs in frilly tea-gowns. Then another massive meal took place in company with the guns, after which the females disappeared to bathe and change. They chatted or played games until the summons of the 'dressing gong' at about seven o'clock, when you went up to change for dinner which took place about eight. You walked into the dining-room arm-in-arm with your designated male and sat down to tackle the chief meal of the day – soup, entrée, joint, game or poultry, sweet and then the savoury, not to be eaten by unmarried girls. How people ate all this and still achieved – as some did – an eighteen-inch waist, I cannot imagine.

Jos was still spending his days in the City, always a vague term and never more so than when employed by him. Together with a partner called Dawson he invented a motorcar which, like the diamond mine, was bound to make a fortune and could not, at any rate financially, go wrong. A prototype was built which ran splendidly downhill, much less so up, or even on the level; it became known as the Grunt and Dawdle car. The money that had survived the diamond mine was further eroded.

Almost exactly a year after her marriage, Nellie gave birth to her first and only child at her parents' home in Sussex Square. Soon afterwards, her mother had a stroke. An independent dwelling for Jos, Nellie, the child (myself) and the inevitable nanny became essential. But where, and how to pay for it? Nellie had made friends with a young woman of her own age who had a house in Mayfair and an estate in Sussex; as the daughter of an engineering, contracting and oil tycoon, Weetman Pearson, who became Viscount Cowdray, she was very rich. Her husband, the third Baron Denman, was a Liberal peer with political ambitions. On her estate at Balcombe there was a charming old farmhouse called Stone Hall, and this she let to Jos and Nellie for a small sum. So, for the first time, Jos had a fixed address, if only a rented one. From Haywards Heath he could commute daily to the City, while Trudie Denman and Nellie went into partnership in an enterprise congenial to both: the purchase, training and sale of Welsh ponies.

We got a cattle-truck of ponies, sixteen, from Wales, and escorted them from Haywards Heath station like a pack of hounds. They were unbroken and wild as hawks, and full of lice. Some could only be caught by driving them into a particularly muddy gateway where they stuck. After some preliminary training we broke them to the saddle by strapping on a children's pony pannier and strapping Elspeth into it – she must have been about three – and putting the pony on a lungeing rein. The pair careered round and round, Elspeth chuckling with delight and poor Nanny Newport rushing and screaming round the perimeter.

The pony project proved a great financial success. The cattle truck of ponies cost us £50 and we had a sale at Tattersalls the Sunday after the Derby. Our top price was £36, and the other ponies averaged about £20 each.

Poor Nanny Newport! No pram-pushing in Hyde Park for her – she had fallen among savages. At about this time her charge was invited to a party at one of the grand London houses Nellie had frequented as a débutante. I made (I have been told) straight for the rocking-horse and began to search in its mane. 'What are you doing, dear?' Nanny enquired. 'Looking for lice' was the reply.

*   *   *

Affairs in the City prospered less than the Welsh ponies; in fact, they did not prosper at all. Gradually it became clear to Jos, as to everyone else concerned, that he was not cut out to be a City gent. His thoughts turned again to Africa. To go forth and make a fortune in the Colonies was then quite the vogue among those whom fortune had eluded at home. There was talk at this time of an exciting 'new' country, recently opened by an adventurous railway, and offering favourable terms to settlers, called British East Africa. Already it was famous as a paradise for big-game hunters; a number of wealthy sportsmen had returned with tales of great expanses of plain and forest untouched by plough or axe, a healthy climate thanks to the high altitude, land going cheap, and great opportunities. Some had taken up land themselves, following in the footsteps of Lord Delamere, that redoubtable pioneer.

For a while, the failing health of Nellie's parents postponed a decision. Her mother died early in 1911 and her father little more than a year later. Then Jos and Nellie were free to start a new life overseas: a freedom rooted in sadness, for Nellie's parents and her home were gone, her brothers scattered, and she had to leave all her relatives and friends. Thanks to his father's sacrifices, her elder brother Hughie had inherited Motcombe free of debt, and had returned to live there, manage the estate and enjoy its revenues. He had married a very beautiful girl called Gladys Nixon whom he had met in Ireland – it was said that he fell in love, proposed and was accepted within four days. Charm, looks and wit were hers but her sophisticated London background and circle of friends could not have been more different from Hughie's.

The decision to emigrate to Africa made, Nellie set about preparing herself for the life of the pioneer. She enrolled in a course in poultry-keeping, and took rooms in a farm-house in Oxfordshire for herself, myself (then aged five), and Nanny Newport. Poor as we were, not to have a nanny was unthinkable. I remember all too little of her but she left a memory, as almost every nanny did, of kindness, love and constant care. Children reared by nannies never, or almost never, went short of love and attention; those of today reared by busy, often harassed parents are apt to find these qualities more spasmodic, and sometimes less lavishly bestowed.

As Nellie was to venture into savage places where she might even have to cook her own food, or at least explain to the savages how to do it, some instruction in the art of housekeeping was arranged. At Fonthill, in Wiltshire, her aunt Ockie lived in solitary state in a huge house built in the Scots baronial style, amid magnificent woods, and within sight of the ruins of William Beckford's famous tower. She invited her niece to learn at firsthand what went on beyond those long passages that led from the panelled dining-room to a labyrinth of kitchens, pantries, still-rooms, dairies, laundries and servants' quarters, complex and dark enough to conceal some modern Minotaur.

Every morning, from the enormous kitchen garden, there arrived in the kitchen baskets of perfectly grown vegetables, which would be perfectly cooked by a Scotch cook and her staff consisting of a head kitchenmaid, second ditto, a scullerymaid and a still-room maid. The vegetables found their way with other dishes, six or seven courses in all, into the dining-room where my aunt Ockie and I were waited on by a butler and two footmen, Ockie nibbling perhaps at a wing of partridge. She was a tiny little woman, with a tiny appetite to match.

Then there was the laundry with a staff of three laundrymaids, where each pillowslip was goffered by hand with a pair of tongs. Many housemaids were presided over by the housekeeper – I think the indoor staff alone numbered seventeen. The waste was of course enormous, but the goal of perfection achieved. Even though I had no idea of what life in East Africa would be like, I had a strong feeling that the domestic economy at Fonthill would not prove to be a useful guide.

Nellie's father had left nothing at all in his will to his daughters; he had, indeed, little to leave, since the land and everything at Motcombe went to Hughie. Nor had he been able to bestow on them the smallest marriage *dot*. Nellie was at first literally penniless; but her father's death did free for her £5,000 left her in trust by a godmother, and this was to be their capital in the new land. Jos salvaged from the City a similar sum which was set aside to be a 'stocking', a final reserve, under the care of trustees. This brought in about £150 a year and was their sole income. In East Africa they had no friends or even acquaintances. Nellie knew a family in Somerset who had interests in a sisal company near Mombasa and gave her an introduction to the manager; that was all.

It was winter when they left. Nellie paid a farewell visit to her old home, now re-opened: Gillie and Blanchie were there and the three of them took turns to sit up all night at the death-bed of Gillie's much-loved lurcher, so the occasion was doubly sad. On their last night in England they were taken to a musical. 'It was a kind of nigger minstrel show with a fat black mammy in green satin – I would much rather have seen a well-acted play, perhaps by Bernard Shaw, whose plays were being staged then for the first time.' Next day they were off, by train to Naples and then in a German ship, accompanied by 'some good saddlery and indifferent kitchen utensils, Escoffier's cookery book, a reproduction of a favourite French dressing-table, a sofa, two armchairs, two mattresses, and a crate of Speckled Sussex poultry, one cock and five hens.' Their only child they left behind

27

in the care of one of Nellie's friends until such time as they had found their patch of Africa and built some kind of dwelling on it. Coming events cast no shadow before. They did not know that on that winter's day in 1912 they were saying goodbye for ever to the world of privilege and stability into which they had been born.

Chapter 3

The ability to reach your destination in, let us say, six hours instead of three weeks is commonly supposed to be one of civilization's major advances. There is a price to be paid. Not only does such briskness deprive travel of excitement and romance; it draws, as it were, a scarf over the eyes and understanding of the traveller.

A man stepping out of his aircraft, briefcase in hand, will feel as if he had merely completed a commuter's journey rather longer than his normal one. The office to which he is whisked from the airport, his hotel bedroom in a Hilton or equivalent, these are just the same, and he has no reason to suppose that the people, their outlook and their problems will not be much the same too. He will be wrong, nevertheless.

In former times, three weeks' steaming eastwards created an altogether different frame of mind. Hour after hour, day after day, your vessel took you farther and farther from familiar sights and people into the sights and sounds of the unknown. Port Said, with its oft-described gully-gully men, the fish-like naked boys diving for pennies, all the allurements of Simon Artz's emporium, even if your ship arrived at midnight; then the canal with its brown, harsh banks and the baking, barren sands beyond; Port Sudan with its camels coming and going from the immense deserts of Upper Egypt; the wire-haired Negroes; Arabs in their fringed head-dresses, swathed in burnouses, their women muffled up in black with slits for eyes. (Generally you had a camel ride at Port Sudan.) Then Aden, that bleak outpost, and the huge 'tanks' to which the visitor was conducted, as well as to the stuffed 'mermaid' in a glass case.

Here you were a world away from everything familiar; Asia and Africa with all their mystery lay before you, and above all there were the smells, so pungent, so evocative and strange. Goodness knows what elements were mixed in them: spices and oils, dried fish and goat-dung, camel and the chewing-twig *mira'a*; sand and seaweed, sweat and resinous shrubs, perhaps even frankincense and myrrh; smells prosaic enough in themselves but, mixed together, endowed with a power to make the imagination soar. Then round Cape Gardefui where the sea grew choppy, and the rocky Somalia coast lay low on your starboard beam as you steamed south on one of the oldest sea-routes in the world, traversed since the time of the Phoenicians by little creaking wooden dhows with lateen-rigged sails, running before the monsoons to link Asia and Africa.

Sunsets over this barren coast of Africa were breathtaking in their royal flaring colours, crimson and purple and gold. Moonlight on the silvery, ever-moving Indian Ocean in that warm caressing air was no less disturbing; it was beyond description, like the music of some great symphony heard not through the ear but in the heart. By the time you reached your destination you were emotionally prepared for a great adventure and keyed up to a pitch of wonder and excitement that even the realities you would soon meet with – dust and dirt, fleas and mosquitoes, prickly heat and fever, rawness, harshness, sores, bites, the foreignness of Africa – could never quite dispel that first impact on the senses. A deeper apprehension of reality was thus imparted than the modern traveller can expect to gather from six hours' reclining in an aerial capsule. Africa is in truth a long way from England, and its people, the products of its rocks and sun and history, are not the same as those of Northern Europe.

Mombasa Island, reached from the ship in a small row-boat, was a place of enchantment with its brilliant flowering shrubs and creepers half smothering palm-thatched wooden bungalows, all shaded by big mango trees that had been planted by the Arabs. Mombasa was still an Arab town, the old harbour crowded with dhows, the narrow streets between tall, honey-coloured buildings lively with coffee-sellers, the villainous-looking sailors in bright turbans and the craftsmen in open-fronted dwellings plying their trades. Already a new town was taking shape with the offices of European firms. There was a spacious, cool-veranda'd Club, also the Hotel Metropole, customs sheds, and house for Protectorate officials who wore white uniforms and topees, and swords on ceremonial occasions. You moved about in open trolley-cars which ran on miniature railway lines and were propelled by hefty African pushers.

Armed with the letter of introduction to the manager of the sisal plantation beyond Nyali, Jos and Nellie stayed in a wood-and-corrugated-iron bungalow full of hornets' nests, millipedes and, after dark, droves of mosquitoes. Each visitor was provided, as was the custom, with a Swahili servant, a haughty-looking Moslem in the long white *kanzu* that was the uniform of the coast. Nellie's attendant 'carried a frightful knife under his *kanzu* which clattered to the floor at odd moments; both were first-class servants but soon got ill from the highland air and returned to the coast.' On their first night the newcomers were taken out to dinner; as they reached the trolley 'Jos threw away his smart white tropical dinner-jacket and then, cursing loudly, his trousers – odd behaviour it seemed, but of course it was *siafu*,' those devilish biting ants that can reduce strong men to the verge of hysteria, and kill with their vicious mandibles any living creature too small to escape. (They are sterile, and completely blind.)

* * *

The departure of the daily train from Mombasa to Nairobi was an event. It did not simply slide out of the station as a matter of routine. Large crowds of chattering, gesticulating relatives and friends, bearing gifts of pawpaws, mangoes, chickens, eggs, sugar-cane, lumps of porridge rolled in banana leaves and goodness knows what else, came to see off the adventurous travellers. The locomotive, fuelled by eucalyptus logs that spat like angry cats, and needing long drinks at every station, hissed importantly, as if gathering strength for its heroic journey.

First-class carriages were for Europeans and the more affluent Asians; second for lesser Asians who filled them with enormous families; third-class for the indigènes who sat all night on wooden benches chattering and eating, surrounded by *kikapus* (large, hand-woven baskets) full of fruit and yams and every kind of eatable, the women generally with babies on their backs or toddlers at foot. The servants of the Europeans bore rolls of bedding which they spread on the seats when the train stopped at Voi for dinner. Their employers dismounted from the coach and walked to the dak bungalow to be served, by the light of paraffin lamps, with a dank meal of tinned soup, tinned hash and tinned fruit, and drinks watered down with tepid soda-water. Then the long train with its panting locomotive, emitting a plume of sparks that got into passengers' eyes

31

and ears and often started grass fires, began its long, hard haul to the highlands, climbing over five thousand feet in about fifteen hours.

With the dawn came enchantment. You looked out of the window to see great rolling plains, pale gold in the early light, each tree-shadow sharply defined, speckled as far as eye could see with the most wonderful collection of wild animals in the world. How many different species might you see from the carriage window? I do not know whether a count was ever made – perhaps between twenty and thirty. All moving, grazing, welcoming a new day, at peace with each other, heedless of the creeping, snake-like train that bore no menace. Lions might be lying down if not with lambs, then with their equivalents, the waggle-tailed gazelles and shiny antelopes that, when the lions' hunger stirred them, became their prey. Elephants in family parties might amble across the plain, rhinos browse in gulleys, zebras and wildebeeste proceed in phalanxes, ostriches stride along shaking their feathers, giraffes nibble at acacia tops, and so on. There were tens of thousands of animals, all on the left-hand side of the railway because they were protected there, whereas on the right-hand side they could be shot. It had taken them a very short while to discover the difference.

The tribe that shared these enormous sun-drenched plains with the wild animals, the Masai, never ate their flesh, and therefore hunted only the lions, which took their hump-backed cattle; the predation of the Masai kept the lions in balance with other species making up this harmonious network of life. Man, at that time, formed part of that balance and that network which he was later to destroy. Technology in the shape of the rifle, greed in the shape of trade in tusks and hides, science in the shape of medical skills that enabled the human species to dominate and eventually destroy the others, were only just beginning. Travellers to Nairobi in 1912, wiping from their faces the red dust that had coated them and their belongings during the night, never dreamed, as they peered from the windows, that before they grew old all this would have vanished, save for small, precarious pockets, from the face of the earth: or that they would be among the agents of destruction of the thing they loved.

*   *   *

Like most intending settlers, Jos and Nellie made straight for the Norfolk Hotel, the solar plexus of settlers' Nairobi.

Its front was largely taken up by the bar, and behind was a row of loose-boxes called bedrooms. Just outside the bar was a row of hitching-rings; local patrons often took morning exercise on mules or horses, and a row of patient animals would await the return of their riders from a search for refreshments inside. Rickshaws in plenty were also lined up, and a few rupees would persuade rickshaw-boys to hold races up and down the dusty Government Road, between two rows of run-down Indian *dukas*, with here and there a stone-built British store.

A genial, blue-eyed countenance above an Old Etonian tie was almost the first sight that met our eyes in the bar. This was Jim Elkington, who had been at Eton with Jos. We were invited to stay at Masara, about six miles out, and accommodated in a roomy tent for the approaching January races. Within a couple of weeks we had bought from our host five hundred acres of potential coffee land at Thika for £4 an acre, also two mares, one a discarded remount from India, White Lady, the other a bay Arab, Wee Woman.

Jim Elkington was master and owner of the Masara hounds, a pack of imported English fox-hounds which met every Sunday morning to pursue the jackal. Jim was a most impressive sight; he had a beautiful seat on a horse, a beautiful sixteen-hand chestnut to sit on, and a beautiful Savile Row red coat and white breeches. The hunt servants had red shirts but eschewed boots, preferring to cling to the stirrups with their toes. The most junior member of the hunt staff was the kennel-boy, a *toto* earning five rupees a month for cleaning out the kennels. His name was Njombo, and he was to become our greatly trusted and beloved headman for many, many years.

Jos and Nellie's five hundred acres of promised land lay about five miles from a place called Chania Bridge, later to become Thika, which was in turn some thirty miles north of Nairobi. It was quite undeveloped, that is to say the soil lay as nature had made it, under a rough cast of veld grass, scrub and bush. On it was no cultivation, no human habitation, no road or even track – only a few narrow footpaths that wound like snakes through the vegetation. To ride about was treacherous because of hidden holes dug by wart-hogs or by ant-bears; small buck would spring up almost beneath one's feet, and sometimes larger animals, zebra and *kongoni* (hartebeeste), would come up from the plains below. Leopards were about. In the dry season, the sun scorched the harsh grass to a dry biscuit colour, and you could see heat shimmering over the ridges ahead. The scarlet blooms of erythrina trees, which flowered on leafless branches, startled the eye. Doves cooed tirelessly from their branches, yellow weaver-birds chattered, and sometimes you could see a bustard, good for the pot, strutting through the grass.

No one knew what this land would grow and what it wouldn't, how it should be treated, what pests and enemies it concealed. But virgin land, it was assumed, was sure to be full of untapped fertility. All you had to do was to tap it by means of a plough and other implements; nature, directed by European skills never before applied in this part of Africa, would do the rest. On top of all this, pioneers believed themselves to be the torch-bearers of civilization, bringing light into dark places and infallibly doing good to the native population. Optimism was the prevailing mood.

Before settling in on their five hundred acres, Jos and Nellie decided to take a quick look at Uganda, where prospects, it was said, were even more promising than in the East Africa Protectorate.

We heard of a wonderful bargain, a dairy farm going cheap, about forty miles from Kampala, whose owners, a European couple, supplied the whole of Uganda with butter – they even sent it once a week on runners' heads to Gondoroko on the Nile. We did the forty miles in one day by rickshaw, with four rickshaw-boys in relays, changed every ten miles. They never dropped out of a trot except on steep hills and never once stopped singing, the burden of their song being that the white man had the brains to invent rickshaws, but not the brawn to pull them.

At the dairy farm, the floors were covered with about a foot of loose grass which was constantly on the move from millions of white ants. Every form of insect lived there, rustling day and night. We got up at 3 am to watch the butter being made. It was made all night, then put into a wire-netting cage cooled by water dripping over charcoal until the following night, when it was despatched in earthenware pots on the heads of runners. This was a brave enterprise, but held no attraction for us. The unfortunate couple died soon afterwards, both of them, of blackwater fever, on the farm.

On All Fools' Day 1913, a little cavalcade set forth from the Norfolk Hotel, bound in the first instance for the Blue Posts. A cart drawn by four very small but very tough humped oxen was piled high with a great variety of objects, including the Speckled Sussex hens and their mate, and surmounted by a lavatory seat on which was perched a monkey Nellie had been given. (She never took to it.) Jos rode a borrowed mule and Nellie an Abyssinian pony, also on loan, whose hide was scarred from flank to shoulder by the claw-marks of a lion that had sprung upon the pony, dragged off its rider, and killed him.

The cart could get no further than the Blue Posts, and here a halt was made and porters recruited to carry the loads, which included tents, to the future farm. How to locate it was the first problem, solved by hunting about in the long grass until the angle-irons planted there by surveyors and numbered, were found. Nellie's household staff consisted of Juma, the Swahili from the coast, still in his *kanzu*. 'He was a Muslim, and when a small buck, a reedbuck perhaps, or duiker, was shot for the pot, he would rush towards it, draw his knife and cut its throat before it died – or so we hoped.'

Once on the site, a patch of bush was cleared and the tents pitched above a small stream called the Kitimuru, after which the future farm was named. 'The grass all round was five feet high. It quickly started to rain, and continued almost without a break for a week. Everything was sodden and muddy. A little trench was dug round our tents and filled with ashes from the camp fire on which poor Juma cooked our meals – he hated every moment of it all. The trench was to keep the *siafu* at bay.'

The next stage was to take on some of the Kikuyu, who lived in their huts not far away in what was then called the Reserve, to start clearing the land of grass and bush. Few of them, at that time, spoke any language other than their own, although the kitchen Swahili that was to form the lingua franca of the country was making inroads. Moreover they were shy, and unfamiliar with the ways of the Europeans. Jos had been advised that an effective way of making contact with them was to tie a safari lamp to the top of a post, and plant the post beside the camp. When darkness fell, and the light shone forth, people would be drawn by curiosity, human moths to the flame, and come to stare. Strange as it seemed to Europeans, these Africans had evolved no form of lamp themselves, not even the simple kind known to the Egyptians over two thousand years ago, nor those in use for centuries among Arabs of the coast. So a lamp was to them a thing of wonder, like many other possessions of the Europeans.

The suggestion worked, and in due course a number of young

Kikuyu men laid aside their spears and wooden clubs to be armed instead with *pangas*, those all-purpose slashing tools to be bought at every *duka*. When the rain stopped a rhythmic chant, always an accompaniment to manual labour, could be heard rising from the bush where Jos had pegged out several level acres to turn into a coffee *shamba*.

Soon other tents sprang up in the bush, and other clearings; not many, but enough to attract the attention of a young assistant district commissioner touring the area on a mule. Pointing with his riding-crop towards one of the camps, he asked to whom it belonged. 'Bwana Kichanga', was the reply. (*Kichanga* means bracelet.) Roy Whittet, our nearest neighbour, wore a gold bangle on his wrist. 'And that?' 'That is Kichuhi's' (the word for ear-ring). Nellie wore, in most unsuitable conditions, a pair of pearl ear-rings which had been a wedding-present. 'Good God, I've come to Hatton Garden!' exclaimed the young man. The name stuck, and later became attached to a polo team made up of Jos, Nellie, Roy Whittet and another neighbour. By European standards they were not close neighbours, but contact was maintained by means of chits, carried as a rule not in a cleft stick but in little leather snuff-holders dangling from the neck on a chain forged by local smiths.

*   *   *

Once the land had been cleared of bush, long grass, termite mounds and trees, the next stage was to plough it. This, again, was by no means easy, because the oxen who had to draw the plough had not been trained. The great experts at handling oxen were the Afrikaners, or Dutchmen as they were generally called. You could see them everywhere on winding red roads that were either thick with dust or deep in mud, in their weather-worn khaki clothing, slouch hats and home-made *veldschoen*, walking beside their long teams with long whips in hand. These whips, although frequently brandished and cracked, very seldom lashed an animal; the tip just flicked its back as the driver called out its name, and the beast would almost leap forward. Every ox had a name. Nellie observed that the slowest and stupidest of their beasts was called Granti, the sleekest and strongest Delamere. Such was his lordship's fame, owing to the amplitude of his flocks and herds, that most ox-teams had a Delamere. The smartest outfits were those of the King's African Rifles, with brightly painted wagons and matching teams, all black, all white, or all brindled.

If you could afford to buy oxen trained by Dutchmen, half your troubles disappeared – only half, as the drivers were not trained either, and had no experience. Nor did untrained oxen take kindly to yokes and traces. One suggested method of taming them was to climb a tree, yoke in hand, and drop the yoke on to the neck of an ox driven underneath. So far as I know, this was not tried at Kitimuru, although it might well have appealed to Nellie. But women's clothing of the day was against agility. For riding, and outdoor work generally, she wore a long divided skirt over her breeches, which had at all costs to be concealed; a blouse with a high, tight collar and long sleeves; and a heavy felt hat called a double terai – all most uncomfortable, and unpleasantly hot.

While the land was being cleared and ploughed, a house, of sorts was built. It was made of mud and wattle, thatched, lined with papyrus reeds, and had a floor of beaten earth. Such dwellings were built exactly like the huts of the Kikuyu except that the living quarters were rectangular instead of round, though as a rule the separate bedrooms were circular. The Kikuyu were accustomed to this kind of building, so the work went ahead quickly; indeed by native custom the thatch, always hauled and laid by women, had to be completed between sunrise and sunset, lest evil spirits should get in. In the case of dwellings for Europeans, this rule did not apply; doubtless evil spirits would get in but, at this period, white men were thought to possess many kinds of magic, unknown to Kikuyu witch-doctors, that would keep them in their place.

But first, before Jos and Nellie's dwelling, a stable for the ponies had to be built. This was because of horse-sickness. Nothing was known about this disease, except that it was almost always fatal, but it was assumed (correctly, as was subsequently found out) to be carried by mosquitoes; these insects flew by night, and therefore it became the rule that ponies must be in by nightfall, and stabled in mosquito-proof buildings. When the stables were completed, Nellie got a lift to Nairobi in a mule-buggy in order to collect the two mares she had bought. Then with Dolly Miles, a friend who had just arrived on a visit, she set out to ride the ponies to Kitimuru. Nellie's mount, White Lady, had not been saddled for a year.

Soon after we started she bucked wildly, and landed sideways on a heap of gravel. At first she seemed all right, but got lamer and lamer as we went on. We had to go on, to get the ponies in by nightfall, so I walked most of the way, and we arrived in the middle of the night. White Lady had split a pastern and was never any good any more. Later I sent her back to Masara to breed, but the vet killed her with the wrong injection for glanders. Wee Woman died in July from horse-sickness in four hours. So my first venture in horse-flesh was very, very sad.

The Kitimuru was a small stream but it had a waterfall with a pool below, and Nellie soon had a vegetable garden going on the bank. Here also she started a nursery to raise the coffee seedlings which were to be planted in rows on the cleared land above. There was said to be a python living under this waterfall, which emerged at intervals to throw its coils round goats and sheep coming to drink, or even round women drawing water in fat yellow gourds.

Nellie was sceptical about this python; she spent much of her time down by the river and had never seen it. But one day she did. It lay coiled on a rock next to the spinach plot, a handsome brown and grey reptile perhaps twenty feet long, glistening in the sunlight and gazing, she thought hungrily, in her direction. Hastily scribbling a note, she sent a garden-*toto* up the hill to summon Jos with his rifle. Back came the messenger, staggering under the weight of a double-barrelled ·450 bore, with the reply 'Shoot it yourself'. 'I had only once fired a rifle, and this one went off half-way to my shoulder. The python fell into the river in a thousand bits, and I cursed the garden-boy because he wouldn't go in and collect them. Nothing would have induced me to go in myself.'

Groceries had to be fetched from Nairobi by ox-cart. This took two and a half days to get there, stayed one day in town, and needed another two and a half days to get back. So it was advisable not to run out of matches. In the rains, and before the branch railway line to Thika opened early in 1914, you were cut off altogether; there was a large hole in the road where a camel was said to have drowned. Shopping was done by means of chits to be settled when you next went to Nairobi. You could not lock up an ox-cart, and, although it stood about all day in the streets and was out-spanned by the road-side on the journey, nothing was ever stolen.

Although our housing was primitive, and we were always short of ready cash, in some ways our standard of living would in later years have been considered high. The average household consisted of a cook – a Goanese in 'grand' households, a Baganda next down the scale and a more or less untrained local at the bottom. There was a kitchen-*toto*, and a personal boy for each member of the household. Each pony, too, had its own syce. In up-to-date households cooking was done on a wood-burning Dover stove, but often three large stones constituted the range. These supported battered, blackened *suferias* (pans) which were never properly cleaned. Considering all this, the meals were passable, though hardly up to Fonthill standards.

To get about, we either rode our ponies or drove forth in the mule-buggy, along very rough tracks orginally made by lopping away the most obvious obstructions with *pangas*. Once, soon after we'd invested in a new mule-harness, we went out to dinner with Kichanga. The harness was left in the buggy when the mules were unspanned and taken to the stables. We emerged after our evening's entertainment to find no harness, and no upholstery in the mule-buggy either. The hyenas, not to be outdone, had had a dinner party too and eaten the lot.

On 4 June 1913, Jos and Nellie went by mule-cart to the capital for an Old Etonian dinner and the King's Birthday Ball at Government House.

We stayed with Jack Pixley, in a house near the Norfolk he shared with Denys Finch Hatton, who was generally away trading in Abyssinia or the Northern Frontier District. There were such a lot of bachelors in those days: Jack and Denys, the Kilima Kiu trio – F. O'B. Wilson, Frank Joyce and Archie Lambert – Jack Riddell, Mervyn Ridley, the Cole brothers Berkeley and Galbraith and Alan Thompson who puts us up sometimes at Karura, a hovel where you sat on petrol boxes, your feet on loose dusty floors inhabited by myriads of fleas, and ate the most divine things out of tins from Fortnum and Mason.

*　　*　　*

Nellie grew tired, after a while, of hovels with floors of dust infested by fleas and also *jiggas*, those nasty little insects that burrow under human toe-nails and there deposit little white sacs of eggs. The sac must be dug out with the point of a needle, or else the eggs will hatch, the baby *jiggas* burrow deeper and the toe will turn septic, possibly gangrenous.

So the bold project was formed to build a stone house. All but the richest settlers contented themselves with mud and grass, and no one could have called Jos and Nellie rich. But the banks were positively urging overdrafts on newcomers, and Mr Playfair, the manager of the National Bank of India in Nairobi, became a kind of friendly god, whose blessing was invoked before the launching of any new enterprise, and who was propitiated at intervals by social calls and weekend invitations.

If the country could not have developed without sympathetic bank managers, nor could it have done so without Indian *fundis* (artisans). They cut blocks of stone from the hillsides, put up sheds and houses, made furniture, laid water-pipes, installed machinery to process coffee, and other crops, and did all the jobs for which Africans then had no skills, and at which Europeans would not have been able to make a living.

Two *fundis* were engaged to cut stone from the river bank, and a European contractor undertook to supervise the actual building. Like many another, his finances were shaky; he preferred to conduct his business in the open air, if possible on the steps of his bank, where he would placate pressing creditors with the words, 'I have the National Bank of India behind me'.

So the stone house, a gabled bungalow, arose above the river bank at Kitimuru, with a view across the valley to the ridges beyond; far, far beyond these, on a clear morning, you could see the white-clad peak of Kenya Mountain softly pencilled against a blue sky. Wisps of cloud swathed its lower slopes so that the peak appeared to be floating in the heavens, unattached to land. Visitors to the country were impressed by an ability to stand on the veranda in the glorious, gentle early morning sunshine of the African highlands and look at snow, less than a hundred miles from the Equator. Some were impressed also by the grandeur of a stone house in the wilds, approached by an avenue of stripling flame trees, though the house was not as grand as all that – by later standards it would not have been considered grand at all. It had three bedrooms, a dining-room, a sitting-room, a bathroom and a small veranda. The bathroom had a tap. Only one, to convey water drawn from the Kitimuru by means of an ox-cart that creaked its way down a corkscrew track to the river and back. In the rains, the water was chocolate coloured, and at all times populated by tadpoles, small frogs and other aquatic wildlife. There was no hot tap; water was heated in the kitchen in *debbis*, four-gallon paraffin or petrol tins used for diverse purposes: for carrying water, for measuring harvested crops (coffee pickers, for instance, were paid so much a *debbi*), for storing grain and, when flattened, for roofing huts. In fact, in their humble way, *debbis* were almost as essential to development as Dutchmen, bank managers and Indian *fundis*.

The single tap and a proper bath, not a tin tub, were all the amenities. To visitors from England, accustomed to indoor sanitation, Nellie would say primly, in the language of the day, 'Now I expect you would like to see the geography of the house'. She would open a door leading to the outside world and announce, 'You have all Africa before you'. Actually there was a path leading to a clump of bushes about fifty yards away which concealed the 'garden house' with a deep pit latrine. This little hut was inhabited by centipedes, spiders, beetles and other creatures who sometimes alarmed visitors, but so far as I know never did them any harm.

Chapter 4

'Safari is what is good for one's immortal soul, little else', Nellie wrote to a friend. 'The shooting part comes up to [fox] hunting for excitement.' An acquaintance called Jack Kirkwood offered to initiate them into the safari life when the planting season was over, and a lull occurred in the activities of the farm.

It was, of course, all foot-slogging in those days, and the first step was to recruit porters. Even the simplest safari needed an army of these, for they would be marching beyond the confines of what was generally called civilization, where nothing could be bought or bartered, and everything that would be needed for perhaps a couple of months must be borne on porters' heads. This must include the porters' own food. Two and a half pounds of *posho* (maize meal) plus salt was the ration for each man, supplemented wherever possible by game meat. As the safari progressed, the *posho* dwindled, to be replaced by trophies of the chase; and one of the arts of safari management was so to calculate supplies that you did not run out of *posho*.

There was a race of professional porters, mostly Swahilis, who were remarkably tough and efficient; they were also expensive, and mainly in the employ of a firm called Newland and Tarlton, who catered for rich sportsmen from overseas. They wore long, navy-blue jerseys with the letters NT stitched on in scarlet, and marched with a pair of stout boots slung around their necks. Each porter was entitled, whether by law or by custom, to a pair of boots, but not compelled to wear them. They were much too valuable in his eyes to be spoilt by use, and were kept for display when the safari was over.

Local settlers could not afford porters like those, or boots, but were content with amateurs drawn from up-country tribes like the Kikuyu, who were by then accustomed to being called upon to carry loads for Government officers when touring their districts. In the beginning, the Kikuyu had been appalled by this demand for male porters; carrying loads was strictly for women, and it was as humi-liating for a Kikuyu man to carry one as it would have been for a British man to have his belongings humped by women. The British were then in the ascendant, and so won the day. The Kikuyu bowed to the inevitable but carried the loads on their heads, not on their backs like their women, whose burdens could weigh twice as much as the load Europeans considered proper for men. The hip-bath was the most unpopular load, with tent-poles a good second.

*   *   *

Everything was assembled at Kitimuru, porters signed on, and away went the safari, gently at first to average about fifteen miles a day. After a while they entered the dense aboriginal forest clothing the slopes of Kenya Mountain – dripping, dark and treacherous, where you stumbled into holes made by the feet of elephants, slipped on rotting tree-stumps, and trod on fallen branches that gave way. Also you might, at any minute, drop into a cunningly concealed game-pit and on to a pointed stake below, or you might encounter a herd of buffaloes invisible until you were a yard or two away.

We were about six days getting through the forest, and wet to the skin every day, owing to the endless streams we had to ford. I had three pairs of boots with me, and used almost to sob every morning wondering which pair would hurt the least.

There was one thrilling day, following up a herd of elephants. Jack Kirkwood went in front, then his gun-bearer with a ·450, then me, then my gun-bearer with my ·450. Soon after leaving camp, there was a great crash in the forest just ahead; I turned round to snatch my rifle and found the gun-bearer bolting out of sight. The crash actually was only a giant forest pig – very rare; the bolting gun-bearer was sent back to camp in deep disgrace; Jack carried his own rifle and gave me his gun-bearer.

We followed an elephant track, the droppings indicating that the elephants were about half an hour ahead. I looked up, and saw an elephant almost tower-ing above Jack, who was examining the spoor. I shouted 'Look out!' and turned round to seize my rifle – again, the gun-bearer was bolting away with it. I hared after him and seized it. Meanwhile, Jack had had to fire point-blank at the elephant, which was a cow with a calf, about ten yards away. Mercifully the bullet glanced off her skull and she turned and went. If she had charged in that narrow path, she would probably have got the lot of us.

We all went up different trees to see if we could find any more elephants, and discovered that we were in the very middle of a large herd – masses of them in every direction, standing stock still, with ears out listening, the only noise that of their tummies rumbling loudly. [In fact so-called tummy rumbling, a most distinctive elephant noise, was eventually discovered to emanate not from the stomach, but from the throat, being a kind of vibration of the vocal chords, possibly a method of communication between members of the herd.] So we had to get down our trees, and slink back along our path in fear and trembling of a general charge. When we thought ourselves clear, we stopped and had a drink.

Jack then told me to stand by a certain tree while he went back to try and spot a bull. By the noise of trees crashing, we could tell that they were feeding again. After what seemed a long time, there was a terrific pandemonium; they got his wind, and the whole herd crashed back past me. My tree was non-climbable, so I shivered miserably trying to keep it between me and elephants in every direction – one came within fifteen yards. They cleared off, and Jack said he hadn't spotted a bull.

Next day, we went off to try and find them again. We left camp at 5 am and walked and walked and walked, up through the forest belt and into the bamboos. The ground was covered with fallen bamboos; if you thought one would give way it tripped you up, and if you thought one would support you, it let you down. Finally we got up into the open, giant heath country, with sheets of everlastings; most lovely, but the height, probably fourteen thousand feet, made me feel sick, and the elephants had gone for miles. So we had to go back to camp, which took us, without a stop, till 8 pm – a hard day. We never got on to their spoor again.

We found Meru a gay scene. There was a big safari in, the Hodgkinsons, she was almost the most celebrated 'fairy' of the year, very beautiful and blonde, and not Mr Hodgkinson's wife at all really. The DC, E. B. Horne, threw a great party, and we got up a game of polo on the golf course – four ponies, four mules, four polo sticks and four brassies. I had a mule and a brassie, and gave Hugh Welby, Horne's assistant, a fine crack in the ribs with my only shot. We broke all four brassies I am afraid. Then we set out for Archer's Post.

Elephant, lion, buffalo, rhino and leopard – these were the 'big five' that everyone wanted to bag.

One evening, Jack spotted a lion slinking into a swamp near our camp, so next morning Jos and I set out to see about it. The lion heard us, and moved off down a buffalo path through the reeds. This was *our* path, and we met face to face. Jos was in front, and I wanted him to get the first lion, but he wanted *me* to. I considered that the question had been settled before we left camp, but when we met the lion, Jos politely and unselfishly stood aside, and said, 'You shoot', I said, 'No, *you* shoot'. He replied, 'No, *you* shoot'. I said, 'Shoot, you bloody fool'. Jos said, 'Don't call me a bloody fool'. The lion, which had stood like a lamb about twenty-five yards away all this time, couldn't bear the language and sloped off. Jos had a shot at his backside, but missed, and although we hunted hard through the swamp, we never saw him again, and got a good ticking-off from our white hunter.

However, one morning our tracker rushed in while we were having breakfast to say there were three lions on a kill about half a mile from camp. Jos and I seized our rifles and dashed off, and saw them on the kill about 150 yards away. The two lionesses went off at once, but the lion stood there. We hurried through the bush to get up to him, and by the time we got there, I was puffing like a grampus. This time I took the first shot and shot over him, shot again below him, shot again behind him. Jos then fired the ·450 and shot in front of him. I then fired again and hit him in the paw. He growled and limped off, sadly waving his paw. Jos tried to fire but the left barrel missed – it often did. So we had to follow the blood spoor into thicker and thicker bush.

After about two hours of this so-called pleasure, the tracker said, 'There he is!' – in a bush. Jos sank on one knee, and took the longest aim anyone has ever taken, and fired just as the lion emerged from the bush. Frightful lion noises, the lion up in the air, apparently charging. Very bravely, I fired at him in the air and hit him in the spine, but actually he was already dead from Jos's ·450 bullet in the chest at fifteen yards.

*　　*　　*

The safari camped on the banks of the Ewaso Ngiro river, about a mile from a store kept by a lone European at a spot called Archer's Post, just within the Northern Frontier District. If a ramshackle store in the heart of the bush purveying blankets and *posho*, beads and knives, tobacco and sugar and *ghee*, to the few Africans passing by on this route to the north, could be described as civilization, Archer's Post was its last out-post before the traveller reached the Abyssinian highlands. As a rule, these outback store-keepers were Asians rather than Europeans. They were said to live on the smell of an oil-rag, and Europeans tended to despise them, but I thought them brave. They were peaceful people, and carried no arms, but lived with their families among tribesmen who generally carried spears which custom demanded should be blooded. Wherever you went, miles from the railway or the *boma* (district headquarters), there was the little Indian *duka* with its rusty corrugated iron roof, its narrow veranda for the customers, its bags of grain and pulses and array of cheap goods like mirrors, mugs, combs and *suferias*. Over all was a pervading smell of spices, and at the back the womenfolk and their very numerous children dwelt in considerable squalor.

If trade flourished, other Indians came; a second *duka* arose beside the first, then another, and another; a sewing-machine appeared on the veranda, its owner in his *dhoti* and round cap tirelessly treadling away; then a shoe-maker perhaps; a tinsmith who could turn old cigarette tins and, of course, *debbis*, into all sorts of useful objects. In time there grew from the earth two rows of *dukas* with a 'street' in between, alternatively dusty or boggy; and so a little township was born. Some were stillborn, or destined to fade away; but others, like Thika, grew and grew. And that is how they all started, as a little Indian *duka* in the bush or on the plain.

At Archer's Post, the safari turned back. On their last day (in September 1913) they marched thirty-two miles across the fire-blackened, powdery Nanyuki plains.

... hard going, but we were all very fit by then. Our porters did wonderfully well. On the way back we met a grand Newland and Tarlton safari whose porters were nearly dying because they refused to eat game meat, and had run out of *posho*. The plains were stiff with game so unlimited meat was available, but they wouldn't touch it although they were starving. If we hadn't been able to give them *posho*, I think they would have died.

* * *

Sometime in 1913 a childhood friend of Nellie's, recently widowed, arrived on a visit. She brought quite an entourage: a maid, myself, and a governess. The arrival at Kitimuru of three more females enormously enhanced Jos's prestige among the Kikuyu. It had not hitherto been suspected that he was so rich as to have no less than four wives. But only one *toto*? Three of the wives barren? Evil spirits must have been at work; clearly, he must change his witch-doctor. Nellie was comforted to hear that she remained the senior wife, but less happy with the reason given, that she was the fattest.

Of the governess I can remember nothing, but she was not a success and did not last long. Nellie's judgement was that she was dank and had religious mania. Nellie's judgements could be harsh, and in retrospect I felt sorry for the governess, pitchforked into this rough and ready household where nothing was tidy and in order, no gloves and no hats. We had a mule called Margaret who used to wander about the veranda and into the grass house, looking for sugar and not always minding her manners; and an assortment of undisciplined dogs and cats. Being religious, if she was, must have made things worse. There was no church nearer than Nairobi, and no way of getting there. Now and again, a parson came out to the Blue Posts to hold a service in the bar, in a not very reverent atmosphere. Jos and Nellie did not often go, but there came a Sunday when, perhaps because of the governess, they decided to attend.

I donned a spotless white linen dress and tidied up generally. We were about to start when an African, unknown to me, arrived with the forefinger of his right hand dangling by a thread of skin. There had been some rock-blasting nearby, and he thought that a detonator or two, suitably flattened, would make a good ornament. I must admit I was somewhat baffled, but seized the dangling bit, popped everything into a solution of permanganate of potash, and strapped the two bits of bleeding finger together. They did join up, and after a few dressings he had a perfectly good forefinger again. But alas for my spotless white go-to-meeting dress, all bloodstained! No church today.

When guests arrived from England, they expected to be taken on safari. Daisy was no exception, and Nellie nothing loath. Safari life had got into her blood, as it did into the blood of so many Europeans. It had a fascination impossible to explain. The cup of tea in the dark beside the smouldering embers of a camp fire with dawn just lightening the sky behind a black line of hills; the setting forth through dew-soaked grass, rifle in hand, treading softly, towards a salt-lick or watering-place, every nerve taut. The rising of the golden sun, the silvering of grass-heads swathed in glistening cobwebs; the flute-like descending cadence of the rain-bird and the chattering of weavers in sweet-smelling acacia trees. The flash of a brightly coloured hoopoe or hovering sunbird; the sight of an antelope – bushbuck or waterbuck perhaps – standing with head erect, horns uplifted, pelt dew-spangled, muscles tensed, and then the sudden bound as it vanished as if a magic wand had touched it and conferred invisibility. The long, hot trudge through bush that bit and sand that

slithered; the herds of tommy, grantii or *kongoni* that, never panick-
ing, kept their distance and receded as you advanced; the search in
dongas for spoor, perhaps of buffalo, lion or rhino; the flat-topped
thorn-trees with the mild-eyed, velvety giraffes nibbling their tops;
the sudden flare of scarlet aloes from pale grass, the sweet smell of
wild jasmine, the tang of dust. And then the camp at evening, that
golden evening with long shadows laid across the grass, the cool and
relaxation, the call of guinea-fowl, the chattering of monkeys, and
darkness swiftly falling, stars emerging in their myriads, the camp
fire crackling, sparks flying, the soft sound of African voices, a smell
of cooking, a hot bath in a tin tub and the comfort of changing into
dry clothing and soft shoes. The habit, which became a firmly rooted
custom, of changing into pyjamas and dressing-gowns for dinner
probably arose from the safari life.

Daisy had led a sheltered existence, but met with no concessions
from her childhood friend. On a shoulder of the Aberdare mountains, at an altitude of over nine thousand feet, they hunted buffaloes
from dawn till dusk for days on end and never got a shot, let alone
a trophy. Poor Daisy was quite severely wounded – not by a buffalo
but by a venomous spider which bit her on the backside. A more
congenial experience was a New Year's party in 1914 to celebrate
the opening of Muthaiga Club, which was to attain some fame in
later years.

There was only one band in the country, that of the KAR, so the music had
a strong martial flavour. Everyone was in high spirits. The crowd by modern
standards was tiny, and I don't suppose there was a soul in the room, barring
visitors, who didn't know everyone else. What a crowd of eligible young men,
and no young things for them! It wasn't at all an alcoholic party – all that
came after the war.

Daisy's visit had, for me, a most satisfactory aftermath: she left
behind two ponies. One, a bay Arab called Lucifer, became more
or less mine. On most Saturday afternoons, all three of us would
ride to a sisal plantation on the plains whose owner, Mervyn Ridley,
had imported a pack of English fox-hounds. Early on Sunday morning we would set forth to hunt jackal if possible, if not a steinbuck,
and occasionally some less orthodox quarry like cheetah, serval cat,
wart-hog or even porcupine. 'We used to hunt all Sunday morning,

and ride back the sixteen miles after lunch, not a bad effort for a
kid of six, but you never seemed tired.'

By mid-1914, sixty acres of coffee had been planted and land prepared for more. Planting was a laborious affair. First the *shamba*
had to be marked out with sticks to indicate a place for each seedling;
they were spaced nine feet apart. 'Marked out all the blessed day',
is an entry in Nellie's diary in April 1914. 'Mr Taylor helped in the
afternoon. We did about thirty-six acres.' Next day, 'Up at 5.45 am,
marked out fifteen acres till noon'. Then came the planting of the
seedlings, carried out often in the rain and with great care, since it
was essential that the little tap-root should be absolutely straight.
'I remember writing to my sister to say I had planted out five thousand seedlings that week. She replied: "What a wonder you are!
Eighteen hollyhocks nearly killed me." It was so easy to slip into
the way of saying one had done something, meaning one had supervised it.' By the end of April, 33,287 coffee seedlings had been planted
at Kitimuru.

Everyone's ship was to come home in 1916. Alan Thompson had a lovely
scheme to charter an entire ship to take us all on leave; it was to be tied up
in the Thames until we were all ready to come back again. It was to be filled
on the outward journey with our coffee and sisal, and on the way back with
all sorts of luxuries, champagne and lovely polo-ponies.

War cast no shadow. With radio yet to be invented, no telephone,
and mails that took up to six weeks each way, people were encapsu-
lated in their small world. The shock was all the greater when it came.
Jos was embroiled in some financial enterprise in Luxemburg, as
usual with a partner who seldom communicated. But one day a telegram came, collected by Nellie at Thika post office. 'Nothing doing
European war expected.' It sounded unbelievable. Back at Kitimuru,
Jos and Nellie played a game of tennis on the newly made court.
A neighbour, more worked up than they were, sent a series of chits
from across the river: 'Vienna Bourse closed'. 'Troops mobilizing'.
'War inevitable'. How could he have known? Exasperated, Jos
scribbled on the back of the last chit to arrive 'What war?' and
finished the set.

* * *

On the morning of 4 August 1914 we proceeded to Nairobi by train, Jos in a clean khaki suiting, with a military helmet on which I had sewn, at his request, two red flannel letters, RS. These were taken to mean Railway Superintendent instead of Royal Scots as we had hoped. [Jos was in the special reserve of his former regiment.] He also carried a sword in the hand. On Nairobi platform, we heard that war had been declared.

Everything was in confusion. Settlers were pouring in from all over the country, mostly heading for the Norfolk Hotel. It was very difficult for reservists, militiamen, etc., to know what to do, as no one knew whether German East would come into the picture or not. A Union Castle liner was sailing within the next couple of days, so decisions had to be quickly taken. About half those concerned decided to rejoin at home, and went off. The rest quickly got jobs, or invented them, and the East African Mounted Rifles was soon in being. Most of the settlers had brought their own ponies or mules, and almost everyone had a rifle, so the essentials were already there.

Personally I collected all the cash the National Bank of India would give me, in case there should soon be no more, and returned to the farm. Jos was taken on in the Intelligence department because of his knowledge of German, and after a week or two was given command of 'Railway Troops', which I think consisted of Trevor Sheen and a few Indians.

The task of the Railway Troops was to guard the single-line railway track whose first two hundred miles or so lay in close proximity (by African standards) to the border with German East Africa. The German forces were considerably larger and better equipped than those on the British side. The Germans made several attempts to blow up the line and some of these succeeded, but the damage was quickly repaired. Bridges were obviously vital points, and such troops as Jos had under his command were concentrated on them, particularly on the bridge over the river Tsavo. It fell to him to interrogate a German patrol found wandering in the bush near Voi half dead of thirst. The patrol had been sent to blow up the bridge, but had relied on British maps, which differed in several important respects from German ones, arguing that, in a British Protectorate, a British survey was sure to be the more correct. It was not, and they failed to find the river where it should have been.

In September, Jos joined the Fourth Battalion of the KAR as a subaltern, went to the German border near Taveta and took part in several 'scraps'. Most able-bodied settlers were in the East African Mounted Rifles. Each district had its squadron or troop. 'The most popular was Monica's Own, called after the Governor's youngest daughter. The Governor, Sir Henry Belfield, was an impressive sight at parades in a straw boater and eye-glass, attended by his bulky ADC, Keith Caldwell, in shorts and a cloth cap.'

The Thika troop, numbering thirty-six, drilled first at Makuyu, and on 1 September 1914 Nellie, Kichanga and I rode to Thika station to see them entrain for the war, wherever that might be. They went first into camp at Kajiado and thence to Longido near the German border, where a battle took place on 2 November. The entry in Nellie's diary for 6 November read: 'Heard nine EAMR killed at Longido, so wired to Nairobi for names. Answer came: Drummond, Thompson, Smith, Sandbach, Tarlton and others unknown.' This unsuccessful battle was, on its little scale, a great disaster in so small a community. Nor was the news from home any better. Collecting mail at Thika was no longer a pleasure: 'Heard from Sloper, Geoffrey Pearson killed. . . . Humphrey Stucley killed. . . . Percy Wyndham. . . .' All three of Nellie's brothers were in uniform and Chucks, the youngest, was already in France.

*   *   *

By the end of the year it had become clear that the war would not be over by Christmas, and Jos applied for permission, which was granted, to return to England and rejoin The Royal Scots. So on 15 December his trunks left Kitimuru in an ox-cart and he and Nellie followed in a borrowed car. There was a gay evening at Muthaiga Club – rather forced gaiety, perhaps – where 'A' Squadron of the EAMR was giving a farewell dinner for one of its members, and at two o'clock next day Jos entrained for Mombasa. Afterwards Nellie went shopping with Kichanga, to buy toys for me. Next day she 'rode completely round the *shamba*, set up ploughing etc., did bills, very hot. Sick ox'. The good times were over.

Single-handed, Nellie had to run the *shamba* amid growing difficulties resulting from war. Her best oxen, together with the cart so vital to her transport, were commandeered. Then her best pony went, but Lucifer, the bay Arab, was spared, for he was too old. All her neighbours on the ridge had gone save one, Kichanga. Tuberculosis had been his reason for coming to Africa. Like many others, he had been advised that the dry, sunlit climate of the African highlands might cure him. So it did, but the process was not complete and at this stage he was not passed fit for active service. (He was later on.) So he remained behind, working twelve hours a day and more to look after several of his neighbours' farms as well as his own.

In addition to coping with the coffee and with labourers and their families, Nellie was supplying vegetables to the hospital in Nairobi; budding and grafting newly planted citrus trees (she personally budded over one thousand); and, at weekends, going over to Makuyu to see to Mervyn Ridley's hounds. She had promised to keep an eye on them while he was away. So hunts continued, with a very much reduced field, in which I was usually included. (The governess had departed.) 'Looking back, it seems unnecessary, but people still thought they'd soon be back to pick up where they left off, and Mervyn loved his hounds.' Sometimes she was assisted by Randall Swift, a cheerful young Irishman who had left the war because he considered, quite rightly, that it was being badly run, and spent a few months on his sisal plantation before rejoining the war in Gallipoli. One Sunday, they set up some kind of record. Before breakfast, they hunted and killed a jackal; later on, a buffalo bull was sighted nearby and they went out and shot it; they played tennis after lunch; and after tea, a two-a-side game of polo. 'Now I hate to think of the bloodthirstiness of it', she wrote later, 'but it seemed good, then.'

*   *   *

Christmas 1914 had passed with no end to the war in sight, and Christmas 1915 was clearly going to do the same. Jos had gone to France with his regiment, which was suffering heavy casualties in the battle of Ypres. Communications were worsening. Money was short; capital had been used up, the bank was no longer forthcoming, and the production of coffee had a low wartime priority. Nellie decided that we must return to England, only to find that passages were impossible to secure. German submarines were sinking vessels right and left, liners had been turned into troop-carriers, and the civilian would-be traveller stood a poor chance.

Then came an unexpected cancellation with the news that Nellie and I would have to leave Kitimuru next day. Kichanga agreed to oversee the farm which our headman Sammy, an intelligent and reliable Masai, would run as best he could. Endless details had to be settled in twenty-four hours.

Andrew, the Masai cook, tried hard to come home with me. I told him he would hate it, and besides where would he sleep? He replied: 'Are there not kitchens in England?' I tried to explain that people didn't sleep in kitchens as a rule. He picked up a clod of earth and dashed it to the ground, saying: 'That is how you treat me because I am black.' It was disturbing. He went back to his own manyatta in Masailand and got killed by a lion which he had attacked with a spear.

The train from Thika to Nairobi had to climb several hills; not very steep ones, but sometimes its primitive engine found them too much. The day of our departure was such an occasion. On several hills it rolled backwards to try again, and on one of them it made seven attempts. It reached its destination half an hour before the scheduled departure of the Mombasa mail. All I had with me was a suitcase and a few unsuitable objects that I could not bear to leave behind, such as a stuffed baby crocodile, a Kikuyu snuff-pouch, and the foot of a bushbuck made into a paper-knife. It was a painful wrench to leave behind my two chameleons, George and Mary, and of course Lucifer, although I could appreciate the difficulties of taking him along. We caught the mail train by the skin of our teeth, only to find, when we reached Mombasa, that the ship was delayed and we had to wait five days.

At Djibouti we all had to disembark; bubonic plague had broken out on board. Everyone was in quarantine, and we spent three weeks in a little overcrowded, dirty, pest-infested hotel. Memories of the stifling July heat of Djibouti, one of the hottest places on earth, and of the miseries of prickly heat, linger faintly in my mind.

After Suez, there were submarines, but we reached Marseilles intact and embarked on a long, tedious, most uncomfortable journey across wartime France. All our luggage, save what we carried, had got lost. There were no restaurant cars, no wagon-lits and apparently no timetables. Eventually we crossed the Channel with no reservations, no passes, no luggage, and money that was rapidly running out.

At last, travel-stained, dirty, hungry and, Nellie said – she may have exaggerated a little – with only fourpence left, we reached Victoria Station in the middle of the night, climbed into a taxi, and gave Trudie Denman's address. The pealing of the doorbell brought forth in his dressing-gown a startled but impeccably good-mannered butler, who at first regarded the creatures emerging from the taxi with disguised dismay. But then he recognized Nellie, paid the taxi, and we were translated, by one of those sudden somersaults in circumstance that characterized Nellie's life, from the squalor and discomforts of wartime travel into the considerable luxury of a well-appointed, generously staffed and faultlessly run mansion in Buckingham Gate.

Chapter 5

No. 4 Buckingham Gate was a hive of activity; a body called Smokes for Wounded Soldiers and Sailors was centred there, and in the ballroom cigarettes were being packed by enthusiastic volunteers. Nellie and I took up temporary quarters in the simplified but by no means spartan Denman household. Our luggage never reappeared.

Once or twice, Jos turned up on leave, thinner but still cheerful, despite the dispiriting progress of the battle of Ypres. On 5 November 1915 – Guy Fawkes' Day, as everyone pointed out – he was accidentally blown up by a hand grenade and wounded in the chest, not dangerously, but badly enough to be declared unfit for further active service. In the same year his younger brother Robin, a staff officer of great promise in the Rifle Brigade (he had won the DSO in the Boer War), was wounded in the spine and paralysed for life; and Nellie's youngest brother Chucks, a captain in the Royal Horse Artillery, after winning the Military Cross, was killed on active service in September. So it was not a good year for Nellie, or indeed for anyone, including, on an insignificant scale, myself, for I was consigned to a boarding-school at Aldeburgh in Suffolk.

After the freedom of Africa, and the haphazard attitude towards lessons at Thika, any English school would have seemed a prison at the best of times; in wartime, with increasing shortages of everything, especially the sources of warmth, to be deposited on the coast of East Anglia was like hell itself. Winters cannot have lasted all the year round, although in retrospect they seem to have; my chief memories are of cold, chilblains and at times hunger, since rationing in that war was sketchy, and the school's housekeeping inefficient. I remember, in desperation, eating my toothpaste; the flavour was nice but the actual paste not at all sustaining; I have sometimes wondered since, without ever finding out, what toothpaste is made of.

There were, of course, lighter moments. These included watching a Zeppelin crash in flames near Felixstowe; no doubt the crew were burnt to death but it did not occur to any of us to feel distressed about this, since they were German. A day or two later we were taken to see the wreckage, and picked up little bits of Zeppelin as mementoes. Several of us had these made into brooches. Gruesome as this may seem now, it was, like Nellie's blood-sports, quite in order at the time. Otherwise the war did not impinge upon us directly, but somehow it was always there. Mines were washed up on the windswept shingle beach where we were made, reluctantly, to go for walks, or even more reluctantly to bathe in an icy North Sea during the summer term. Among the dunes were disused, sand-bagged trenches which we could briefly explore, peopling them with khaki soldiers in tin hats and puttees waiting to go to their deaths over the top.

Men in the blue uniforms and red ties of the wounded were seen in the street of the little town along which we marched on Sundays to the grey church. Brothers would come sometimes to see their sisters, clad in their clean and tidy uniforms, neatly pressed, with polished buttons and Sam Browne belts. There were uneasy moments when a pupil would vanish for a few days looking pale and weepy, and we knew that the name of her brother, or possibly father, had been added to the casualty lists. In due course the girl resumed her place and there were no comments; a stone had been dropped into a pool, the ripples died away and all was as before, but somehow, without consciously thinking about it, we knew that another stone lay, its journey over, at the bottom of the pool.

*   *   *

There was, at this period, a vogue for crystal-gazers and soothsayers of all kinds, who might produce those words of reassurance so badly needed by the relatives of men at the front. Nellie returned from a visit to one such person to tell Jos that he and she were soon to go to a city over the water, somewhat south of London, and to live a grand life there among kings, queens and nobles. 'They must be going to crown you king of the Jews', she remarked. A few weeks later, Jos was appointed military attaché in Madrid.

They were met by a colleague from the Embassy who took them for a drive in the surrounding hills while their possessions were being unpacked and installed. This turned out to be a *gaffe*.

There were two military attachés and two naval ones; one of each pair was the genuine article, the other a spy. The man who took us out was the spy attaché, and next morning Jos was summoned before King Alfonso and put on the mat for consorting with him. This was never to be done again, and it never was. When we saw the spy attaché dining at the Ritz or some other smart restaurant with some lovely lady, Jos envied him from afar. The real naval attaché was Oliver Baring, and the spy one Compton Mackenzie, who also had the run of lovely ladies in restaurants.

The British ambassador, doyen of the Corps Diplomatique, was Sir Arthur Hardinge. Jos had barely settled in when the Russian ambassador died, and there had to be a full-dress funeral. Jos in a splendid military head-dress with black cock's feathers walked just behind the ambassador, at the head of the long cortège of diplomatic splendour. It was cold and wet and the streets narrow and muddy. 'Suddenly the cortège halted, and partially disintegrated; diplomats of all nations were leaving their places and seemed to be wandering about. What had gone wrong? The British ambassador had lost one of his goloshes in the mud, and refused to proceed until it had been found and restored to his foot.'

Jos and Nellie took over a flat equipped with a cook, a footman and a dachshund; and they did indeed move among kings, queens and nobles. Spanish meal-times were at first difficult; lunch was between three and four o'clock; tea-parties did not start until about eight o'clock and continued until ten; dinner was from eleven onwards, followed by bridge, and bedtime at about three in the morning.

Polo matches played in the presence of the king and queen were attended in force by the Corps Diplomatique. On one of these occasions, Nellie was presented to Princess Beatrice, a grand-daughter of Queen Victoria, who was married to Alfonso, Infante of Spain, a first cousin of the king.

The Infanta adored riding and also adored one of the king's best polo players. She could persuade none of the Spanish ladies to ride with her, and thought I was the answer – I would go out with her and play 'gooseberry'.

So, a royal car arrived outside our flat at six o'clock every morning. This, to my regret, was the only hour of the day when everyone in Madrid was asleep. A few odd sentries did present arms, but I was never really seen in all my glory. We proceeded to the Campo Santo, six or seven miles outside

Madrid, when the Infanta's boy-friend would appear, and also a rather horrible old man called the Duque de Tetuan, head of the Cavalry School. After a bit, the Infanta and her boy-friend would wander off for a ride on the Campo Santo. The Duque put 250 horses at my disposal, and lovely, lovely horses they were. He proposed that I should take part in a certain exercise, it consisting of galloping in line at a low hurdle just beyond which was a precipitous cliff with a stream at the bottom. Down this you went, and everything depended on the horse keeping in a straight line; the cliff was so steep that the horses used to scrape the skin off the backs of their hocks.

When about twenty officers had completed this exercise – one got out of the straight and went tumbling down into the stream – the Duque invited me to take part in the next descent and to choose my mount. I had carefully marked down a wiry little sure-footed horse and chose that – not for the rider's beautiful horsemanship as he thought. We completed the exercise all right. The high jumping I found more difficult, but I never actually fell off, getting up to 6 feet 6 inches. Going home was a different matter – a shabby cab, but with a bottle of sherry presented by the Duque under my arm. He was rather like a toad to look at, and had a favourite remark: 'Things are put into alcohol to preserve them, I put alcohol into myself to preserve me.'

After a quick bath and breakfast at the flat, I would proceed to the Red Cross work-room where British ladies – even including some of the Untouchables from the commercial community with whom we were not supposed to consort socially – toiled daily from ten o'clock until three, cutting out and tacking together shirts, underwear and pyjamas for the wounded. These were given out to Spanish ladies who machined them up at a cost of about 3d a garment. The British First Lady, Alix Hardinge, a great believer in economy, used to bring yards of cheap flannelette to get shirts and pyjamas made up for the ambassador at a cost of 3d a garment, and had to be watched, lynxlike, to see that she didn't actually use the Red Cross material.

Alix wasn't very good at French but she kept going. Once when I was with her at tea, together with the Spanish foreign minister, she plunged into politics and said charmingly: 'Vous, monsieur, vous êtres neutre, n'est-ce pas?' His reaction was to leap towards the ceiling, almost shouting: 'Non, *non*, NON, madame!'

There was an awful moment when the Duque d'Alva, practically the only *aliadofil* in Spanish high society (he was having an affair with the Duke of Westminster's current wife) threw open his vast and beautiful palace for a Red Cross money-raising reception. As doyenne, Alix was put in the front row in the huge crowded room, with me beside her. Round came a nobleman with a huge golden salver and held it before her. Crash, bang, resounded far and wide as a metal coin, worth I think about 5s, dropped in. I hastily covered it up with all the notes I could muster, giving much more than I had intended, but the point had been made.

*　　*　　*

Spanish society, and especially the army officers – although not the king – were strongly pro-German. This made Jos's periodic contacts with the Spanish army difficult. 'He was greeted by much clicking of heels and German speech. The latter he countered, much to the Spanish officers' surprise, by continuing the conversation in German rather better than their own. They would then attempt to break into their grammar-book English, but Jos would have none of that.'

As usual, the diplomatic community sorted itself out into groups or coteries, which cut across national lines. That which formed around Jos and Nellie, adopting the name of Club des Sales Bêtes, included the French counsellor, the French first secretary and the Romanian minister, M. Coetziano, a jovial man, although perturbed about whether his country would enter the war on the German or on the Allied side. He himself favoured the Allies.

He used to come a lot to our flat, and liked to describe how, if he mentioned our names to the German ambassadress, she would leave the room and go to bed, whereas if he talked of her to us, one of us would merely put a waste-paper-basket over his head. Later we liked to think that Club des Sales Bêtes diplomacy had helped to bring Romania into the war on the right side. I liked a remark he made to me: 'Your French is pretty bad, but nothing like as bad as your English.'

The long evening tea-parties bored Nellie sadly, and she had to give parties in return. Her flat was small, but opposite lay a walled garden belonging to an elderly *marchesa*. Nellie asked if she might borrow the garden for a tea-party now and then.

Certainly, the *marchesa* replied, I could have the full, and free, use of her garden, on one condition: that, when I went back to England, I would take her false hair in the diplomatic bag to be done over by André Hugo, a fashionable hairdresser in Sloane Street. I said 'of course', and the tea-parties I gave in her very pleasant garden were quite a success. In due course, when I went home, I escorted a bag with the noble hair cosily packed inside.

On reaching London, Nellie went to see Jos's chief at the War Office, who praised the thorough way in which the attaché had carried out his duties; never, said this authority, had a more meticulous incumbent of the post been known. Asked to find out the circulation of the main pro-German paper, he had given the figure of 999,999¾ copies. He was doing his own typing.

Summing up, Nellie later wrote: 'It may seem that we were frivolous in Madrid, but all our nonsense was just a barrage against gloom. It was an awful summer anyhow, and the Spanish press invariably made all our defeats and casualties seem even worse than they were, and I was glad to be gone.' She added, with a twinge of regret:

I sometimes wonder what happened to the 'tidy' dresses I had to have in Madrid. I was fond of them and it was the only time in my life when I felt dressed on equal terms with the females around me. I had three evening dresses: a very lush black velvet, a nice green (arum lily leaf shade) taffeta with cerise sash and, grandest of all, a lace dress made from yards and yards of beautiful Carrickmacross lace which had been a wedding-present and never used before. It was made, while draped around me, by a 'little' dressmaker who was a very large woman, Beerbohm Tree's sister, and with my aquamarine necklace it looked really good.

After Nellie left, Jos shared a flat with one of the partners in the firm of Williams & Humbert and learnt a lot about sherry. 'Also he was seduced by Alix, and then went to Biarritz where he had, he said, a most rewarding affair with a glamorous French lady. Also Phoebe was very devoted, so he did quite well. He stayed on as military attaché until 1918 and was taking a Senior Officer's course at Aldershot when the Armistice was declared.'

It was not until many years after his death that I heard of this romantic episode in Jos's life. I remembered then that once he had, very shyly, handed me a poem he had written called 'A Garden in Granada', lyrically extolling the famous Alhambra gardens; and that he had spoken of them with tenderness and nostalgia, and with a dreamy look in his eyes. He had found happiness in these gardens, if of a fleeting nature, walking there with – Phoebe perhaps? She was the wife of a fellow attaché. Some years later, when on one of his rare visits 'home', he took me to see her one afternoon at a house in Surrey. All was correct, they were good friends, enjoyed each

other's company and reminisced about Madrid. I do not think he
ever saw her again.

*　　*　　*

Leaving Jos to his diplomatic duties and his three graces, Nellie
joined forces again with Trudie Denman, who had formed and was
directing the Women's Land Army. Nellie was appointed travelling
inspector for the counties of Hampshire, Dorset, Surrey and the Isle
of Wight, with the task of organizing the billeting and training of
Land Army recruits, and generally supervising their welfare. She was
provided with a second-hand motor cycle, on which she negotiated
lanes and farm tracks, tumbling off now and then, and pushing the
machine through mud and puddles, over fords and into farmyards.
It broke down often, and she did almost as much pushing as riding.
Her headquarters were in Winchester and she lived in comfortless
digs that were no place for lace evening gowns.

One of the hostels in which some of the recruits were billeted was
an ancient manor house. Here the girls were well looked after, well
fed and should have been in clover, but they refused, in a body, to
remain. The house was haunted. Nellie found the ghosts to be unusual; they were dogs. The girls felt tails wagging against their legs,
and heard the pattering of canine feet. Nellie tried to persuade them
that they were lucky: ghostly dogs were better than no dogs at all,
and the animals were evidently happy, since they wagged their tails.
It was of no avail, and the hostel had to be closed.

*　　*　　*

The problem of what to do with me in the holidays was solved by
Nellie's sister Blanchie, who lived on a farm near Shaftesbury.
Cherry Orchard was almost as cold as Aldeburgh, and much wetter
but, by comparison, paradise. Farms in those days were proper
farms, not food-producing factories. No tractors then but big, shiny
horses with tufted heels, deliberate tread and brass pendants, now
adorning pubs, dangling over their wide foreheads. To ride atop the
loose, sweet-smelling meadow hay piled high on the swaying wagon,
and behind the broad-backed horses, was a summer pleasure so keen

that no child is likely to forget it. The search for eggs in dark corners of barns and disused mangers was another vanished pleasure; likewise the patting-up, with wooden Scotch 'hands', of yellow butter, and stamping it with moulds carrying the impression of a thistle, a rose or a sheaf of corn.

Few sisters can have been less alike than Blanchie and Nellie. My aunt could be excellent company and had a mordant wit, but she could fall into fits of gloom which might last for days and even weeks. One never knew what might set her off. She harboured resentment, that was the trouble: resentment against fortune's betrayal. A happy childhood, marriage to a handsome young officer, a gay and affluent start to married life (when she and Jim were living in Cheshire they kept, Nellie recalled, twenty-three hunters) had abruptly ended, without warning so far as she was concerned, in financial disaster and, for Jim, disgrace. He had left the army; the hunters and the gay life went for ever, and they had retreated to this small dairy farm in Dorset as tenants of Hughie's, without such comforts as electric light, a motor car or telephone, and to a large extent cut off by Blanchie's own pride from their 'county' neighbours.

This did not make for a happy atmosphere in the home. Blanchie solaced herself, in the family manner, with dogs. Her fox-terriers were everywhere, especially on the sofas and chairs, and not very clean. Fox-terriers are uncertain-tempered little animals, and at intervals came an outburst of snarls, barks and frantic yells as Blanchie, or anyone else nearby, attempted to quell the fight. A smell of boiling tripe, their staple food, permeated the house. My uncle was away at the war and Blanchie ran the farm, slogging round the fields and through the deep, deep mud of gateways in boots and leggings and a black serge skirt, with the aid of a ruddy-faced, stolid, slow but honest Dorset foreman called Perce.

There were three daughters of the house, two older and one slightly younger than myself. We quarrelled a good deal, but had our diversions, such as making up and acting plays to an audience of Blanchie, Perce, the cook-general and the terriers, and hunting with our uncle Hughie's pack, the South and West Wilts. The only pony on the strength was Buttercup, a fat and lazy animal who drew the dog-cart at a stately pace to Shaftesbury or to Gillingham Station. As only one of us could ride her at a time, we depended on the generosity of local farmers who very often lent us ponies of a fairly rough kind.

The kennels were at Motcombe and my uncle Hughie was a formidable figure of whom we were afraid. He was gruff, and gave a sort of grunt before each utterance, which was generally laconic, and we believed that he detested children. I doubt whether, in reality, he did. I think the fiction was started and kept going by his wife, my aunt Gladys, who constantly decried the war, the brutal behaviour of the Allies and the blood-sports of the Dorset squirearchy. In subtle ways, and perhaps not intentionally, Gladys built up in our minds the image of a monster who, if he did not actually devour small girls, growled at them and did not want them under foot. Certainly he was fierce in the hunting-field and swore at anyone who did the wrong thing, but that has always been the prerogative of the Master. Also he looked rather simian, with flared nostrils and a bony brow.

But sometimes, when on leave, and when there were enough children in the house – as there often were, for Gladys had a lot of nieces and nephews and was fond of children – he would organize a game of hide-and-seek called Fox. Two children were the quarry, one of whom was nearly always my cousin Puck, his only child, who was swift, bold and athletic, and knew every corner of the house. Motcombe was ideal for the purpose, being full of empty rooms, and cupboards, corners and flights of stairs; it was only partially occupied. The rest of us were hounds. He would cast us forward with appropriate cries; eventually the quarry would be sighted and a terrific hunt ensued, accompanied by the notes of his hunting-horn which echoed down dark corridors and through empty rooms. At such times he certainly did not appear allergic, or alarming, to children. But Gladys could not resist taunting and making fun of him before her sophisticated relations and friends. Then he would shut up like a clam and perhaps stump out of the room; the treatment soured him, and the marriage was not a happy one. He was, undoubtedly, a selfish man. Although comfortably placed with his eight thousand acres of Dorset* and the town of Shaftesbury thrown in, he gave, so far as I know, little, if any financial help to his brothers

---

* Two thousand of the ten thousand acres left by his father had already been sold; the rest were to follow.

and sisters, all of whom were having a struggle, not always through their own failings, to survive.

When Jos returned from Madrid in 1918, he and Nellie began to think of the future. They wanted to get back to East Africa as soon as possible once the war came to an end. In October, Nellie left the Land Army and enrolled in a one-year course in agriculture for servicemen and women at Cambridge. So, at last, belatedly, she did get to the University, if only for a short time. This concentrated course delighted her. For the first time she was able to get a glimpse into the scientific method, and into the laws governing the behaviour of the plants and animals that filled her life. She was in the biology laboratory dissecting a pigeon at eleven o'clock in the morning of 11 November 1918. Next to her was General Sir Hubert Gough. 'He had just said to me politely: "Please may I see your liver?", to which I had replied, "Certainly, if you'll show me your lungs", when all the sirens went off and Cambridge went mad. The war was over, and he never saw my liver, nor I his lungs.'

Chapter 6

In 1919, everyone was in the wrong place and wanted to get somewhere else quickly; transport was chaotic, and the Spanish 'flu epidemic made matters worse. Jos managed to get himself into a Union Castle liner over-full of others with the same idea. Nellie was left to complete her course at Cambridge, passing out with high marks and praise from the professors. Then she squeezed herself in to a small, slow vessel going via the Cape, taking among her luggage many packets of seeds, silkworm eggs to start a new industry, veterinary equipment, a sewing machine, a shaving-brush for Jos, and a windmill. This last was put together at Thika, but unfortunately the bore sunk to tap a great supply of underground water produced only a trickle, so while the sails revolved in fine style above, nothing came up from below.

Kitimuru was in a sorry state. The headman, Sammy, had done his best, nothing had been pilfered or destroyed, but nothing had gone forward either. The various bugs, beetles and mildews that delight to prey on coffee bushes had enjoyed a field day, and part of the plantation was in such a state that Jos, acting on experts' advice, which they subsequently contradicted, had cut the bushes down to the roots. Four years had to pass before they would regrow sufficiently to yield a good crop. Pipes had rusted, leaks been sprung, termites rampaged. A great deal needed to be done and there was no money; on the contrary, there was an overdraft. Optimism, however, was in the air, and extended to the banks. They were open-handed, at eight per cent. The Kitimuru overdraft was greatly increased and the work of restoration begun.

*   *   *

I was the third and last instalment of the family to go back to East Africa. It had been decided that I must stay on at Aldeburgh to be educated. This for me was an unwelcome decision. Many years before – I must have been about five – I remember being carried, at night, on the shoulders of a village policeman, through a hayfield; the smell of hay for years reminded me of this. I had formed the project of reaching a sea-port and stowing away in the hold of a ship bound for BEA, where I knew my parents to be. What the letters stood for, or where it was, I had no idea, but felt confident that the slices of bread and butter and cake I had been secreting for several days in a tin box hidden under the roots of a yew-tree in the garden would see me through for nourishment. I had enlisted as my companion my cousin Puck, my senior by two years. We crept out of the nursery after dark and made our way across several fields to a wood where Puck, who was less enthusiastic than I, announced that he was cold and wanted to go home. I was indigant, but cold also, and we decided to sleep in the wood. There, in due course, the policeman found us, and we were restored to the nursery with its agitated nanny.

By 1919 I was old enough to know that East Africa could not be reached like that, but I was resolved to reach it somehow none the less. It did not take great acumen to grasp the point that if I made a thorough nuisance of myself the school would be as anxious to be rid of me as I was to be rid of it. I already was a nuisance, I expect – argumentative, disobedient and erratic in my studies, having no ambition to master those I did not like. Moreover I was going through a craze for horse-racing, at a distance, of course, which died out young. I had entered into correspondence with a well-known trainer. Why he should have answered my letters I cannot imagine, but evidently he did, as these were intercepted and brought horror and dismay to the headmistress, an ample-bosomed lady whose mind was normally focused on higher things.

It was immediately clear that I was on the right lines. I redoubled my interest in horse-racing, widened my correspondence, interested a number of my fellows and even managed to start a book on the Derby, collecting pennies from my classmates and making up the odds – how, goodness knows; the mathematics of book-making are quite beyond me now, and I am sure must have been then.

Before the race was run, all was discovered, and I was removed to the sanatorium, to be isolated as a source of contamination. This suited me nicely. The sanatorium was on the edge of the town and surrounded by gorse-bushes and sand-dunes where I could wander more or less at will unlikely to spread the vice of gambling among the nightingales. Indoors, I read *Dracula*, a great deal more interesting than French verbs. In due course I found myself back at Cherry Orchard amid the fox-terriers, the smell of tripe and the mooing of cows, with a rather grumpy aunt, who felt she had enough of children in the holidays, let alone one on its own in the middle of the term.

Half the battle was won; I still had to get to Africa, and there were anxious moments when the possibilities of other schools were raised. But it was felt that, having been expelled from one, no other was likely to welcome me; anyway it would cost a lot less to maintain me at Thika once I got there. And so it was arranged.

There remained the question of education. This was solved, as everyone hoped, by the engagement of a governess, whose pay would be considerably less than the fees of a boarding-school. Nellie sent instructions to the effect that the governess must be young and active, fond of dogs, horses and poultry, adaptable, good-tempered, if possible a tennis-player, and that she did not want anyone with a moustache. My aunt Elsie paid for our passages, and off we went.

*   *   *

The second governess has been expunged from my memory as completely as the first. I travelled with her to Kenya, as BEA had just become, and cannot even remember her name. She proved to be a total disaster.

Her luggage consisted mainly of six pairs of double sheets [Nellie recorded], and she was prone to wander round our bachelor neighbours' houses at night, which terrified them. One day she sat on your bed and said, 'Which do you prefer, your mummy or your daddy? *I* prefer your daddy.' The end came when Jos found her reading a pornographic novel to her charge. With difficulty, we increased the overdraft by the cost of a first-class fare and she was bundled off, her double sheets unused.

Nellie decided to tackle my education herself, with the help of Jos for French and one of the bachelor neighbours for Latin. This neighbour, Jack Everard, had forgotten most of what he had learnt at school during four or five years in the army. But a Rugby football club had recently been started at Thika and he was a keen player. Our lesson periods soon turned into post-mortems on the Saturday match, illustrated by diagrams, and, I became a great deal more knowledgeable about rugger than about Latin grammar.

Nellie taught me history, with the aid of H. G. Wells's *Outline*, as well as other more off-beat subjects she happened to be reading about, such as a learned critique of the book of Elijah, and a history of the Rosicrucians. 'I am in despair about E's education,' Nellie wrote to a friend. 'Perhaps my view wouldn't be so prejudiced if the damned arithmetic book had answers, and if she could put two words of French together, which she can't.' I liked best drawing maps of imaginary countries and writing historical plays. Nellie had decided, goodness knows why, that I was to become an architect – perhaps because she would have liked to become one herself. As the only architecture one could look at locally took the form of mud huts, Indian *dukas*, bungalows on stilts and hideous labour lines for railway workers put up by the Public Works Department, there could hardly have been a less promising subject to choose; coffee-table books with lovely photographs, which might have kindled an interest, were at that date unknown. Lessons took place in the grass hut to the gentle accompaniment of insects rustling in the roof, dachshunds scratching in the sunshine on the veranda, melodious African voices calling in the distance, and the chattering of yellow weaver-birds.

My education, such as it was, formed only one of many claims on Nellie's time. The coffee factory was one. Coffee cherries on the bough must go through several processes before they emerge as dry, green beans ready for roasting. The machinery involved was, I expect, quite simple, but it did not seem so, and offered a temptation, which Jos could not resist, to improve upon it. 'Jos is the complete coffee-king, surrounded by little engines, but still finds time to invent,' Nellie wrote to Jos's brother Robin. 'The complete Grant factory, with entirely revolutionary processes, won't be ready for a year or two, but he is quite happy meanwhile discovering more, and ever more, criminal failings in the so-called coffee machinery of the present day.' I gave some examples. 'The factory has been going, or rather stopping, for some time now. Something went wrong every single day. The huller collapsed and all the coffee came out, instead of as berries, as one solid black cake, completely roasted. It smelt lovely.'

We've been running the mechanical dryer all day and most of the night [Nellie reported]. This means alternate shifts and is horrible work, as one gets so sleepy. We have a woolly so-called *fundi*, who's become a fairly good engine-boy, and can be left for short periods during the day, but after 5.30 pm either Jos or I have to be here without budging. Jos has plugged up the safety-valve on the boiler, so the needle showing the pressure goes careering round the dial far beyond the safety mark, which is most unnerving. We have largely given up the very late runs, it was too much. Before that, Jos took on until midnight, and I took on from then, till I came to a suitable spot in my knitting when I would put the engine to bed and close down. Jos would then have to spend the next day drying the coffee I had taken out of the dryer, as perfectly dry, at about 3 am. This was not popular ... if it wasn't for the overdraft and bill for the factory, we should be doing quite comfortably. As it is, the colossal wage and paraffin bills during picking leave us with less cash than ever.

*   *   *

I was at this time, I regret to say, very bloodthirsty. With a .22 rifle I shot, or shot at, small buck that lay up like hares in the long grass and scrub; at wild pig occasionally; once, I fear, at a cheetah that had strayed up from the plains. Also I slew a lot of pigeons, some wild duck, and Egyptian geese when rain flooded the vleis. No one, least of all myself, felt any qualms about this, nor did it occur to us that the supply of wild animals to shoot at would ever dwindle. We were, of course, in the main, shooting for the pot, and could have advanced the well-worn argument that if we did not kill the animals, someone else would. Nellie herself, by this time, had given up shooting altogether, and for good, and Jos never really cared for it.

It is strange, on reflection, how we drew a line between creatures of the wild, meat fit only to be slain, and tame ones, on whom we lavished almost inexhaustible love and care. Now and again a wild animal might pass over from one category to the other and qualify for the love and care given to dogs, cats and ponies. Most households had, at one time or another, a pet duiker, gazelle or even lion. Reared on bottles, they grew up, when they did, to be adorable, although the antelopes became a nuisance in gardens, and most of them came

69

to a sad end, wandering off to be killed by Africans or leopards, snared, speared, or just dying. I myself had a pet duiker called Twinkle whom I loved, but I was always afraid that one day she would disappear, and one day she did; Njombo said that she had gone to join a mate, and I could only hope that this was true; but the life of a small antelope I knew to be short and precarious.

Ponies were an anxiety because of horse-sickness. No vaccine or drug then existed to prevent or cure the disease. We took the ponies' temperatures every morning and, at the least sign of a rise, out came *debbis* and sponges for the cold-water treatment, the only treatment there was. This had been introduced to combat malaria among his human patients by Dr Burkitt, famous throughout the colony for his ruthless, eccentric and humane professional behaviour. The theory of his treatment was simple. The microbe causing fever thrives only when the patient's temperate is high. Lower his temperature, and the microbes cease to multiply. This, of course, is treatment of the symptom, not of the disease, but it worked. All over the country, in Dr Burkitt's day, naked people with chattering teeth were being sponged down in cold water by relays of helpers night and day; babies were being slung in hammocks in draughty places and turning blue with cold; and ponies were shivering in mud-wallows under trees with water constantly dripping over them.

We had a tough little white Somali pony whom we thought must certainly be 'salted', that is, recovered from the disease. He was called Moyale after the place on the Abyssinian frontier whence he came, walking right across those northern deserts where you had to be tough, man or beast, to survive. I thought sometimes, when I rode him, of a story told me by a man who had served in those deserts with the KAR. He had come upon a group of human skeletons around the ashes of a fire, their trade goods beside them; their camels must have made off or been captured, leaving them in the wilderness to die of thirst. If Moyale had come safely through conditions like those, I thought, surely horse-sickness could not defeat him. But one day Moyale's temperature soared, he stood shivering under a tree for three days and then lay down and died.

Next, my own pony got the disease. He was called M'zee, which means 'old' in Swahili, and old he was, but very game and wise, a shiny chestnut; he would shake his head knowingly when I spoke to him and, when introduced to the kind of polo we played, proved nimble and clever. He was sponged for nearly a week, his eyes sinking deeper and deeper into their sockets, his bones jutting out, every rib showing. To make matters worse, Nellie got a severe bout of malaria at the same time; her temperature soared as high or higher than M'zee's, and there was consternation indoors and out. Nellie refused to be sponged, and recovered; and so, at last, did M'zee, though it was some time before his coat shone again. A fortnight later our third and best pony got the infection and died. Two out of three was a heavy loss, as well as a personal sadness.

*　　*　　*

'Colonial hospitality' had become a byword, a useful one for visitors from Britain, since it entitled them to suppose that they would be welcome anywhere and could stay as long as they liked. Some, obviously, were more welcome than others, and some overstayed their welcome, since their entertainment cost money and interfered with the work of the farm.

One guest who never overstayed her welcome was Cockie Birkbeck, who had come to Kenya with her husband Ben under the post-war Soldier Settlement Scheme. She shared with Nellie a great love of jokes and fun, and had the gift of turning the most commonplace statement into a funny remark. If she was merely describing, say, a visit to a hairdresser, everyone would be in fits of laughter. Parties seemed to spring up spontaneously wherever Cockie was. She and Nellie had met at a New Year's Eve dance at Muthaiga Club. In the room in which the dance was held, a clock was fixed high up on the wall. Someone put a ten-rupee note on top of the clock and invited the two ladies to race for the prize. The room was cleared, bets were laid and Nellie and Cockie came under starter's orders. Cockie was the younger by seven years (Nellie was by then thirty-five) but her rival was the tougher. They dashed across the room, piled chair on chair and grabbed the bank-note simultaneously. It tore in two.

Some of our guests were humble, occasionally some were grand. At Makuyu, Mervyn Ridley's fox-hounds had been revived, and polo, of a sort, was played at weekends, on ponies of many sizes

71

and shapes. Now and again there were tournaments, and players would be billeted on us at Kitimuru. Quite a stir was caused by the arrival of Lord and Lady Francis Scott, accompanied by Lady Cromer. The Scotts were building a two-storeyed mansion, a thing hitherto unknown among settlers, in a district called Rongai.

They were really very nice indeed, though they spent most of their time in bed [I reported to my uncle Robin]. The ladies of the party didn't get up till well after twelve. In the afternoons they had to go and watch the polo, but I believe when they were in Nairobi they went to bed again all the afternoon and most of the evening too.

They brought a brace of maids, which impressed us more than words can describe. When Lady Francis had finished her bath, the maid had to come and pull up the plug. Their arrival was most prolonged. First of all one maid arrived with a car full of luggage. Then another car, with more luggage and another maid, started from Thika, but the back axle broke under the load, so we had to fetch them in the Chevrolet. [We had just acquired this car, a cumbrous second-hand box-body; it was known, following a bad pun of Jos's, as the goat-in-milk.] Eventually the party themselves arrived in another huge car, the Governor's Cadillac, also full of luggage. It was most exciting. The Scott party's one word was 'wo-o-o-nderful', very prolonged. Everything was wonderful (prolonged), down to the boys spitting over the wall just underneath Lady Cromer's bedroom window, which was 'so much nicer than the cockney voices one hears at home'. They were painfully polite.

*   *   *

Now and again, Jos and Nellie became guests in their turn. Sometime in 1922 all three of us rode up through the forest and over the flank of the Kinangop peak in the Aberdare Mountains, and down into the Rift Valley on the other side. We were heading for Njoro, an embryonic township on the railway, and lying at the foot of the Mau Escarpment which formed the opposite wall of the great valley. There Trevor Sheen, Jos's former colleague in the Railway Troop, had settled to 'grow wheat and overdrafts' as he put it. He had sent word of a great opportunity to buy 'marvellous land going for a song' (there was always land like that somewhere), so we were going to have a look.

On our first night we camped on the forest's edge, and next day followed elephant tracks, first through dense undergrowth and then through a belt of bamboos that lay between the cedar forest and the moorlands on the summit. Long, slender bamboo trunks arched muddy paths like the vaulting of a Gothic cathedral, and the filtered sunlight had an eerie greenish tinge. Sometimes the crashing of elephants – surely the noisiest feeders in the world – came to our ears, making the ponies nervous, but though we were close enough to hear their 'tummy-rumbles', we did not see them – nor they us, fortunately. Shortly before dusk we emerged on the other side, crossed a stretch of tufty moorland and, as darkness fell, walked into a barbed-wire fence, somewhat optimistically hailed as civilization. The startled owners of this remote ranch provided us, our ponies and our syce with food and shelter for the night. It was cold at that altitude, eight to nine thousand feet, and we were glad of a roaring cedar-log fire to sit by in pyjamas and dressing-gowns after our meal. This consisted of steaks from one of our host's young steers that, he told us, had been killed the night before by a leopard.

Next day we rode down into the Rift Valley, as hot as the forest had been cold, and spent a night with Lord Delamere's manager at his ranch, Soysambu. Bobby Roberts, a jovial and hospitable man, was following the Delamere custom of inviting in, after the evening meal, as many of his Masai herdsmen as wished to come. They stacked their spears on the veranda and sat on the floor in their short ochre-dyed cloaks, their greased and plaited ringlets hanging down, their mutton-fat-anointed skins shining like copper in the lamplight, and talked of their beloved cattle, the warp and weft of their lives. Not long after our visit, Bobby Roberts met with a tragic end. One of those swift and sudden grass fires that, in the dry weather, sweep across the plains trapped his wife and sister-in-law. He went to their rescue and saved the sister-in-law, but he and his wife were burnt to death.

After five days' riding we reached Njoro, stayed with Trevor Sheen and were taken by the owner of the marvellous land on a tour of inspection.

Algy Cartwright led us at full gallop over it, up hill and down dale. Large pig-holes gaped, and hidden logs had to be leapt over. There was no one living on the thousand acres he wanted to sell. Algy provided the ponies, which mercifully were used to his ways. In among the trees was a tiny little square, wooden bungalow, full to the brim with maize illegally grown by Tom Petrie's illegal squatters. The Njoro river formed the upper boundary of the land. Forest came down to the river bank and was full of game, buffalo and waterbuck and bushbuck, and of course leopards; there were Colobus monkeys, and masses of hyraxes which screeched all night, so that when I got the farm I called it Gikammeh, the Kikuyu name for them.

It was all quite different from Thika: the enormous view over the sun-drenched valley to mountains beyond; the fat and multi-coloured clouds that threw shadows over plain and hill; the tall cedars bearded with grey lichen; the emptiness, the sense of space and freedom. Nellie fell in love with it at once.

During her service in the Land Army, she had suggested to Trudie that an investment in East African property ('marvellous land going for a song') might be of interest to her. Now Nellie wrote and told her friend of this opportunity. The price was only £5 an acre. Trudie immediately bought the thousand acres, and presented it to Nellie. For the next forty-three years it was to be her challenge, her centre, and her home.

Chapter 7

The land was Nellie's; but where was the money to turn it into a farm? Kitimuru's overdraft now stood at around £10,000. Coffee was flowing from it to the London auctions in satisfactory quantities, but interest on the overdraft swallowed all the profit, and it would take a lifetime, at least, to pay back £10,000. Kitimuru must be sold.

For the next year or so our lives were confused. Nellie departed for Njoro, Jos stayed on at Kitimuru to run the coffee plantation and I was billeted on a kindly Cape Dutch family in Nairobi in order to attend the Government European School, which was accommodated in dilapidated wooden sheds, roofed with corrugated iron and ravaged by termites, in a part of the capital known as The Hill. On Saturdays I went by train to find M'zee waiting for me at Thika station, to take me either to Kitimuru or, with Jos, to the weekend hunt and polo at Makuyu.

Nellie went by train to Njoro.

I duly arrived at the station with camp equipment, two Siamese cats and three dachshunds, Primrose, Foxglove and Hollyhock. (Primrose was taken by a leopard from a neighbour's veranda when I left her there in 1928; Foxglove disappeared out hunting in Tanganyika in the same year; and Hollyhock was killed by Kavirondo labour hunting in a wattle plantation.) To my amazement, also there to meet me were six of our Kikuyu labour force. Without saying a word, they had gone ahead, so as to be first on the spot to ask for *shambas* and grazing for their goats on the new farm. Among them was dear old Njombo, whom I quickly made *neapara* (headman); there was also a former house-boy, so domestic staff arranged itself.

My new neighbour Tom Petrie had very kindly sent a small ox-cart to meet me. About half a mile from the station ran the Njoro river, still unbridged, but fordable except in the rains. The ox-cart crossed it – the dogs and I were walking – but slipped backwards on the steep bank and capsized into the river, throwing everything out. My first thought was for the Siamese cats in their cage, the second for a case of gin and a case of French vermouth on board. Thank goodness, all three were safe.

Eventually everything arrived at the 'house'. Tom Petrie had cleared the maize out of one room for me to settle into; maize still occupied the rest. The room had no door, no glazed window, no floor-boards and no chimney; and it was very, very cold. So it remained till I got hold of some Indian *fundis* who quickly built a chimney; there was plenty of wood all round to burn. The two ponies arrived by road, so I was all right for transport.

After a few days, I was measuring the sitting-room for floor-boards when something happened to my back – a slipped disc, perhaps. Suddenly I found I couldn't get up from from the floor. Somehow or other, by degrees, I got myself into a chair – the only one – where I spent the night. Next morning, I had a pony brought to the door and was heaved on to it, rather painfully, and I rode the two or three miles along a forest track to my nearest European neighbours apart from Tom. These were the Lindstrom family. It was rather an odd introduction to dear Ingrid, who at once massaged my back, and gradually mobility was restored.

Ingrid remembers an earlier meeting, that had slipped Nellie's memory. The Lindstrom family had emigrated from Sweden, impulsively, in 1920, with a clutch of children ranging in age from nine to three. Gillis Lindstrom had been an officer in the Swedish cavalry. Four years of wartime mobilization without action had made him restless, and when it was over he went to East Africa to seek adventure. Like others, he fell in love with the country and bought, or booked, about a thousand acres at Njoro, on which he intended to grow flax. Everyone, at that time, was going to make a fortune out of flax. Then, after sending instructions to Ingrid to sell everything in Sweden and follow with the family, he went on a long hunting expedition with his friend Bror von Blixen.

When he got back from safari, the flax boom had collapsed. He cabled to Ingrid telling her not to come after all. She was by then in Paris with four children and a governess, waiting to join a ship at Marseilles. Money had begun to run out and they had moved to a cheaper hotel, omitting to leave the new address. So the second cable never reached her. In due course they all arrived at Mombasa, and the die was cast. 'Have you any money?' was Gillis's first question. 'No, it is finished', Ingrid said. The family spoke little English, Gillis was often away, Ingrid had no transport, and the eyes of the governess were permanently red from weeping. One Sunday, Ingrid decided to pay a call on Tom Petrie, her nearest neighbour, about three miles away. She dressed in her best, an ankle-length skirt, embroidered blouse and big straw hat. The small girls were attired in frilly white dresses and Nils, the boy, in a white suit, and all wore white pith helmets bought at Simon Artz. In single file, in the hot mid-day sun, they followed a game-path winding through bush from which at any moment a herd of buffaloes might emerge.

Unexpectedly, a car came lurching down a track that led to Njoro. In it were Nellie and Trevor Sheen. 'They thought they were seeing visions', Ingrid recalled. A few words were exchanged, and the Lindstrom family marched on to Tom Petrie's dilapidated little bungalow. He was not at home, and they marched back again.

*   *   *

As at Thika, the first step at Njoro was to prepare the land for the plough.

The clearing of the land – oh the clearing! The most colossal stumps of cedar and olive had to be hauled out before the plough could go in. My ploughs kept on hitting hidden stumps for years. Goodness knows what it cost to get the first hundred acres cleared. I had to get in extra labour, and at one stage had a gang of fifty from Kisii. They were at a very primitive stage, never having ventured before from home, and the Kikuyu hated them.

After a few days, they fled in a body back to their homes. The DC sent them back to me to complete their three-months' contract, but they were a very tricky labour force, and I was terrified that there would be a show-down with the Kikuyu, whom they greatly outnumbered. If they had turned nasty they could have carved up the Kikuyu in a most unpleasant way.

Gradually the house was enlarged a little, and given windows and doors. A track was made to the river to bring up water in a cart. A kitchen was built: what was cooked therein it is hard to say. 'I must have eaten something', Nellie agreed, but she couldn't think what. There was plenty of game on the farm but Nellie left the animals alone. It was lonely on the forest's edge. Hyraxes shrieked all round the house all night, an eerie, grating sound, and often she heard leopards calling in the forest. Her three dachshunds were her constant companions. Dogs are a favourite food of leopards, and when the dachshunds rushed out barking at night – she slept with her bedroom door ajar to allow them to come and go – she was afraid for their safety. She did not seem afraid for her own.

77

On Sundays, there was polo at Njoro where a club had been started, and contact could be made with other farmers round about. At times, even this was impossible. 'I remember my hands were both in bandages for weeks and weeks with veld sores: why did we have them? Some mineral deficiency?' I remember them too. They came for no discernible reason, grew larger and larger, suppurated, and hurt; the only palliative – scarcely a cure – was to paint them with Stockholm tar. Africans came continually for this rough-and-ready treatment. Had veld sores been the trouble with Job? Why did they come and why, eventually, did the whole affliction disappear?

At last Kitimuru was sold. It was sad when the house, of which we had all been rather proud, had to be stripped and much of the furniture disposed of. Some ten years later Nellie revisited Kitimuru and reported an unexpected change.

The poor little house is now tortured by a jostling crowd of wild beasts' heads. There is a particularly fine specimen of a hyena – not even a laughing one – over the dining-room door, and when, overcome by sentiment, I staggered to the sideboard to accept a gimlet, I found I almost had to drink in a sitting position, owing to the interference of a greater kudu.

Like Nellie, I loved Njoro from the first. There was a freshness in the air, an exhilarating sparkle in the sunlight. To wake each morning to regard that great, spreading view across the Rift, with the turquoise gleam of Lake Nakuru far below, was a delight daily renewed. Or almost daily; sometimes it rained, of course, there were fogs and hailstorms, and it could be very cold. After dark we had hot baths, changed into pyjamas and dressing-gowns and sat round a blazing fire of cedar logs, nibbling salted peanuts and sipping short drinks. The Kikuyu were delighted with so much fertile land for nothing; a small village of round thatched huts soon appeared, and the women hoeing in the *shambas* looked happy and fat.

The time came when I had to leave for England to complete such education as I had. To no one's surprise, I failed to pass the Cambridge entrance examination, falling at the hurdle of Latin. Our rugger-playing Thika neighbour had never really tried to recapture his memories of the language and pass them on to me. In Nairobi my teacher, while quite a good scholar, was distracted by his courtship of the matron, which took up a lot of his time. Only one other pupil was sitting for the examination, so we formed a class of two; there could hardly have been a better pupil/teacher ratio, but as against that, two were unlikely to get up to serious mischief if left alone for long periods in favour of more interesting ploys. This suited us as well as him, so we made no complaint. Nellie, I fear, was disappointed; like other parents, she would have liked her child to fulfil ambitions she had been obliged to lay aside herself. But universities were not as fussy then as they have since become, and a place was found for me at Reading, which was to achieve full University status in the following year.

So there had to be a parting, sad like all farewells. The night before I left Njoro, there was a fancy-dress dance at the club. We all went, and enjoyed a merry evening with sing-songs and champagne. Dawn was not far off when we got back to the farm. I changed and took my rifle (which I am glad to say was not used) and followed a favourite forest path beside the river bank which, in a mile or so, reached an open glade. The sun came up and threw long golden shafts between the tree-trunks across grasses silvered with dewdrops caught on innumerable tiny cobwebs. All was astir. A bushbuck doe and her fawn picked their way across the far end of the glade; they had not seen me, but some whiff came on the air; she raised her head, sniffed, and in an instant, with a short, sharp bark, was gone, her fawn beside her. A tree-top shook with a commotion; monkeys no doubt. The soft note of a rainbird dropped through the air, like water from a bottle, in a descending cadence: the last time that I should hear it for I knew not how long. I thought, perhaps, as long as three years. It was to be nearly eight before I saw the forest glades again.

*　　*　　*

The township of Njoro, consisting of about a dozen *dukas*, stood at the bottom of an escarpment which blended into a wide plain that formed the floor of the Rift Valley. This valley was almost treeless and might have been made for the plough, but it had no water, therefore no human habitations. Lord Delamere, who owned much of this land, had a pipeline laid from springs on the escarpment above. Then he had the plain surveyed into five-hundred-acre sections, planted on each a patch of quick-growing black wattle for firewood, installed water tanks, and leased them all on very easy terms.

Nellie managed to secure a three-year lease of two adjoining blocks. She hoped to make enough profit from maize in those three years to pay for the development of Gikammeh, which was costing much more than she had reckoned owing to the expense of clearing the land. Also she planned to feed some of her maize to pigs. Her pig-sties went up first, next her simple dwelling, which became known as Piggery Nook.

It was in the middle of a wattle patch and was shady and cosy. Quite a lot of neighbours all round. Two were from the navy, and as co-midshipmen had been among the very few survivors when HMS *Victoria* was rammed and sunk during naval manœuvres. Odd that they should find themselves next to each other at Njoro! One of them used to watch me ride out at seven o'clock each morning and nip over to help himself to my whisky before I got back.

Jos, meanwhile, was in Tanganyika. There had been rumours of a new railway to be built to open up that country's 'southern highlands' and link them with Dar-es-Salaam. Here lay riches, everybody said; untapped fertility, virgin land, lots of rivers, a healthy climate: another Kenya, in fact. True, there were no roads, no telegraph, no doctors, no supplies, but all that would come, and now was the time to get in on the ground floor. The prospect was irresistible.

So we went – a cavalcade of ten of us in a procession of battered old cars and one lorry. We camped as we went, by the roadside, and after a week's fairly hard going arrived at a very primitive rest-house at Iringa. Jos and I went on to stay with my cousin Mick Billinge and her husband about thirty miles farther south. They knew the ropes, having come up from Rhodesia some years before.

We bought a bit of Mick's land, suitable, they said, for tobacco, which had a house of sorts, and leased another five thousand acres, very cheaply, from the Government. I leased a waterfall miles away, as I thought I could make a go of grinding wheat when people started to grow it. Also it was a beautiful waterfall. The farm was called Saa Mbusi, the hour of the goat – goat o'clock. I got a lift back in a lorry, but Jos stayed on and started to plant tobacco. Unfortunately he went all out for the Turkish variety, which fetches better prices but isn't so hardy. The whole of his first crop was destroyed by frost.

Jos suffered as well as the tobacco. 'Here I am with a leaky roof, no doors or windows, no beds, chairs are petrol-cans with a petrol-case table – quite all right in the dry season but rather horrid in the rains. The mails are a bit uncertain as the railway is two hundred miles away and the roads often impassable for weeks at a time.' Jos was by then in his mid-fifties.

Nellie, at Piggery Nook, had turned into a contractor. New farmers on the pipeline were short of equipment and looked round for help in ploughing their land. She had by then built up several teams of well-trained oxen with an experienced driver in charge, and acquired some three-furrow ploughs. She went into partnership with two friends.

Max put up most of the capital, Pelham-Burn supervised the actual work and I supplied most of the tackle and did the accounts. We engaged a Dutch boy as team supervisor, we had my excellent Kavirondo driver, and everything went well. It was a lovely sight to see ten teams, each of sixteen oxen beautifully driven, in action on the level pipeline land where the going was easy. But later, when we took on jobs in Sabukia on rough land, things weren't so good, and we lost several oxen, some through falling into hidden game-pits, some through disease.

All the same, we broke 7,000 acres in one year, harrowed it, and in some cases cross-ploughed, all with oxen. But tractors were beginning to come in by then (1928–9) and I acquired two second-hand Holts. Afterwards I sent one down to Tanganyika driven all the way by that marvellous head driver Amupala to help out with the tobacco project. Amupala stayed down there, and I was glad to hear made a packet and had lots of wives. We wound up the 'MPG Syndicate' the year Max died. We remained friends with all our clients *and* got paid. But, alas, nearly all my share of the profit went into Tanganyika and never came back.

At Piggery Nook the maize thrived, but then came disaster. 'I got almost the whole of the two farms, nearly a thousand acres, planted up with maize. It grew splendidly, and in six months was in cob and very promising. Then along came a hailstorm, and I sat shivering in the car at one edge of the field watching the destruction of the whole crop. But we tried again.' 'We tried again' more or less sums up Nellie's life in Africa.

*   *   *

Farther west along the forest boundary from Gikammeh was a lovely farm, or ranch, called Larmudiac, large even by African standards, belonging to a Welsh couple called Harries. He was known as Black Harries because of his big black beard. Their life-style was eccentric.

They lived like the pigs they grew, only didn't house themselves as well as they did the pigs. But inside an awful house – if you were bold enough to go to lunch there – you found an enormous, genuine refectory table, about sixteen really good Chippendale chairs, Black Harries carving a colossal hunk of meat at one end of the table and Ma Harries dismembering innumerable fowls at the other.

Black Harries was immensely strong, and once pulled a wounded leopard backwards by the tail out of a bush, saying: 'It's a cat, so it will pull away from me.' Then he finished it off by a blow on the head. One day, I was having trouble putting some of my young stock through the cattle dip. Harries happened to come by: he picked up a three-quarters grown steer which had got back to front in the dip, lifted it right off its legs, swung it round to face the right way and pushed it into the dip.

The savagery they lived in! Such a mixture. Fierce dogs biting guests on arrival, the lovely Chippendale chairs, and dirt everywhere. Worse was to come when they moved from Larmudiac to another vast holding in Solai. You walked up to the house, or hut, ankle deep in animal bones. When you sat down to a meal, you had to push Muscovy ducks off the Chippendale chairs. A hatch was opened between kitchen and living-room and an indescribable, utterly horrible stench belched forth, followed by the food. The Harries' bedroom, a large rondavel, was shared between the marital bed and a large, probably 500-egg, incubator. The roof above was lined with a tarpaulin to keep the incubator, not the Harrieses, dry.

By contrast there was Deloraine, the Francis Scotts' residence; as civilized as the Harries *ménage* was savage. From the wide veranda you looked over smooth, sprinkler-watered lawns with great clumps of bougainvillaeas and flowering shrubs. The rooms were high-ceilinged, spacious and cool, with polished hardwood floors. The imported furniture was beautiful and cared-for; the long mahogany dining-table shone like a mirror and was set with family silver and crystal cut glass. Lord Francis limped from a war wound in the foot that never healed and always pained him, giving rise sometimes to fits of irritability too transient to detract from his great charm and courtesy. His laughter, his perfect manners and the sparkle in his pale blue eyes was the impression that remained. Eileen Scott, daughter of a former Viceroy of India, reclined among velvet cushions surrounded by books and small dogs, exclaiming 'Oh, François! François!' in mild protest if some remark of his disturbed her. The servants, in spotless white *kanzus* with crimson sashes glided silently about, served the excellent courses correctly, and never joined in the conversation, as Nellie's quite often did.

Their transport was not up to the standard of their housing. In early years they had a T-model Ford, whose driver had to keep his foot pressed hard down on the clutch pedal to hold the car in bottom gear. The track leading to Gikammeh was steep, winding and, in the rains, skiddy, and on one occasion Francis ran into a bank and overturned the car. Everyone was thrown out on to the bank, luckily unhurt. Another peculiarity of the T-model was that if you were obliged, as you often were, to clean the carburettor, you had to lie on your back underneath the vehicle. Francis took the opportunity to clean the carburettor while the car, for once, was on its back and he was on his feet, while Eileen sat on the bank, surrounded by cushions and dogs saying 'Oh, François! François!'

The Lindstroms at Sergoita were Nellie's closest friends. Because, no doubt, of their kind-heartedness, cheerful spirits and easy-going ways, they became a magnet for African squatter families who soon clustered round them in a feudal sort of way. They called Gillis *Bwana Samaki*, meaning fish, detecting, in his pensive demeanour and slightly protuberant eyes, a piscine expression. So Fish he became to all his friends.

Quite a lot of Scandinavians settled in Kenya and most of them, it seemed, were related to the Lindstroms. Birthdays were frequent and each one called for a party, when varied and delicious Scandinavian dishes appeared. Now and again, relatives from Sweden arrived to stay. One such, Nellie thought, talked rather strangely. 'I couldn't quite understand your cousin', she said to Ingrid when the guest had gone. 'She seemed to talk a lot about being on the rack; you surely don't have tortures in Sweden?' Ingrid gave her wide, face-crinkling, beaming smile. 'She has a great imagination; just now she thinks she is a suitcase, making a journey round the world.'

A frequent visitor to Sergoita was the Baron von Blixen-Finecke, well known both as a white hunter and as the husband of Karen, or Tania, whose fame as a writer, under her maiden name Isak Dinesen, was later to spread throughout the world. Blix was known also for his charms as a philanderer, and for his shaky finances. On safari, he chased lions and sometimes ladies, but in between his creditors chased him. Sergoita was his favourite hide-out. Its farm track wound down a long hill, steep in places, and approaching cars were often out of sight when zig-zagging up to the house. A creditor might therefore take the Baron unawares and serve a writ. This situation, Fish decided, must be remedied. Mobilizing his plough-teams, he drove a track straight down the hill, eliminating bends. Approaching vehicles could then be seen scrambling up in good time for Blix to take refuge in the forest behind the house. In the rains, the track became a river which swept soil down to form a quagmire at the bottom. Then Blix was even safer; his creditors could not only be seen but could be seen to be stuck. The same, of course, applied to other visitors and to the Lindstroms themselves if they wished to leave their farm, and they were often cut off from the outside world for days, sometimes for weeks, at a time.

*   *   *

The railway that was to open up Tanganyika's southern highlands proved stillborn. (Nearly half a century was to pass before one was built, by the Chinese.) Saa Mbusi clearly had no future. Jos sadly abandoned it, and Nellie her waterfall, all the capital invested lost and gone. Piggery Nook, when the lease expired, closed down too, and Nellie returned to Gikammeh, no richer for all the hard work and successful development of the pipeline farms. She was cheered up by a visit from Trudie Denman, described by Evelyn Waugh, who was in East Africa gathering material for his travel book *Remote People*, as 'a prominent feminist devoted to the fomentation of birth control and regional cookery in rural England' (untrue, but perhaps his way of indicating that she was a founder of the Women's Institutes.) Jos and Nellie, Trudie, her daughter Judy and Evelyn Waugh made a brief foray together into Uganda. Evelyn was young then and often very funny; he had not yet become the crusty, eartrumpeted character of later days.

The next few years, the early thirties, were sad and grim. Three devils launched an offensive against the country: drought, locusts and the collapse of world prices. This was the period in history when coffee was used to stoke locomotives on Brazilian railways. In Kenya, the price of maize to farmers fell to two shillings (ten pence) for a two-hundred-pound bag, considerably less than the price of a gallon of petrol, and farmers sometimes harnessed oxen to pull their cars. Jos and Nellie's ancient Ford was converted to run on paraffin; the engine spluttered and stopped more often than it ran; journeys were frequently completed on foot and oxen sent to retrieve the car for yet another cleaning of plugs and carburettor. All three ponies had been sold to raise cash, so polo ceased, also Sunday morning rides up into the forest, and most other pleasures.

The reason given for the collapse of world prices was over-production. There was said to be too much of everything, and markets were choked. Was there anything, Nellie wondered, that was *not* over-produced? She cast round for possibilities. In South Africa, she read, almonds were successfully grown; Kenya imported almonds; surely this was a gap that might be filled?

When planning a new project, Nellie always made a thorough study first of all available literature on the topic; she was a dedicated reader of pamphlets, reports and scientific papers. Several varieties of almond tree, she learned, must (as with apples) be planted together to ensure cross-pollination. After correspondence with growers and research stations in South Africa, a selection of the right kinds of young almond tree arrived and were planted in the right order.

They thrived – in fact, too well. Njoro's fertile soil and winterless climate stimulated them to go on growing instead of stopping, as they should have done, for a rest. They observed no dormant season. And so they flowered as the spirit moved them, now one tree, now another, instead of all together. There was no cross-fertilization, or very little; and instead of tons of almonds, Nellie harvested only a few hundredweight.

At about this time, she was appointed to a Government committee to consider how best to tidy up the squatter labour situation, which had got out of hand. (The committee, Nellie wrote, 'consists of the Hon. Attorney General, the Hon. Acting Chief Native Commissioner, the Hon. Canon Burns, the Hon. Hugh Welby, the Hon. Mrs Grant and plan F. O'B. Wilson, H. Clay and Kenneth Archer'.) It met in Nairobi, and the expenses of the journey were paid. The cost of fuel had put visits to Nairobi out of court until then. Now she set off with her almond samples in a shopping bag and, in the lunch hour, hawked them round to Nairobi's grocers and confectioners. (There were three.) They reported that her almonds were of the highest quality, and she returned excited by their undertaking to buy all she could grow.

Determined to subdue the wayward trees, she pruned them to the roots. Rain brought a splendid flowering, all together.

Now we're off, I said. The little birds had other ideas. They came at dawn and attacked in millions. I put on relays of *totos* as bird-scarers. That worked all right until I got a tummy bug and some kind of fever and had to stay in bed for nearly a week. So, it seemed, did the bird-scarers, and nearly all the buds were stripped off the trees.

She tried again. There was another flowering, and the birds were more or less kept at bay. Then, one afternoon, there came a hailstorm which proved even more destructive than the birds. She persevered for three or four years, and then uprooted the trees.

This experiment failed; others succeeded. Nellie was not the first Kenya grower of pyrethrum, whose flowers are used to make an insecticide, but was probably among the first half-dozen. By 1933, she had ten acres planted out. Drought was the snag: no rain, no flowers. In the early thirties the rains failed more often than not, and farmers watched their crops wither, their grass turn to straw and from straw to powder, their animals become walking skeletons. Hot, dry winds seemed to suck sap from the trees and marrow from the bones; grass fires raged, dust-devils raced in a macabre ballet across the plains and tempers were stretched as taut as strained wires. At such times, hope alone kept farmers going. Tomorrow, rain would fall.

Chapter 8

It was, I am afraid, a disappointment to my parents that I did not return to Kenya on completing three years at the university (one of them at Cornell in the USA). At twenty-one you have flown the nest and have no wish for an immediate return; there will be time enough later. Much to my surprise, a job came my way which offered independence, interest and experience in journalism, in which dubious art I had already made a start as polo correspondent for the *East African Standard* (as I have related in *The Mottled Lizard*). So at the end of 1928 I took up residence in a bed-sitter in Ebury Street and went to work for a body called the Empire Marketing Board.

My pay was £5 a week, a sum then not merely adequate but generous; the standard weekly rate for typists was, I think, thirty-five shillings. My £5 a week enabled me not only to keep and clothe myself but to run a little Austin 7 open two-seater, painted silver like a racing car; go away for weekends when invited, take an annual holiday, frequent the cinema, and generally enjoy life. Economy, of course, was needed; you fed in cheap restaurants and tea-shops (and cheap they were), walked to save bus fares and spent little on clothes; but economy, within limits, could be in itself a minor pleasure, offering many triumphs, small but satisfying, when you got something for sixpence less than you had reckoned to pay.

That I should, after an interlude in London, return to Kenya, was the general assumption. Two things intervened. The first was the Slump, or World Depression, which started at the end of 1929. It accelerated gradually at first, but before long jobs were falling like skittles in all directions, and we heard of Jarrow, hunger marches and starving miners in South Wales. The response to this predicament was different from that of later generations: wages, instead of going up, went down; civil servants took a cut of ten per cent and the 'Geddes axe' was applied to the root of the tree. Everything was cut back and my own branch was lopped off altogether. By that time, the second intervention had occurred: I had married. We shared the same branch, and my husband, too, was threatened by the axe.

Gervas and I had met, unromantically perhaps, in the dingy government offices in Queen Anne's Gate in which the Empire Marketing Board was housed. He occupied a superior position as head of the publicity division, I a humble one as unfledged assistant in its press section, which consisted of Patrick Ryan, the able and incisive press officer from whom I learnt all I ever came to know about writing for newspapers. (He had come from the *Manchester Guardian* and went on to a distinguished career on *The Times*, just missing the editorship.) Gervas was some thirteen years my senior, so I was naturally flattered when he invited me to visit him one Sunday at a house near Abingdon where I found him painting a green-house. Thereafter our acquaintance ripened; we shared a taste for country walks of a Sunday, and would return from tramping over the South Downs (there was a good deal of Belloc in the air in those days) to a delicious supper at L'Escargot in Frith Street, then a small and virtually unknown restaurant run by M. Gaudin where one might spend as much as 10s for the two, plus a bottle of good burgundy for 3s 6d.

At this period, something called the Marriage Bar existed; married women were totally debarred from employment in the civil service. So, when you married, you resigned. To resign from a department by that time doomed to extinction obviously did not matter much, but the end of the department mattered a great deal to Gervas, who bore the stigma of being 'unestablished', and therefore without hope of being transferred to another branch of the bureaucratic tree when his own was demolished.

So there we were, or thought we soon should be as the Depression ground remorselessly on, faced with unemployment and no dole. But Depressions, like everything else, are unpredictable. They can even generate jobs. This one generated a job, quite unexpectedly, for Gervas. It concerned tea. Like all other primary products, tea was down and out; thousands of chests of it clogged warehouses in Colombo, Calcutta, Batavia and elsewhere, over-produced, unsaleable, unwanted. In all the tea-producing countries, planters were going broke, companies passing dividends, coolies being laid off. It was a familiar story, told of many other things besides tea.

Someone, at this sorry stage, conceived the notion that if tea consumers could be persuaded to drink more of it, and those who did not drink any be persuaded to do so, some at least of the warehouse-clogging chests could be disposed of in a better way than being thrown into the sea. It was a bold idea, and the difficulties of acting upon it were immense. However, after strenuous efforts, a body called the Ceylon Tea Propaganda Board came into being, based in Colombo, but intending to set up a headquarters in London and to operate in half a dozen countries of the world. Someone was needed to run the show, and by great good fortune Gervas was offered the job.

Good fortune indeed: the task involved travelling in North America, in Australia, in South and East Africa and Egypt; in India and Ceylon; in the Netherlands East Indies (as they were then) and in parts of Northern Europe. The air age was dawning but had not quite arrived, so comfortable, well-conducted ships took us about the world. We packed our bags and set forth in January 1933. It was to be five years before we unpacked them under our own roof again.

*   *   *

I had been lucky too. At the end of 1931 Lord Delamere, who for thirty years had bestridden the Kenya scene as pioneer and politician, died at his home outside Nairobi, and I was commissioned to write his biography. As I could not tackle this while travelling round the world, it was arranged that I should base myself in Kenya while Gervas moved about, returning in due course to pick me up. So on a cold winter's day we parted, sadly, at Marseilles, he to take a steamer for Colombo, I a different one, Mombasa-bound. We had been married for just over one year.

In February 1933 I was back at Njoro, to find things not so greatly changed. Njombo was there, grinning from ear to ear, and Mbugwa, one of his sons, a stalwart young man with a stutter who had been a *toto* when I left, was now a married man and Nellie's houseboy. The house had been smartened up; the small sitting-room had been panelled in an attractive local wood, and Vera, Robin's widow, had carved bunches of fruit and flowers in the Adam style over the fireplace to frame an attractive little painting Jos had bought in Madrid, referred to as the 'neo-Goya'. There were plenty of dachshunds.

Out of doors, there was an interesting market garden; Nellie was working up a 'basket trade', delivering *kikapu*-fuls of fresh vegetables of many kinds to her customers in Nakuru once a week. I was invited to meet 'the hairy Peruvian'. A guest? A pupil? Possibly a goat or mule? He turned out to be a grass, said to possess every grassy virtue. In a row of home-made hutches crouched a number of snow-white, silky-furred Angora rabbits. Two partners on the slopes of Kenya Mountain had imported a stock, and were said already to be making £1,000 a year. They had undertaken to buy all the fur Nellie could produce, indeed all that anyone could produce, and to find a market for the fleeces of three million Angora rabbits.

Nellie had not changed much: only a few more wrinkles, a few grey hairs and considerable stiffness in the knees. Jos, too, was much as ever, drawing reflectively on his cheroot; now and again a dreamy look signalled that some scheme for making money, which could not go wrong, was gestating in his mind. One such scheme centred on a hotel on Mombasa Island, in essence a good idea but, as usual, he lacked capital. A partner was found who proved, like others, to be unsatisfactory. In due course the partner swallowed the hotel and Jos lost all the money he had borrowed to start it with. The lender this time was not a bank but his sister-in-law Vera, and he was striving hard to pay the money back. He had scraped up £9 for a course in short-story writing, hoping to 'turn out tripe for magazines, earn a little money and so pay you back by degrees', he wrote to her. Alas, it was not a success. His mind seethed with plots but he was weak on characterization. I thought, myself, that some of his stories were neat and clever; he liked a twist at the end, in the manner of O. Henry. But this was not in fashion, and he never sold a single one. His only little triumph was to win first prize in a Christmas story competition run by the *East African Standard* – prize money: £5.

*   *   *

For the next few months I was on the move, sometimes at Njoro but more often at Loresho, near Nairobi, where Delamere's widow

Glady lived. Hers was a compelling personality. Her wiry, black hair surmounted a chalk-white complexion; her voice was deep and rather husky; the general effect was positive, forceful, dynamic. She had first come to Kenya on safari as the wife of a rich baronet, Sir Charles Markham. After the marriage came apart she returned on a visit, and espoused Lord Delamere, some thirty years her senior, whose son was her contemporary. This was in 1928. Delamere died three years later.

At Loresho, Glady entertained many lively friends, and gave excellent parties. Also she took a vigorous part in local politics, and was to become a somewhat improbable Mayor of Nairobi. Every minute of the day was filled with some activity. She seemed to be running away from something – perhaps her own company. She was not one of those cut out to live alone and should have re-married, but the man she loved and was her lover eluded her. This was her tragedy.

Loresho was a delightful perch. Glady followed the current fashion for employing tall Somali servants who were handsome, haughty and efficient, and she had an excellent cook. There was always, in her sitting-room, a smell of madonna lilies, and a gramophone played softly from a corner, tended by one of the silent, softfooted Somalis. If ever I hear the sentimental tune 'Under a Clover Moon', I am reminded of Loresho. I was given a desk to work at, all the papers Glady had – not many – and any help in contact-making that I asked for. Glady never interfered. 'The family' is often a biographer's bugbear, but with Glady there was none of that.

*   *   *

Much of my time was spent in Nairobi. Despite the Depression, it was a cheerful little town, at a half-way stage between pioneer squalor and the urban sophistication that was to transform it when the age of tourism arrived. It had as yet no skyscrapers, but the streets had been tarmacked and there was one relatively tall building, Torr's hotel, a foregathering-place for pre-lunch drinks and evening revelries. The Indian bazaar remained unchanged, its scruffy *dukas* crammed with merchandise and customers and smelling of spices and humanity. Everything there was wonderfully cheap, and suits and dresses could be run up for a few shillings almost while you waited.

This was the age of brightly coloured clothing, then a novelty; sea green, cobalt blue and claret corduroy trousers for both sexes, silk shirts in brilliant hues, and big terai hats with fancy trimmings, such as twists of leopardskin. Rickshaws had disappeared, to be replaced by box-body cars, forerunners of estate wagons, coated in dust or mud according to the season and packed with kit, dogs and Africans. The grandest car, apart from the Governor's, was a large yellow Rolls-Royce with a rhino horn mounted on the bonnet, which swept along with the princely figure, white-crested and mahogany-complexioned, of the Chief Game Warden, Archie Ritchie, at the wheel.

Whether responsibility lay with the times, the climate, the people or (more likely) one's own youth, I do not know, but one felt a sense of glamour. There appeared for the first time, in places like Torr's and the New Stanley, fit-looking young men with pilot's wings stitched over their breast-pockets and a hitherto unfamiliar insignia on their caps: Imperial Airways pilots and crew. The London to Cape Town run had only just been opened, after years of pioneering; the first passengers flew the route in April 1932, taking ten days. Flying over Africa was still an adventure and pilots were seen as bold, resourceful fellows, as indeed they sometimes had to be.

In June 1933 Gervas, who had proceeded from Ceylon and India to South Africa by sea, decided to save time by flying up to Kenya from Johannesburg. When I arrived at Nairobi airport to meet him at the scheduled time, I was told that his aeroplane was lost in the bush, no one knew where, probably in Northern Rhodesia. The navigator, flying with a map spread on his knee – no radar aids to navigation then – had lost the way, the plane was running out of petrol, and nothing but bush, bush and more bush could be seen below. In the nick of time a small clearing appeared and the pilot pancaked down in a maize-patch full of burnt tree-stumps, which damaged the machine but not, by great good luck, the passengers. With the radio out of action, there was no way of communicating with the outside world. Fortunately the owners of the maize-patch appeared, disappeared, and returned with eggs, chickens and gourds-ful of water. For three days crew and passengers camped by the plane, disturbed at night by elephants, until spotted by one of the light aircraft sent out from Salisbury to look for them, and taken off, with some difficulty, one by one.

Undeterred, Gervas booked passages for us both from Nairobi to London, which took six days. You felt more as if you were starting off on a prolonged picnic than on a prosaic journey. Crew and passengers were all in it together; your captain was no disembodied voice from the intercom but a cheerful young man with whom you shared meals and drinks, hopes and fears and sometimes mishaps. If someone spotted a herd of elephants, the pilot would come down to a few hundred feet and circle round while passengers took photographs; there was a herd near Bor in the Sudan who must have got very tired of this treatment. If you overslept – although there was not much chance of that, with so much pre-dawn bustle and cups of tea – the aeroplane would wait for you. There were disadvantages; no pressurized cabins, which grew exceedingly hot, and you flew at low altitudes, so that it was very bumpy and most of the passengers were sick. No food was served on board, so you bumped down to earth to eat while the plane was being refuelled. But that was all in the day's work and scarcely counted against the interest, excitement and sight-seeing opportunities provided by the trip.

Six days, and many stops; Africa unrolled before you. Breakfast at Kisumu, lunch at Entebbe, tea and your night-stop at Juba on the Nile. Here tribesmen with peculiar hair-do's, some like firemen's helmets fashioned from their own entwined, mud-plastered locks, strolled hand in hand beside the quiet-flowing river with its crocodiles. Your aeroplane was called Horsa or Hannibal, and its maximum speed was about a hundred miles an hour. Then came the immense Sudanese desert, getting hotter and hotter, bumpier and bumpier: Malakal, Kosti, then Khartoum, laid out in the pattern of the Union Jack with General Gordon's statue dominating the square. At Luxor time was allowed to see the Valley of the Kings before breakfast; crossing the Nile by boat at dawn still remains an enchanted memory.

At Cairo you changed to a graceful flying boat, Sylvanus, and slept at Alexandria. The next day was all sea, with stops at Crete and Athens and then Brindisi, where you took to a train; and such a comfortable train, with excellent meals *en route* and a pause at

93

Milan long enough to see the cathedral. On through the Simplon tunnel, more good meals, Paris for breakfast, and one short hop to Croydon and a welcome from friends eager, or at any rate prepared, to hear the saga of your adventures. How sad that technology, advancing like a juggernaut, has crushed these little pleasures lying in its path.

*   *   *

After June 1933, when Gervas and I reached England, I kept nearly all Nellie's weekly letters. There were, of course, gaps; sometimes I was in Kenya or – though much less often – she in England and our correspondence was suspended.

Jos and Nellie went to the East Africa Protectorate as pioneers in what was then regarded as a great and honourable enterprise. 'Wider still and wider, Shall thy bounds be set' was a statement of intention, not then recognized as arrogant, about the British Empire, not merely the finale of the last night of the Proms. By the time Nellie left the independent Republic of Kenya, the hour of midnight had struck; pioneers had turned into colonialist oppressors, white settlers into land thieves, administrators into lackeys of imperialism, even do-gooders into paternalistic stooges. (There are signs that they may be taken back into favour again.)

Because Nellie's fifty-three years in Africa spanned these profound changes, and because the recent past seems now so far away, I hope that these extracts from her letters may hold an interest for a wider world, even though they are glimpses from the wings rather than a view of action on the stage. The novelist fills in the picture of the characters he creates with details, small events, changes of mood. Nellie created her own character, warts and all, by the same means.

PART II

Letters from Kenya
1933–65

1933 – 6

After seeing Gervas and myself off at Nairobi airport on our return to England, Nellie returned to the farm.

26 June 1933 I left Nairobi at 11 am and had a peaceful run to Nakuru, where I stood myself and Kabucho a cheap matinée of *Congorilla*. Kabucho rocked with laughter all the way from Nakuru back to Njoro. It was his first 'pictures'. He liked best the newsreel with a carnival in New York featuring the inauguration of George Washington as first President of the USA, though a monster New York fire with twenty firemen overcome by fumes was good, also a female swimming race. Near Njoro he said: 'I must say I've had a lovely day, what with seeing the inside of the *ndege* [literally bird, used also of aeroplanes] this morning, and this show *maridadi kabisa* [altogether splendid] this afternoon.' A heavy thunderstorm appeared, so at Njoro I put on chains. Near the Plant Breeders the Ford stuck. It was pitch dark, I had no torch to work by and pouring rain, so I just walked home, getting in at 8.30 pm soaked to the skin with sore, suppurating heels and very tired and cross. Walked back with six oxen next morning and got the car going. It was a bloody homecoming. Luckily the little dogs were very well – bored but fat. They had eaten the major part of poor Hugh Douglas [a bull] during my absence.

14 August 1933 The Masai country is in an awful state of drought. They really are in a fix, as they have to pay Sh 20/- hut tax, and their cattle are so thin they only get about Sh 9/- per beast. ...* Jack Dawson [the district commissioner] has a district three thousand square miles, larger than Wales, to run with one ADC, nine native police and eleven tribal retainers. Narok is a funny, rather wild little *boma*. ... A few nights before we got there a lion had pulled down and eaten a waterbuck exactly thirty yards from my bedroom window. The

* The Kenya unit of currency is the shilling. There are a hundred cents in a shilling.

window was large and very low, so I felt it would have been most agitating keeping the lion out, and the dachshunds in.... It is very parky these days, all blue hands, except when black. The naughty herd has lost an ox which was pulled down and eaten by hyenas in the night, poor devil. That cost the herd Sh 30/-; it was utter carelessness.

17 August 1933 Set out for home, heavy rain, no helper with me so decided not to get into a muddy mess by putting on chains, and take a chance and see how far I got. I got further than expected, and only stuck because the car did a terrific skid and landed in a bush about a mile from home. There was a pale moon through the rain, and you should have seen the peke's face when it realized it would have to abandon the front seat of the Ford and take, in its feathered paws, to the mud and rain. The staff refuse to believe it is a dog, but say it is 'something out of the forest'*.... Divine rain every day this month and lovely planting weather. Have got out ten acres of pyrethrum and can plant one acre a day when the weather is suitable. Have also picked my first few *debbis* of flowers which is very exciting.

7 September 1933 Masses and masses of rain – we had thirty-nine days running of rain and could do with sun now. Lovely blossom on the almonds.... Reggie Pelham-Burn has flown out suddenly to square H. E. Uganda about his scheme to catch crocs and fish on Lake Victoria. He lunched here Sunday and talked a *lot* about fish. If the crocs eat the fish, you catch the crocs; if the monitors – large lizards – eat too many croc eggs, you catch the monitors; if neither crocs nor monitors are hungry, you catch the fish.... Have just made a cake, which Karanja [the cook] wants to ice with the alum I got to put in the hydrangea pots.

At this period in colonial history, the Africans inhabited a number of native reserves, one for each tribe, whose inviolability was secured to them in perpetuity by official pledges. White settlers lived on land similarly set aside for them by the government, mainly on 999-year leases. The object of establishing these native reserves (later known as native land units) had been to protect each tribe in its own area and prevent tribal lands from being bought or leased by aliens, whether European or Asian. Population pressure had not yet made its appearance; but

* Nellie was looking after a peke for a friend; her own pack were dachshunds.

whereas a great many blacks lived and worked in the so-called 'White Highlands', those who had their own shambas *being called squatters, no whites, except for missionaries and the transient officials, were allowed to live in native reserves. So very few Europeans took any interest in what was going on there. That, they considered, was the affair of the missionaries, and of officials who did not normally encourage too much wandering around by Europeans lacking official status. Nellie, however, was interested in everything, including what was going on in native reserves. A lot was going on, in point of fact; district commissioners and their colleagues were laying the foundations of local government which, because they were laid in time, enabled Kenya to make the transition to independence a generation later without upsetting the apple-cart. One of her former neighbours at Thika, Hugo Lambert, had joined the Administration, and Nellie took a few days off to visit him and his wife at Kiambu, near Nairobi.*

21 September 1933 It is such a lovely holiday. I breakfast in bed at 7 am and read lovely things to do with native administration. Hugo lent me the minute book of the Local Native Council, which is entrancing. Yesterday we attended the Local Native Tribunal and met Koinange and all the nuts. Koinange has an amazing face. The tribunal was great fun, a terrific case going on between a very old man and a very old woman. The latter is easily the best woman speaker in Kenya, and if I was one-tenth as good, I should return to the EAWL [East Africa Women's League] and flatten out Ailsa. [Mrs Ailsa Turner was the League's chairman.] Yesterday we had a gorgeous day in the reserve. We called on Chief Waruhiu;* he has an incredibly nice house, much better than the old Grant home, spotlessly clean, lovely rat-proof stores, meat safe etc. – almost an Electrolux – and a marvellous garden with gladioli up to show standard. He is a charming man. We discussed squatters for a long time, me talking Kisettla† and Waruhiu perfect English.

28 September 1933 Had a heart-to-heart with the very genteel PMO [Principal Medical Officer] about health. The conversation was entirely about worms and latrines. It seems the only way in which one

---

* To be murdered by Mau Mau nearly twenty years later.

† A form of kitchen Swahili, spoken by up-country tribes and by most Europeans, the lingua franca of Kenya.

must *not* uplift the Native is to provide a seat, one must encourage the squatting position. I am now an authority on yet another aspect of the squatter problem.

3 November 1933   The Mau Mountain Wool Farm is now in existence; forty-eight angora rabbits arrived on Sunday. Have worked out that we reach the six-thousand mark on 1 January 1936. Do you suppose anyone has done any research on the best feeding to make the hair long? Or indeed on wool rabbits at all?.... Everyone is short of feed, the lack of rain is again awful. Picking pyrethrum gently and delivered the first bag, fifty-two pounds worth Sh 65/-. There'd be masses if only it would rain.

23 November 1933   Walker the pyrethrum expert said he had seen the first bag I delivered and it was excellent, good flowers and very well harvested. ...

14 December 1933   I've sold my poor pigs for Sh 1/- each. ... Cockie [Birkbeck] rang up last night to say could she come for two nights and bring Kiki Preston. This little house wasn't built for international drug fiends [Kiki was a heroin addict], it will be hard on the electric light engine, and the little dogs will doubtless disturb her mid-day slumbers, but it is at her own risk.

22 December 1933   Well, it happened, and we laughed a great deal. Kiki said we must be the three funniest people in Kenya. Of course it meant an all-night session and we went to bed at 4 am, but I won Sh 15/- at backgammon. Kiki really is a marvel; she was very well here and had an egg for breakfast, which hasn't occurred for years, and got up for lunch. (She's very clever with her needle, Cockie says.) I went to bed at 12 pm as absolutely couldn't stay the course and left Cockie and Kiki to it, extinguishing the light engine as I went. They actually got up and left at 8.30 next morning, looking very healthy.

27 January 1934   Have just read Cunliffe-Lister's* speech at Nakuru. Would you believe it, he said we were all very courageous

---

* Sir Philip Cunliffe-Lister, then Secretary of State for the Colonies. He became Viscount Swinton in 1935.

and that is the Spirit That Makes the Empire What It Is. No wonder he gets septic throats if his vocal chords have to cough up tripe like that. Grogan has just rung up asking us to dinner at Muthaiga as he wants an 'intelligent woman' to sit next to Sir George Tomlinson. We go. ... G. is having a terrific walk-out with a very young man. Dolly Miles was staying nearby with the Jexes and said she was going over late one night to use G.'s telephone. Muriel Jex said she'd be sure to find G. in bed with a poached egg, but it wasn't a poached egg.

12 February 1934 Nearly two months since rain. The water tanks are all but empty, the first time I've ever run short. The marvellous pyrethrum carries on, almonds ripening off.... Have just agreed to go with Cockie to Clouds tomorrow for one night only, as Dina wants moral support in facing Donald [her husband, who was given to fits of violence]. Anyway shall get some garden loot even if Donald does shoot us all.

Clouds, the residence of the famous Lady Idina, was in the so-called Happy Valley, which lay on the slopes of Kipipiri, part of the Aberdare range. Lady Idina was then at the peak of her fame. Donald Haldeman was her fourth husband. The previous ones, in chronological order, had been Euan Wallace, Charles Gordon and Josslyn, Earl of Erroll, later to become the victim in a notorious murder case. After Donald Haldeman came Vincent Saltoe, an airline pilot, and then James the Sixth. Nellie was firmly convinced that Dina was barred from marrying James legally by a law placed on the statute book by Henry VIII which forbade anyone to have more than five spouses, so as to ensure that no subject could equal or exceed the monarch's record. I think Nellie really believed this.

25 February 1934 The heat, dust and drought are terrific; everybody in hot-weather frame of mind, snappy and strung-up. The Coast is a mass of red locusts, the Wa-Digo [an African tribe] eaten out and starving. Old Ali* has just given them £1,000.... I spent two days with Cockie in Nairobi. What a life – Americans, Swedes,

* Sir Ali bin Salim, the Liwali [Judge], or leader of the Arabs of the Coast Province, then the Protectorate (as distinct from Colony) of Kenya.

Danes, rushing in and out all day and all night. Kiki and Gerry (Preston) were finally too over-alcoholized to drive themselves away so flew to Naivasha. Cockie's front yard was so full of abandoned cars that she and I thought of having a sale.

11 July 1934   Please, please, get me some Johnson's tea. It sounds the most marvellous thing. You drink it at breakfast with Ryvita, and the rest of the day let yourself go as you like. Nina Lindstrom, who was so fat her aunt wouldn't take her to Stockholm, lost five pounds in one week and was allowed to go to Stockholm. Perhaps it only happens in Sweden, but *do* find out.... Beckley said my pyrethrum was better coloured than anyone else's – this is the Njoro climate not me – and a first-class sample.... Delivered 112 lbs almonds in the town today, value Sh 183/-.

18 July 1934   Am picking hard all and every day, also planting up misses, and hope to get the forty acres of pyrethrum consolidated by the end of this month.... A foul hyena came one night and dragged my very best heifer calf out of the calf house and ate it, and the next night finished off the poor old ox it had worried before. Its lair is in the forest, and I've got leave to put down poison there.

25 July 1934   I had a lovely time yesterday. I've planted a vitex forest at the lower corner of my maize, and a *brayera* forest at the edge of my bean *shamba*, and a vast mixed forest all along the top of the ridge. Queenie Ritchie just back from Rhodesia sent me seeds of a wonderful native tree, *Securidaca longipedunculata*, which has large bunches of blossoms that smell just like violets.... Forgot to say, it's Janssen-té, not Johnson's, I'd be *very* grateful for three or four pounds.

15 August 1934   Marjorie Dudgeon was full of Nairobi Race Week doings. The pageant really does sound marvellous. The Government House party were all rather ailing, the ADC having been too clever about the cocktails the night before, so when the scene arrived when the Portuguese had plague in Fort Jesus and were very ill all over the place, someone said in a loud voice, 'They must have been dining at Government House.' Mervyn went to sleep just when Vasco da

Gama's wooden cross was put up. When he woke up he said: 'When am I?' Someone replied, 'Two hundred years later.' He blinked at the wooden cross and said loudly: 'Then what have the white ants been doing all these years?' Glady scored a great success as an early settler arriving at the Norfolk in a rickshaw.

29 August 1934 The postmaster rang up with a telegram from Jos [in Mombasa where he had started a hotel] and I got heavily struck with lightning in the ear; there really was quite a bruise. Started a lovely rock garden. It *is* lovely and it cost Sh 1/20, i.e. two old men two days. I told Mrs Gilfillan with pride it cost Sh 1/20, to which she replied 'How ever did you spend *all that* on it?'.... A hospital meeting 2.30–7 pm. A successful gold-miner who wishes to remain anonymous (I wonder what his chances are – it is B. F. Webb) has given £500 to help meet fees people can't pay. The Govt. pays for completely indigent ones, but most people can't quite rank as that, and outstanding fees are nearly £1,000.

11 September 1934 Ingrid [Lindstrom] was very sweet about Viveka's trousseau for Europe.* She said Harriet had made her a red satin evening frock and 'a little white silk tennis frock'. I said: 'I suppose that is for the winter in Sweden?' She said: 'But no, we leave the winter in Sweden to the people of Sweden. It worked very well last time.' So Viveka's trousseau is now complete.... The German line are running a wonderful trip to England tourist class £40 return.

25 September 1934 This week has been largely devoted to getting old Fordi to go.... Everyone seems to be agreed that Kenya's financial position is disastrous. Business has never been so bad, the N'bi business houses have had one long drain of capital out of the country and say they can't last more than six months. There has been no rain, and the promise of bumper crops – whatever they're

---

* To avoid confusion, the Lindstrom family may be clarified here. The parents, 'Fish' and Ingrid, had four children: Nils, the only son; Harriet, who was to marry first Philip Barnes and then Bertie Geohegen and live mostly near Nairobi; Nina, to marry an American and live in Philadelphia; and finally Viveka, who after her marriage to Hans Stjernswärd was to live and farm at nearby Rongai.

worth – has vanished. Pyrethrum does seem to be the one bright spot. David Petrie has started a small acreage of it next door, and took on some Luo to work it. One enormous Luo nearly cut off his leg with a *panga* and was carried here for me to tie up, which was messy.

17 October 1934 Telephones are a scandal, last year the PMG admitted to making thirteen per cent on rural lines. About half the Njoro subscribers dropped out last year, and this year all but four people are going off. I gave in our notice with much regret, I must say, and on 31 December they will remove the plant.... The Petrie Luo who cut his leg so badly has made a wonderful recovery on my home-made dressing of Kerol and grease, and refused to go to hospital. Now all the Luo community come for medicine every day, which is a curse, *and* their wives have been stealing Ingrid's maize, so I have to cope with that, and daren't try my own methods on these sophisticated visitors. My own methods, I hasten to say, are purely compensatory (fines).

24 October 1934 Yesterday I started a new scheme of preparing pyrethrum for planting out. I've had a trench dug, and am dividing up and heeling in sufficient plants for the 35,931 little sticks already in beautiful lines two-by-two feet apart. This does 3.3 acres of land. I've already sent off twenty-four bags this month, my record so far.... Cecil Soames arrived to stay after a District Council meeting with a Creamery one next day. He looks beastly, but one knows that no good gardener could really be, and his dogs are very fond of him.

30 October 1934 Graded rabbit wool all morning, and an unknown girl arrived about 4 pm. She is a daughter of a pseudo-friend of my youth who married a half-wit of the great Cecil clan. She got engaged to someone considered unsuitable, so was sent out here for a year. At first I thought she was an awful girl, very pleased with herself, long-winded and platitudinous, but when she got on to describing the awfulness and fatuosity of her mother, I liked her better.... Gall-sickness is terribly bad now, I lost two cows and two calves last week. Absolutely no rain which is damnable, how long the pyrethrum can go on as it is I tremble to think. I have over thirty thousand plants in a trench waiting to go out, and haven't had anything approaching a single planting day since August.

20 November 1934   John Henley has recently married Cecil Soames's wife, so C. Soames doesn't think much of Henley's pyrethrum drier. Nor do I really, it is so small and the pyrethrum a bad colour. Henley's place is the most divine I've ever seen, just like the place described by John Buchan in *The Lodge in the Wilderness*, situated at 9,100 feet on the very edge of the Mau escarpment, with a two-thousand-foot drop from the garden. Every bulb and flower does marvellously at the top, and at the bottom of the escarpment is almost tropical forest.

11 December 1934   Wednesday last was Joss Erroll's meeting at the Club to explain British Fascism. There were 198 people there, no less, and a very good-tempered meeting, as everyone cheered to the echo what anyone said. British Fascism means simply super-loyalty to the Crown, no dictatorship, complete religious and social freedom, an 'insulated Empire' to trade with the dirty foreigner, higher wages and lower costs of living.... All questions and answers cheered to the roof, especially Salvadori who gabbled furiously in unintelligible English and no one heard a word. Whenever Joss [Erroll] said British Fascism stands for complete freedom, you could hear Mary Countess at the other end of the room saying that within five years Joss will be dictator of Kenya. There was one of those grim suppers afterwards, we got away as soon as we could.

5 January 1935   I got second prize at Nakuru Show for my pyrethrum, and very complimentary remarks from the judges on the sample. It was very close to first and 'perfect' colour.... There was a leopard in the garden two nights ago; it jumped on to the roof of one of the huts. I kissed Sweet William [a dachshund] goodnight last night, and he bit me in the face, quite deep, and very sore.

16 January 1935   We put two gallons of petrol into Ingrid's car and all proceeded to lunch with the Mohrs, which was a great treat. They had some marvellous delicatessen from Norway, and salted trout from their New Year safari in the Aberdares. She then let me see her pictures, which was a great concession, and made a lovely afternoon. She paints in the spare room about ten by twelve feet with no light at all, and has about eighty pictures parked under her bed. She sold two pictures to a Norwegian who made £4,000 in December alone on the Musumba goldfield for £60 which paid her bill for paints and canvas....

23 January 1935   I've marked all the breeding rabbits' ears, which is a loathsome job, and makes one feel sick. Two squealed which was awful. You do it with lamp-black, so my hands and the rabbits' ears were the same colour as Suya's face.... I've developed a passion for book-keeping. I've tackled it most seriously, and find all sorts of exciting things happen that you wouldn't expect. I did the rabbit accounts thoroughly. Without depreciation, we made a profit of Sh 40/- odd, and with depreciation a loss of Sh 35/-. I have started the most lovely books for 1935 and think I shall pursue my studies even unto accountancy. It does instead of crosswords, up to a point.... Do you know the 'sinic conception of Yin and Yang'? You ought to, it's fun.

1 February 1935   The terrific news this week is that we have had *real rain*, which is too marvellous. Yesterday about 4 pm a black cloud considerably larger than a man's hand appeared in the Rift Valley. I watched it anxiously; it moved over Nakuru and I thought it had gone forever; when it reached Menengai it put in its reverse, having apparently met a gale advancing from Lower Molo, and together they charged the Mau. The wind was terrific, the rain was very gentle at first, but as the wind dropped, the rain got heavier, and finally settled down good and proper, and we had 1.78 inches, and not a drop wasted. Am going to plant out pyrethrum tomorrow, and this should start it off flowering, thank goodness.... Connie Coke has wired to ask if she can stay Monday to Friday, so she must, and Marjorie Dudgeon has proposed herself to lunch on Sunday. so willy-nilly must be social. I've given up smoking now for three days, and hope I shall continue, as I've worked out that if I stop for a month I can afford the new Botanical Journal Kirstenbosch is fathering, so have subscribed to it trusting to luck about the non-smoking.

13 February 1935   Old Fordi is constantly puncturing now, tyres being at the end of their lives, such a curse. A small spring has gone in its ignition and its battery is finished. Really, these cars.

2 March 1935   The Jacks came to stay in a new Dodge with a special carburettor [adjusted to run on paraffin]; apparently the Dodge's 'hot spot' is so efficient when new that it vaporizes all the paraffin before it gets to the cylinders, so the car doesn't go until you throw cold water over it. Unluckily they didn't know this, so had to be rescued at frequent intervals. Then, on the escarpment, three washaways, torrents pouring over the road, boulders crashing down with torrents, so cars queued up expecting to be stoned to death at any minute. The Jacks left N'bi at 9.30 am and got here at 9.30 pm, the last scene being a complete stop down the road when Jack switched over to petrol and found he hadn't any. Mrs Jack and Monica walked up, Monica asking pitifully if it hurt much to be bitten by dachshunds.

3 April 1935   Jos and I have started the orange cure. Collected a bag of two hundred oranges, a gift from Bo Fawcus, in Nakuru. You have barley water as well. It's lovely having no food to organize, but Cecil Soames has cramped my style by writing to ask if he can stay tonight. He is such a super gardener and so generous about plants that I've organized some food for him, but otherwise people arriving will have *absolutely* nothing and the cook is on holiday. A silver salver, or dish, reposes on the dining-room table, permanently piled up with oranges, and we go and have a dip whenever we feel like it.

1 May 1935   Oh dear, it has been a social week and I am so tired of it! Monday I played in the rock garden all day, so *much* nicer than parties, and did some farming. On Tuesday my left heel turned into a veld sore and something is coming out of it which looks very much like pure gin. Anyway it is a curse as the leg is swollen up to the knee and much throbbing. But I tied a shoe on with an elastic band and played eighteen holes with Francis and beat him three up, and then – we went to a party! Bridge before and after dinner, got home about 2.30 am. Went very early to Nakuru next morning to take in a wretched *bibi* who had started producing and couldn't get on with it. I saw fifty-six gallstones which had been removed by Charters from a patient, each the size of a maize grain, lovely colour like old ivory, funny angular shapes; would make *lovely* beads. Back to lunch and that's all the news.

7 May 1935   Jubilee Day [King George v's Silver Jubilee] passed quietly on the farm; we went over to Donald Seth-Smith's to photograph his dairy herd and stayed to dinner. Made Donald produce some port and sang 'God Save the King' and watched bonfires on Menengai and Mau Summit.... I got a silver medal sent all the way from Buck. Pal., with a nice letter from the King. I'm *not* the only one but there are really very few G's on the list. Mine was for 'social services'.

22 May 1935   I wore my medal at the Trooping of the Colour in Nakuru and it fell off several times. Came home to lunch, but others went on to the ceremonial tree-planting and an Indian bun-and-treacle tea; saw the rockets go up from here.... My best cow has eaten some poison and is expiring, poor thing. A leopard has eaten Karanja's dog.

29 May 1935   A plethora of meetings: Njoro Assn: Executive, Hospital Board, Township Afforestation, pyrethrum meeting in Nakuru and so on. Am also diverting two waterfalls for the Fishing Committee.... Viola [dachshund] got caught in a snare, and rushing to her assistance I took a header into a bed of the most savage stinging-nettles I've ever met. Muchoka is delighted that I'm going away as he adores sitting in the office chair doing labour sheets etc., which he does very well. The garden is so colourful it makes you blink.

In June, Nellie flew to England, where she stayed partly with Gervas and me at our London flat but mainly with Trudie in Sussex, or at Thorpeness in Suffolk, where they played golf. Jos went to his hotel on Mombasa Island to try to sort out its financial difficulties, also those arising from municipal regulations which he had not studied with sufficient care, and from the illness of his partner. The farm was left under the charge of Muchoka, Nellie's headman. (Njombo had retired.) He belonged to the M'kamba tribe, and had a wife, shamba and flocks and herds near Machakos, south-east of Nairobi, and a Kikuyu wife and shamba on the Njoro farm. He was an intelligent and honest man with a great deal of charm, who had taught himself the three R's, got on well with the Kikuyu and was good with the dogs. Nellie returned to Kenya in September, having an adventurous journey.

5 October 1935   Was seen off by Trudie and D., Vera and *the* most awful looking object in rusty black, as broad as long, looking like an unsuccessful tart. This proved to be Sybil. She drew me aside and muttered spells over me, pressed a golden snuff-box into my hand, wept, and said I had altered her whole life. Trudie proved her organizing powers to the hilt by sweeping us all into the very sordid bar and standing us all gins-and-french. ... At Alexandria we were called at 3.30 am and took off in the Hengist, but had to change into the Horsa at Cairo. In the front part were Proctor, Megson, self and two of the most lousy, affected, giggly, selfish English girls you've ever seen, going on a visit to Entebbe. In the after cabin were a sweet American mining professor from Yale, a huge Norwegian journalist, a fat German, a suave Belgian, an Indian, two youths from S. Rhodesia and two dashing Italians with diplomatic passports. Away we went from Cairo, destination Khartoum, coming down at Assiut, Luxor, Wadi Halfa (lunch) and a new place, Kariema. Took off at 6.30 pm from there and on came several *haboubs* [sand whirlwinds]. The machine was chucked about anyhow, the pilot could only just control it; he couldn't get through to Khartoum on the wireless, so at 7.45 pm they turned round to make back to Kariema. This is a tiny place with only one European, the wireless man. ...

Along came the old Horsa, the pilot tried to do a down-wind landing in terribly bad visibility with very sketchy flares, took the hell of a bump, then another, when our wings hit some hillocks or something. Off he fluttered to have another go, had to do a terrific bank to miss a tent, which actually did remove our starboard wingtip light, and caught our left wing in the sand. So when we finally came to rest, it was to find the fabric badly torn on both wings. It was rather alarming because of the extreme dark, and howling wind, and lots of lightning. However, the only casualty was a broken leg to my specs, which got trodden on. We bundled out into the desert. About half a mile away was the wireless man's hut, where he produced three beds, so the lousy ones and I slept in his garden, and the rest on the airstrip, in the tent or outside – most wisely the latter, as there were scorpions in the tent.

There was a marvellous steward on board, a perfect man, he produced enough food and drink that night from the plane (emergency rations). We were called at 5 am and foregathered to embark, the staff having worked all night to mend the wings with the wireless man's shirt and the windsock. But as the pilot was stepping in, he noticed that a strut had snapped off, and examination revealed quite serious wing damage, so we all bundled out again into the sand, and they wirelessed to Cairo for engineers and parts. The steward commandeered a donkey and galloped off to the native village to get eggs etc. We passed the day as best we might.... The poor relief plane – an Avro monoplane – met frightful weather, couldn't find us at all, got knocked all over the place, and finally arrived at Khartoum at midnight with four minutes of petrol left. It got to us next day about 10 am. Meanwhile we'd really had quite a good party.... The lousy girls got worse and worse, wilting and grousing. No one could bear speaking to them, they were so nasty. Finally I had to speak to them sharply.... It turned out that the Horsa was really badly damaged, so the Avro took us three females, the Italians, the German and the Indian to Khartoum and went back to fetch the others with the minimum of luggage – I personally have only what I stand up in. The next thing is, how to get us away.... The Italians had two grand planes waiting for them, and fluttered away quickly to Eritrea. It came through on the wireless that war had begun, though the League of Nations said it hadn't.*

9 October 1935 Back in the old home, and will continue my adventures. That Saturday morning at Khartoum the rest of our passengers were brought in by the Avro. The Hanno, the next service after ours from Croydon, arrived on time on Saturday evening but they wouldn't let anyone on board, it was full to the brim; they took our mail and departed. We gnashed our teeth and settled down to

---

* They were wrong. Italy had invaded Abyssinia, thus starting the Italian/Ethiopian war.

another day at Khartoum.... At 5 pm on Sunday in came the mended Horsa. At 1 am we were called and proceeded to the aerodrome, sat in the plane waiting to go, when the wind suddenly changed, necessitating a completely new set of flares. Then up came a couple of heavy thunderstorms and our cautious, slightly shattered captain had us bundled back to the hotel at 3 am. At 7 am we really did get off; gave Kosti a miss so had to fly mostly at about fifty feet to save petrol, it was definitely bumpy. Got to Juba about 6 pm, to be greeted with the news that the Hanno, hurrying on ahead with our mail, had crashed at Entebbe. A tyre had burst in the air, in the dark. The pilot evacuated everyone to the very back of the plane and did his best, but it was a crash all right. The pilot went through the windscreen, but was only shaken. We saw the poor Hanno yesterday, its nose buried in the ground, both paws missing, one wing hanging by a thread and the two propellers firmly established in the front cabin. They'd had a nasty moment, as one engine wouldn't stop until the petrol was switched off and the exhaust kept billowing flames. It was a marvellous escape.... They sent two Atalantas for us to Juba which we left at 5 am Tuesday and proceeded uneventfully by the usual methods to Nairobi which we reached at 2.30 pm.

16 October 1935 Muchoka did marvellously as manager. He kept all the labour sheets, tickets, etc. finely; the labour turned out for him, he sent off all the pyrethrum and cream, his figures tally exactly with the receipts. No animals died, and several calves were born – mostly bulls, but that wasn't his fault. The *posho* records worked out perfectly. In fact I do think he has been extremely good. So has Karanja in the house. The rain has been awful. There is, alas, little good to report on the general situation. Maize is Sh 2/75 a bag, far below the cost of production, coffee prices miserable, everything pretty bleak. In fact so discouraging that I can't take any interest in anything, except selling all the pyrethrum possible.... The standard of living is coming down well, our batteries are quite dead so we have safari lamps only.... My Californian fuchsias are showing signs of coming into leaf already – marvellous.

Suddenly and unexpectedly, the Italian invasion of Ethiopia generated a temporary burst of prosperity in Kenya, owing to the demand for provisions for the Italian troops.

23 October 1935 Butter has jumped from Sh 72/- to Sh 128/-, people on the plains are coining money through baling veld hay for the Italians.... The bank manager was so on his toes that I positively had to restrain him in the amount of cash he wished to give me for labour.... How long it will take to wipe off the overdraft is entirely a matter of rain.

13 November 1935 Am doing a really savage bant, mostly hot water and veg. I'm interpreting it a little widely – whisky may come from maize, practically a vegetable, and gin has juniper, practically a fruit. But really I'm having very little alcohol, or anything else.

11 December 1935 I did a come-back, also a come-off, in the polo world, as Mrs Tryon wired asking me to take her place in the Mau-Molo ladies' team. Female polo is going very strong. I borrowed a pony to practise on, not having been near a horse for eighteen months. All went well till a young man harooshed past me on a wild yellow beast, which upset my beast. It gave six super-bucks and sent me for six on to a *very* hard polo ground – I was much damaged morally, and slightly physically, and ached all over in body and mind till next day.... The N'bi females are hot stuff, and really play very well. One is the lady tennis champion, another the games mistress at the European school, so very muscular.... Trudie has sent me £15 for Christmas, saying I was to spend nine-tenths of it on gin and one-tenth on a broken window-pane. I replied that fresh air was good for everyone. Actually I'm taking some out in petrol to go to N'bi on Sunday to judge a flower show, one of my secret vices as you know, and to buy a few blankets for the more deserving of the farm and domestic staff.

1 January 1936 On Sunday morning one of Petrie's boys rushed along to say his wife had produced twins in the night, one of the afterbirths had come away but the other hadn't, although they had looked everywhere for it with a stick, and now the woman would do nothing but scream. My midwifery experience couldn't tell me whether twins have one afterbirth each, or if they share one, but I made up a prescription of ergot, quinine, etc. and told the husband to go on giving it till something happened. Late that evening the best happened, and mother and children are now flourishing.... Tomorrow I go to N'bi, which is *very* foolish, to play old ladies' polo again. I do think it silly of me, but also have to do the shopping for the Njoro Club children's party.

8 January 1936 I stayed in N'bi at Chiromo. Lady Mac* was marooned on the Serengeti in floods of rain with seventy miles of black cotton soil on each side of her. Uncle Charles was a tremendous host, however, and gave a succession of dinner parties.... Had three days' polo and our team won the champion female cup, defeating the tiger-women of N'bi by 5–0.

22 January 1936 An Anglo-Indian family, new settlers, arrived to stay. Their favourite spots in India appear to have been Bloody Knout and Buggernigger. He is a sweet little man who hates shooting rioters or anyone else, which is nice in a soldier. Mrs Buggernigger is quite frightful, so hearty I felt in a maze all the time they were here, and got into such depression that I took calomel, but I really think it was Mrs BN and not liver. It rained heavily and their room leaked, and they stuck on the hill. The small child got bitten by fleas and became irritable. Finally the general helped to push the car out of the garage and Jos ran over his foot.... Have kept some grand account books last year, but got tied into awful knots at the end and had to call in expert assistance. Taking correct depreciation into account, the balance sheet shows a net profit for the year of £15 – but it isn't really true, as I only paid myself £70 salary. However, this year should be better....

In June 1936 came an invitation Nellie could not resist, to join a district commissioner, H.B. Sharpe, on a safari to the Samburu and Turkana country in the Northern Frontier District. 'Sharpie' was an unusual DC. *White-haired, rubicund and inclined to stoutness, he had joined the Colonial Service rather late in life and had no wish whatever to elbow his way along the corridors of power to become a chief secretary,*

---

* Widow of Sir Northrup Macmillan, an American millionaire. She lived in some state at Chiromo, a comfortable, well appointed house with several acres of garden in Nairobi. Uncle Charles was C.W.N. Bulpett, an old friend and hunting companion of Sir Northrup.

or even governor of some far-flung Colony. All his interests lay in birds, plants and gardens. Every station to which he was posted he embellished with green lawns, flowering shrubs, indigenous trees and, if he had half a chance, tinkling streamlets diverted from the nearest river. The gardens became bird sanctuaries, full of the song of golden orioles, bright with the plumage of sunbirds and the red-throated, sapphire-blue starlings, so different from the dull European kind. The garden he created at Rumuruti became famous. In green glades in the natural forest grew primroses, narcissi, violets, freesias; in shady corners were ponds covered with water-lilies; there were even peacocks strutting about. Here you might be introduced to Dicksee, the elephant he had reared from a baby who wrestled with him in his sitting-room and browsed on scarlet cannas by the stream. (She went subsequently to the London Zoo.)

The main object of this particular safari was to read the riot act to the Samburu, whose moran *– young men of the warrior age-set – were over-indulging in ritual murders, committed in order to blood their spears. Such murders led naturally to retaliation, and might at any time provoke a flare-up of inter-tribal warfare, always simmering among these nomadic or semi-nomadic peoples of the remote north. Moreover they were often brutal, cowardly affairs; anyone's blood would entitle the killer to carve another notch in the haft of his spear; old women and young children were acceptable spear-fodder.*

So the Pax Britannica must be enforced; but on safari Sharpie carried a plant-hunter's trowel as well as the Union Jack. Northern Kenya was, and no doubt still is, a plant-hunter's paradise. He invited as companions, as well as Nellie, two expert botanists: Dr Jex-Blake, a former Harley Street specialist who had retired to a coffee farm near Nairobi, and his wife Lady Muriel. Nellie took the old Ford which was practically dropping to bits and on the first day out a front wheel came off and the axle broke. Then after spare parts had been fetched for the Ford, the springs of the lorry carrying all the camp gear collapsed.

2 July 1936 So a bullock was slaughtered, and the raw hide wound round and round the springs, and that took the lorry through the whole trip. Next day did eighty-three miles to a camp called Barikoi where Sharpie had a *baraza* [open-air gathering]. The Turkana are a *sweet* people. The old men arrived for the *baraza* with song and dance, hand in hand, such a good idea to brighten up Leg. Co. [the Legislative Council] I think. After the *baraza* they had an *ngoma* [dance]. They imitate all the animals too beautifully – guinea fowl, ostriches, rhino, etc. So sweet. Sharpie gave the Samburu a hell of a ticking-off. The situation is that all the murderers of all the murders are known, but it is impossible to get witnesses. So Slatter, the police-man, has been sent there with a 'levy force' of sixteen *askaris*. This costs Sh 7,000/- a month, which has to be paid by the Samburu out of their cattle. Slatter's job is to prevent more murders, and try to get witnesses for those already done.

The last murder was in March and they have just got one murderer sentenced to death, but there are masses of unconvicted murderers going about, and as far as one can see, unless the Samburu have a change of heart, they will be put out of existence as a cattle-owning people by paying for the Levy Force. It is all rather pathetic, but I suppose Govt. can't allow indiscriminate murdering, and all this ritual business only leads to cowardly murders. At the same time, the Pax Britannica doesn't offer the Samburu anything else. They seem potentially very bright, and two experiments of young men going into the police were very successful. Another problem lies in the fact that the young girls prefer to marry old men and have *moran* as lovers, rather than to wait for single-wife status with a *moran* when he sheds his pigtail etc. and becomes an elder, so it is doubtful whether there are enough girls to go round, and what *is* the induce-ment for a *moran* to become an elder? At present, the *moran* have been given a definite date to become elders by; their paint, hair, spears and earrings have been taken away (by request of the elders) and the youths have got to be circumcised at once. Slatter is rounding them up and chasing them to circumcision ceremonies. We saw some 'youths' who were heavily moustachio'd men. . . .

We started serious plant-hunting there, and the actual camp proved to be full of stapelias of the richest and rarest sorts, some may be quite new. After two days there, we went on 116 miles to the foot of Mt Nyira, where forty-five donkeys were awaiting us. Got to the top next day, and camped at 9,000 feet. It is a *marvellous* mountain, a great slab of a thing surrounded by desert, with glorious cedar and podo forest on top. We climbed from 3,500 feet to 9,000 feet. Next day we went to the very, very top at 9,600 feet. An incredible view, Lake Rudolf [now Lake Turkana] lying at your feet and streaking away out of sight, Teleki's volcano just below, Mt Kulal to the north and Abyssinian border hills just beyond. Collected many plants. We all went out in different directions, each accompanied by an *askari* with a loaded rifle (buffalo all around) and an enormous Samburu tribal retainer armed with a spear. Mine had a spear in one hand and a small trowel in the other, and the *askari* always laid down his rifle to help grub up plants. We got a lovely blue potato creeper, quite new, it is a glorious thing. The Samburu say elephants aren't 'allowed' on Mt Nyira, nor rhino, and lions only for the night. It is given over to buffaloes and leopards, and innumerable gorgeous birds, of which Sharpie knows not only the name, but the notes, of every one.

Was the camp cold! We had roaring fires outside every tent day and night, also rings of permanently red-hot ashes round each tent against *siafu*, who made some fierce attacks. It was rather in doubt as to how we were to get down Mt Nyira on the east side, but someone said they knew a path, so we started off. It *was* a path, the poor donkeys had a terrible time, and often had to be lifted, loads and all, over rocks. We had a lovely camp half-way down, and got to the Horr valley about 5 pm next day. A really hard walk, that was, but my arthritic knees, flat feet and varicose veins behaved marvellously.

Made another camp in the Horr valley, donkeys went back, Barikoi again, then off to the Matthews range to meet Slatter at a camp called Wamba. Going along a *very* bad track, through thick bush, crawling on top gear, I heard an unpleasant noise, and out came a rhino charging like hell. I only saw it when it emerged from the bush, literally ten yards away, and was looking down its throat. Didn't look long, but shot old Fordi into second gear and the rhino *just* missed the back of the car. Luckily it didn't turn, apparently you never know in these parts if an animal hasn't got a bit of Turkana spear in it.

Our camp at Wamba was under some fig trees near pools, the trees were muddy up to ten feet where the elephants had scraped themselves dry the night before. At 7.30 pm twelve of them came to bathe, and we watched them in the spotlight fifty yards from our tents. At length they solemnly moved away in single file, and did the same the next night; it was a lovely sight. Then back to Maralal, to hear that the night before a lion had killed a zebra between the house and the staff huts. At 6.30 pm the din began – and such a din. Between second toastie and coffee Sharpie took us in his car and we saw an old lion fifteen yards from the road. We got the headlights on him, and he crouched there waving his tail for minutes and minutes. Sharpie shouted 'simba' and he moved away, back to the kill. There must have been twelve lions, and a furious din all night. . . . On the way back met awful weather and had a foul trip. Got in at 8; Karanja said, 'You look old and thin as if you had come out of the forest.' I'm really very fit, and all the better for those strenuous walks and climbs. . . . It was a lovely, lovely safari, and I was so lucky to have it. It has been thundering and lightning all the time. . . . Is there a cheap edition of Trotsky's *History of the Russian Revolution*? If so, could you get it for me?

There was a price to pay, however, for the lovely safari. Nellie went down with a bad attack of malaria.

The second go was much worse than the first, and my temperature only got down to normal yesterday, after days of thirty grains of quinine a day, which makes one feel awful. However, my two nurses, Miss S. William and Miss S.U.N. Flower, were constantly faithful in attendance, and I often called in a 'special' from among the half-dozen volunteers seated more or less permanently on the veranda.

Another outcome of the safari was the arrival of a batch of tough little Samburu donkeys, bought for a few shillings each. They were used for rides in the forest, and later put to an original purpose. Nellie had a deep trench dug in the garden and lined with straw, and into it were lowered two donkeys. They disappeared from sight. Every day more straw was added, they were generously fed, and gradually rose up on layers of deep litter; first their ears appeared, then their backs, then the rest of them until they walked out. Nellie's ambition at the time was to grow prize delphiniums, which are greedy feeders. She produced some magnificent blooms.

117

20 October 1936 I've got a very exciting new grass, imported from Paraguay, said to be drought-resisiting. The fruit-cage is a hive of industry, raspberries and strawberries coming on well. I've also planted blackberries, a Pomme d'Or, and grenadillas, and Tom Petrie is enquiring into the possibilities of tomato juice.

26 October 1936 Guests all the weekend, and Karanja rather *distrait* as his wife was having a baby. I used to have a theory that if people proposed themselves, they came at their own risk, but I've altered that now, and think it awful for people to come at all. Jos's reminiscences got out of hand this time, and I thought the weekend gloomy. However, they've all gone now.

Interlude 1937

An idea which germinated at about this time was that I should write a book about the Kikuyu: nothing anthropological, but the chronicle of an ordinary family. The tale would start before the coming of the European, and trace the effects of that revolutionary event on the fortunes of various members of the imaginary family.

Nellie arranged that she and I should live for three months or so in the heart of Kikuyuland, equipped with interpreter, notebook and camera, to find out all we could about the past. Later events we could gather from Njombo and other Kikuyu elders living at Njoro. The provincial commissioner at Nyeri offered us the use of one of the rest camps that were dotted about for the convenience of administrators touring their districts. So, early in 1937, we established ourselves with Karanja and a selection of dachshunds in a location called Murigo's, near the market of Karatina.

Chief Murigo's permission had first, of course, to be obtained. He was an impressive figure, heavily built, dignified, and always to be seen in his wide-brimmed chief's hat with its Kenya emblem, a shiny rampant lion, and carrying his brass-knobbed chief's staff. He wore as a rule a stern and rather dour expression, despite his wealth in goats and cattle, his nineteen wives and his innumerable children.

If ever a countryside could be described as smiling, this was it. Here the generous rainfall seldom, if ever, failed. Above arose the great mountain, from whose forests this fertile land had been won, and from whose snows issued many clear, sweet streams that rippled down between red ridges to the thirsty plains below. All up the sides of the ridges – quite unterraced then – were *shambas* of maize, millet, sorghum, sweet potatoes, groundnuts and other crops, haphazard and higgledy-piggledy, with women hoeing assiduously among them. (Hoeing and harvesting was always done by women; the men's sole agricultural task was to break new ground with pointed digging-sticks; ploughs had not yet been introduced.) Cattle and sheep and goats with tinkling bells browsed on juicy grasses and sweet white

119

clover. A purple-flowering shrub, *muthakwa*, and a golden gorse-like cassia dotted the scene.

Here and there a big fig tree, sacred to ancestral spirits, threw shade over a party of elders seated on the ground, drinking home-brewed beer from cattle horns. Each circle of round thatched huts, enclosed in a wooden palisade, sheltered a single family, in the widest sense of the term. Each wife had her separate hut and her granary, a smaller round thatched hut built on stilts to keep out rats and other vermin. The whole presented an almost idyllic pastoral scene; the sun shone, goats bleated, children called to each other, women pounded grain with their wooden pestles in mortars made from hollow logs; the air had a sparkle in it, you could almost feel the sap of growth in your blood. These Kikuyu were indeed fortunate in their habitat.

Would they, however, welcome a pale-skinned interloper asking questions about their private lives? They were by nature a suspicious people, and it was a toss-up whether they would accept us, or shut up like clams. Murigo broke the ice by bringing us a present of eggs and a chicken, and by attaching to us one of his *njamas*, members of his council, with instructions to smooth our way.

We were lucky, too, in Robert, the interpreter lent to us by the Church of Scotland Mission. He spoke fluent English and quickly grasped our aim. Karanja was able to vouch for our bona fides, and I have no doubt that the local people knew all about us in a very short while. And then, most elderly gentlemen like to recount the exploits of their youth; the difficulty is usually to find willing listeners. Here we were actually inviting reminiscences. When we got on to cattle raids and skirmishes with the Masai in pre-colonial days, a light came into their eyes, their voices grew resonant and one could almost see the spear trembling in the hand and hear war-horns echoing across the ridges. Several elders brought out their insignia from the dark recesses of their huts for our inspection: spears, swords in red leather scabbards, *rungus* (wooden clubs), anklets and head-dresses. It was as if one had invited members of the Cavalry Club to re-live for our benefit the battles of Abu Klea and Omdurman.

Once we had settled in and made a number of acquaintances, it seemed that no secrets were withheld. Some were, no doubt, but there was no suggestion of resentment at our curiosity. The local witch-doctor allowed us to sit in at a number of customary cere-monies, of which there were many, since no one could go on a jour-ney, or undertake almost any enterprise, without first making sure that he was not, in some fashion, giving offence to his ancestral spirits, and if necessary securing a charm to protect him. No event, to the Kikuyu, was fortuitous; if you fell ill, or broke a limb, if one of your cows died, or your wife miscarried, there was no natural cause; you had offended a spirit. The question was, how had offence been given, and how could matters be put right? Only a witch-doctor, an inter-mediary between the living and dead, could give an answer. He would, for a fee, identify the source of the *thahu* – a form of uncleanli-ness – and conduct a ceremony of purification.

To witness this ceremony was a duty and certainly no pleasure, because of the cruelty to the sacrificial goat that was entailed. The goat's legs were broken and its stomach slit open to extract the un-digested contents, a necessary ingredient in all such ceremonies, while it was still alive; in fact it was essential that it should remain alive while this was being done. The spectacle was horrible, and Nellie refused to watch. The witch-doctor and his clients remained totally unmoved by the goat's agonies. Compassion for a suffering animal appeared to be unknown. The Kikuyu were themselves most stoical in face of pain, and doubtless expected animals to be the same.

We were invited to witness a girls' circumcision ceremony, and this also was a sign of trust, since the Government, as well as the Missions, disapproved of the custom. This, too, was a cruel and brutal spectacle, but conducted with decorum; and, as in all initia-tion ceremonies, the initiates gave no sign of pain. To cry out, even to wince, was so deep a disgrace that the shame of the boy or girl would never be forgotten or erased.

Our camp was on the foothills of the mountain, and we felt very much under its lee. The temptation was too much for Nellie. Above the forest belt grew interesting, semi-alpine plants. It was agreed that time could be found for a quick dash up towards the snow-line. We had no idea of trying to reach the top – the peak is 17,058 feet. The idea was just to get as far as we could, and look at the scenery.

We recruited half a dozen porters, borrowed a light tent, packed some food and set off, at first following elephant tracks through the

121

forest. Then came a belt of tall, feathery bamboos, forming a kind of pointed arch overhead, from which we emerged on to a bleak and windswept expanse of heathland. Grass grew in thick, slippery tufts, waist-high or more, and horrible to walk on; you had to raise each leg at every step as if going up a ladder, and your feet slid off the tufts into soggy channels in between. At frequent intervals you fell flat on your face in black mud. Then came tall lobelias and giant groundsel, cabbages on stalks: a weird, uncanny sort of flora, so big, and rather intimidating, like something from another planet.

Our second camp, at about 11,000 feet, was the last spot where we could collect dry stalks of the giant groundsel for firewood. We huddled round the blaze, and water froze solid in its *debbi* a few yards away. Next morning, leaving the porters, we set forth just as dawn was breaking for our final climb, at first among the slippery tufts, and then, as we toiled upwards, along a rocky col between two gorges, covered with scree. The view was stupendous, and frequent stops to admire it enabled us to regain our breath. Above us the twin white peaks Batian and Nelion were shrouded in cloud.

We marked as our target a huge rock that towered above our col, under the invisible peaks. And there was the snow: not very deep and even, but undoubted snow, thinly coating the slithery scree. At the rock's foot we ate some chocolate and turned back, thankfully, I am bound to say, in my case. Nellie never liked turning back, but we were not equipped for rock-climbing. Without an aneroid we could not check the altitude but knew that the snow-line at that time of year – it varies with the season – lay at about 16,000 feet. Not high by Himalayan standards, but quite high enough for me. We reached camp soon after dark, and never had the warmth of a fire seemed more welcome, nor a mug of hot Bovril. The Kikuyu, very sensibly, never tried to climb their mountain; their god dwelt in its peaks, and to approach too close would have been sacrilege.

When our time was up at Murigo's we walked back over the Aberdare range of mountains to Naivasha in the Rift Valley, following a track that had been used by the Kikuyu to carry loads of produce down into the valley for barter with the Masai, obtaining in exchange goats, cattle, and sometimes brides. There was a good deal of Masai blood in the Kikuyu, which could be seen in their features. The loads, of course, were carried by the women, and very heavy they were, perhaps a hundred pounds or more; the men walked ahead with spears.

Back on the farm we found everything brown and bare for lack of rain, and seven cattle dead. Nellie diagnosed East Coast Fever. All the cattle were driven once a week through a dip to kill the ticks that carried the infection, but if the chemical in the dip was not kept strictly up to strength, some ticks would survive. In her absence, this had occurred. 'The eye of the master fattens the beast' is an old English farming adage. The absence of that eye, in Africa, often killed it.

In April, Nellie and I returned to England together. Jos had to stay behind to grapple with the affairs of his Azania hotel at Mombasa. Nellie spent part of her time with us, part of it with Trudie and the rest with her sister Blanchie in Wales. Nellie's family had dwindled, in practice, to Blanchie and her three daughters. Hughie was alive still but they did not meet. He had more or less cut himself off from the rest of his family by the sale, in 1925, of the whole of the Motcombe and Gillingham estates. Fox-hunting was his passion, and the South and West Wilts not good enough; he wanted to become Master of one of the crack packs in the Shires. This was an expensive ambition. He and Gladys had parted company, although they were never divorced. Their son Puck came of age in the same year as the sale of what should have been his inheritance. What upset Nellie was the remembrance of the sacrifices her father had made to keep Motcombe clear of debt and hand it over intact to his heir. Now that heir had sold his birthright, as it seemed to her, for a mess of pottage.*

So Hughie sold up, to the consternation of his tenant farmers, and went on to be Master of the Fernie Hunt in Leicestershire and Northamptonshire, also to keep a string of race-horses and a yacht. All this brought him little joy in the end. He took great pride in his son, who had inherited his father's love of sport and toughness, together with his mother's looks and charm. He was three years my senior, and I remember him, on the rare occasions when we met, as a most attractive companion, with a great zest for life and sense

---

* The property, 8,103 acres with numerous farmhouses and cottages, several villages and a wood, sold for a total of £180,350 – an average of just over £22 an acre.

of fun, and no trace of condescension towards an uncouth female cousin. At Oxford he had got his degree, despite keeping two hunters while he was there; he rode his father's horses to success in several major races and finished eighth in the Grand National when he was only twenty-two. Added to that he was a skilful flyweight boxer, and took up ocean racing to such purpose that when, in 1927, only two vessels survived ferocious storms to finish the course in the race from Cowes to Fastnet Rock and back, he was in the winning crew.

He also took up flying, bought a Moth, and in it made the first solo flight round Australia – 8,000 miles, flying by map with no such aids as yet-to-be-invented radar. (He was then ADC to the Governor of South Australia.) The next project was to be an attempt to break Kingsford-Smith's record from Australia to England. But when travelling as a passenger on a short routine flight, something went wrong and the aircraft nose-dived into Sydney Harbour. The bodies were never recovered. Puck was twenty-five. 'We looked on him', wrote one of his contemporaries, 'as the particular star of our generation.'

In October 1937, tea business took Gervas to Paris, Belgium and the Netherlands, and this time Nellie came too. It was perhaps the best holiday she had enjoyed since childhood. We saw many, many pictures, enticing shop windows with elegant clothes, gardens and palaces, Leyden and Bruges, Amsterdam's canals mirroring autumn foliage, the cheese market at Alkmaar, the fishermen at Volendam in traditional costume not yet donned only for tourists. And we had some superb meals. Years later, Nellie lovingly recalled a burgundy we drank in Brussels – a Corton Clos du Roy 1919, at one shilling and four pence a bottle.

In an attempt to get some kind of order into the material I had gathered about Kikuyu tribal life, I enrolled that autumn in a course of seminars at the London School of Economics held by the famous Professor Malinowski, whose classic study of the Trobriand Islanders had caused a sensation in anthropological circles. (The men, he found, had failed to connect their sexual activities with the procreation of children.) Social anthropology, then in its early days, was strange to me, and bewildering, and I was glad to find that one of my fellow students was himself a Kikuyu. I sat next to him at the first seminar and we broke the ice by exchanging a few sentences in Swahili, and a phrase or two – I knew my accent was poor – in his native tongue. After that he could not have been more friendly, and we lunched together several times at a Chinese restaurant in the Strand. This was none other than Johnstone Kenyatta, as he was then known. His reputation among colonialists was that of a dangerous focus of subversion, in fact a revolutionary, probably secreting bombs. He had spent a year in Russia, which had imparted to him, in the eyes of many Europeans, an almost diabolical aura. So I was intrigued to meet this burly, bearded and most articulate 'agitator', as future national heroes and founding fathers were then known.

Johnstone Kenyatta acted his part to the full; he loved an audience, and had embellished his appearance with exotic touches such as a ring with a large semi-precious stone worn on a little finger, a staff with a jewelled top, and flashy check trousers. There was something a little intimidating about him, despite his joviality and deep belly-shaking laugh; he had bright, quick, penetrating eyes that put me in mind of the Ancient Mariner, but it may well have been his reputation that imparted a kind of sinister patina which possibly he did not merit. But he had not yet become the mellow *M'zee* [Elder] of later years. He was then in his early forties, in full vigour, and actively embroiled in various pan-African and anti-colonial movements.

Curiously enough, our motives in enrolling in these courses under Malinowski and Dr Raymond Firth were basically the same. Both of us were writing books about the Kikuyu, he from the inside, an anthropological study published in 1938 as *Facing Mount Kenya*; I from the outside, a documentary novel published a year later as *Red Strangers*. As a student he was alert, intelligent, self-confident and concerned, I thought, only with those aspects of the discussions that bore directly on his purpose. He gave an impression of a mind subtle, keen but closely channelled. The Kikuyu people, not the world, were his oyster. He did not return to Kenya until 1946, after an absence of seventeen years.

Nellie, meanwhile, had gone back to find Jos depressed about the failure of his hotel, and the farm ticking over rather than forging ahead. 'It has been a disappointing year', she wrote. Crops were indifferent, 'the cattle dip much under strength, which is alarming'. The primary school she had started on the farm had run into difficulties. 'The teacher Douglas was a dead failure and no one came. Jehosophat was very popular and numbers rose to eighty.' He, too, had left, and now there was a stop-gap; trained teachers were hard to find. Gikammeh was drawing children from several neighbouring farms as well as from her own. 'I must keep the school going somehow, as the tots swarm to it.'

Life was enlivened by the arrival of Louis and Mary Leakey, struggling and as yet unknown young archaeologists. In a prehistoric burial ground near Nakuru they had unearthed skeletons dating back to about 2000 BC. (This site became known as Hyrax Hill.) 'The Leakeys are entirely without cash for the job, and want only £60 for six months.' The editor of the *Kenya Weekly News* opened a public subscription for them and Jos and Nellie each gave Sh 5/-.

Up in the forest and beside the river, Nellie discovered a cave. The Leakeys came to investigate and found bones, ornaments, pottery shards and evidence of cremation of the dead. (Subsequent radiocarbon tests gave a date of 960 BC.) The Leakeys camped on the farm and Nellie built them a *banda* in which to sort their finds. Like many others, she was captivated by Louis Leakey's eloquence, enthusiasm and power to make prehistoric people, or even hominids, seem alive and real. In the evenings, by the fireside, he would make string figures of extreme complexity, and he tried to teach her *guithi*, the Kikuyu version of the game played all over Africa with beans and shallow depressions in the ground, or on a board, so complicated that very few Europeans have mastered it. Nellie was not among them; she continued to prefer backgammon. Louis was working, at intervals, on his monumental study of the Kikuyu, which was to run to seven hundred thousand words, and failed to find a publisher for over thirty years. After the author's death the Academic Press, assisted by the L. S. B. Leakey Foundation in California, published it in 1977 in three volumes as *The Southern Kikuyu*.

During his stay on the farm Louis told Nellie about aspects of tribal life she had not suspected, although she had lived among Kikuyu people for twenty-five years.

You must never ask a man *directly* his name. If you do, he is bound to lie to you, because he cannot put himself in your power. Always ask a third party. There is no 'I am sorry' in Kikuyu. If you have offended in etiquette you say nothing, but offer some small bead or ornament from your clothes, which is accepted in silence and the incident is closed. Spitting on the hand in greeting means that you have transferred some of your life to the other chap, so would not cast the evil eye on him, or you would be doing yourself down.

I went fully and frankly into the matter of sex. It is a dreadful disgrace for a man not to give his wife complete satisfaction. Leakey says this is true of all African and Indian people, and accounts for the popularity of coloured lovers among white women. The man is taught thoroughly how to do it and how not to do it, and the bride-to-be is also given full instruction in positions etc. by her mother, so that they have a wonderful sex life. Homosexuality is absolutely unknown; there were no rules about it, it simply did not exist. The first two wives were always love marriages, and there were five occasions on which any girl could back out of a betrothal without disgrace if she wanted to.... The poor Leakeys are held up for wages money and only have two months work in sight on the skeletons, and need two years. They live on the smell of an oil-rag themselves, work all day on the site and up to eight or nine o'clock at night sorting and labelling the day's finds.

The event of the year was the arrival of the first wireless set, a very different affair from today's transistors.

It is too wonderful, and the greatest possible success. We cut down two blue gum trees and put up the poles buried three feet in the ground, with thirty-one feet out of it, stayed with wire. The wireless sits on the writing-table with its two batteries underneath, all very neat. We rushed to it at 6 pm to have our first session alone with it, and the most awful chug-chug-chug noises occurred. Jos with great skill diagnosed the electric light engine so we stopped that, and then reception was perfect. We heard all about poor Ramsay Mac-Donald and Kenya in the House of Commons etc. I finally abandoned it at 10.45 pm and went to bed, when Jos rushed along to say I must listen to the pipes from Glasgow.

The year ended with a request for pamphlets on caponizing cockerels and on the breeding of Minorca hens, and for twelve dozen corks for bottling rhubarb wine.

1938−9

During this, the year of Munich, international tension was mounting, and tremors reached Gikammeh through the newly installed wireless and the press, represented in Nakuru by the Kenya Weekly News. *Nellie passed on the warnings.*

9 January 1938 By the way, Frank Couldrey [the editor] says the state of the USA is far more serious than China, or Spain, or Germany. The most bloody civil war is about to break out on an unprecedented scale, accompanied by complete economic collapse. Need Gervas go? [He was about to leave for the USA.] They'll be drinking blood all summer, not tea, according to Frank.

30 January 1938 Cockie has arrived in a hired car with no lamps as she hadn't put them on properly. She wants me to go with her to Babati in Tanganyika for four days to fetch an inkstand. I say it is rather too much to go 400 miles and back for an inkstand, but she says she wants the inkstand.... A lovely letter from the Harper Adams man about crossing poultry to get back broodiness. He says my idea is quite in fashion and is being done in England, and the recommended cross is with Silkies, the only chickens I really like. They have turquoise blue ears,* and are *sweet*.

20 April 1938 Easter Sunday I had planned a quiet day, with a nice friendly game of golf in the afternoon. The day worked out like this. At 10 am the Seth-Smiths looked in on their way to fish. At 11 am Louis Leakey arrived on his first camp removal trip. At 12.30 pm Mr Ball [an agricultural officer] rang up to say could he bring two intending settlers up to talk farming in the afternoon. So at 2 pm I did a hasty trip to the club to scrap golf. At 4 pm they arrived, a strange pair of men, one one-armed and called Marseilles (really).

---

* Not really. They have turquoise blue lappets at the base of the ear.

They had lived for twenty-five years in China and Japan and knew less about any form of country life than you would think possible. During the afternoon both Leakeys arrived, to stay. While we were at tea, a mere seven, the Conduits arrived with a girl staying there, and that meant much gardening. At 5.30 pm Ball and the future settlers departed and the Conduits stayed to drinks – they always do. At 6.30 Fish and Ingrid arrived on their way back from fishing and they stayed for dinner. So that was my nice quiet day.

4 May 1938   You must admit that the enclosed chit was rather startling to have handed one by a full-blooded, almost naked Masai while doing a little quiet accountancy in the office about 9.30 on Monday morning. 'Dear Grant, A Kikuyu named Wakuha said to be living on your farm among your squatters, knifed young Jack White an hour ago to death. Police are called for, will you please make all enquiries among your squatters. Jock Harries.' The poor lad White was a very harmless boy, whom everyone liked, and the really astonishing thing is that he should have been knifed and not Harries. This farm became a sort of base for the police. The murderer Wakuha went off across it into the forest with one of my ex-squatters whom I sacked because he was a real bad hat. We were bristling with *askaris*, in and out of ambush.... They arrested both men at 8 next morning and brought them here, a really good piece of police work, getting the murderer within twenty-four hours with all these hundreds of square miles of forest. He was a discharged inmate of Mathari [the mental hospital], so presumably lost control beyond the normal.... On Tuesday I took myself off to the forest with the Leakey party. The little dogs had a lovely day and I saw two fine bushbuck. The Leakey finds now include some basketwork never before found south of the Sahara.

14 June 1938   My White Silkies were the sensation of the poultry section of the Show. The 'breeding trio' got second in a very strong class, and a hen 'highly commended' in a very strong class – Open Imported. People were thrilled with them – mostly they seemed to think they had something to do with Angora rabbits. I've booked enough orders to last me for years, but am going to work up my own stock first.

In August Gervas and I flew to Kisumu, where Jos met us and took us to Njoro. The Leakeys were there and we visited the caves; Njombo gave a beer party to welcome us; Silkies, turkeys, pigeons woke us in the morning; a tree-planting programme – podocarpus, Cape chestnuts, jacarandas, munungas, brayeras – was in full swing. Gervas went off to visit tea plantations and I had lessons on the farm in trapping moles from the Dorobo, and in Swahili from the schoolteacher. The wireless brought nothing but bad news from Europe. In September Gervas flew to South Africa; the Munich crisis worsened and we expected at any moment to have to hurry home. On 28 September German mobilization was announced for 2 pm next day and a cable came from Gervas to say that he was flying back from Durban. On the 29th the crisis began to subside and on the 30th it was over; the Munich agreement had been signed. Gervas went back to South and Central Africa and we arranged to meet at Moshi in Tanganyika for a quick safari to the Serengeti plains with Jos and Nellie and the Lindstroms, on our way home.

The safari belongs to another story; it was a week of enchantment. On 31 October Gervas and I entrained from Rongai (near Njoro) on the start of our return journey – not by air this time but first by train to Namasagali in Uganda, then by paddle steamer to Masinda Port, bus to Butiabu on Lake Albert, paddle steamer down the Nile to Nimule, overland again by car to Juba, back into another paddle steamer and through the Sudd, four days days of it, nothing to be seen but papyrus on all sides in which our flat-bottomed boat stuck continually, and had to be pushed out with giant punt-poles. It was excessively hot, and full of mosquitoes, and at Malakal great swarms of locusts appeared. At Kosti we left the boat and reached Khartoum by train. Another train, scorchingly hot, took us to Wadi Halfa on the Egyptian border; another boat to Aswan; another train to Luxor; then a car to Cairo with tea business on the way. At Alexandria we embarked on an Italian vessel which took us up the Adriatic to Venice (wet and cold for a change); the Simplon–Orient Express took us on to Paris, and finally an aeroplane landed us at Croydon, on 1 December. The whole trip took exactly a month. Another gap therefore occurred in Nellie's letters, but in November they were resumed.

19 November 1938 I sacrificed my Sunday morning long lie, most reluctantly, to see some native sports at Njoro. Rather an odd thing, organized by a small committee of 'Independents' at Kiambu to show how they *can* organize. All for Kikuyu *totos*, masses of them coming in by train from Kiambu and Thika even, and all the farm schools entering teams. There are twelve *totos* from here. No sign of schooling for weeks – only drill! The fathers, most unwillingly, have spent Sh 1/50 each on amerikani shirts with green and red stripes, and I've given them each a ditto sash, Karanja says that *maridadi* will win many marks. I asked him who was the judge? He said it was like our House of Commons – everyone was to judge. Karanja has bought bread and butter to put up a feast. Every single soul on the farm is going or gone.

25 November 1938   The sports were organized by the Independent Schools Association at Thika, and very well done. There was a big drill ground curtained off with hessian, a Royal Box for the six elders who were judging, other seats according to price, a steward's box, printed tickets, etc. Thousands and thousands came. There were eight teams in all. Ours came third. The *totos* from Fort Hall won. Karanja was *the* lad of the village. It was just a big drill display, on the whistle, not terribly good perhaps, but the organization was *very* good. Leakey says they hold these shows to demonstrate that they can organize without the European. He also says that not all Independents are bad at all, and the Independent Schools Assn. is a reputable body. They only want to get free of Mission education, to have their own schools run by themselves, non-sectarian, and to stick to polygamy. Well, I thought Njoro ought to make a gesture, so horned in on the Royal Box and invited the elders to tea on Monday morning. And did they come. They were very sweet indeed. Five quite old, obvious elders, one of them very keen and alert, and one much younger, very intelligent man. They said they'd rather speak Swahili than English. I gave them tea under the small olive, with cake and bread and butter, and then asked them in and gave them cigarettes. Njombo was one of the party. It was rather a squash, but two got quite comfortably into the big armchair. We discussed every war in the world, Germany's claim to colonies etc. They think no colonies should go back, as the British Empire is a great force for good in the world. Then we went to see the school, drying shed, etc. They were sweet about flowers, pounced on every one they didn't know and asked if it grew from cuttings, etc. They had lovely manners, and said they appreciated a gesture from settlers very much. They asked me to stay any time I liked.

28 December 1938   The Farm Produce Show and Sports is over. Marvellous entries for the Produce Show, about thirty. Karanja's wife won, with fourteen different kinds of produce, Kupanya's second with thirteen. Gitau had a lovely exhibit of real popcorn; I have booked some seed. The Dorobo put in a grand lot of bows and arrows. Everyone showed everything they had – an alarm clock was included. Next came the babies, then sports. A sheep race for the elders was very popular. There was a vast crowd. I had a steward for every race, and two handicapping committees. They were much quicker on the uptake, and altogether brighter, than the committee running the club's children's party. At 4 pm prizegiving and a scramble for oranges among the children, somewhat restricted as the spectators had pinched fifty per cent of the oranges. The party then had free cups of tea, bringing their own cups. They got through twenty pounds of tea and fifty-six pounds of sugar. It cost about £5, but I feel it was a good move.

After Hitler's invasion of Czechoslovakia on 16 March, even the sturdiest optimist had to face the inevitability of war. In Kenya, the general gloom was worsened by a devasting drought. A scheme to settle on the land a number of Jews who had escaped from Germany had been sponsored by a body called the Plough Settlement Association. Nellie volunteered to take a couple and give them hospitality and basic training.

14 March 1939   Well, the Jews arrived this morning. I was nearly sick with apprehension after the wire came to say they were coming. But so far, so good, we have really been very lucky. He is a Jew from East Prussia who had his own farm which he lost, and was put into a concentration camp last November. She is nineteen, very clean and pretty, from Bavaria, absolutely unaffected. I should say he was a competent man, quiet, and looks very ill and sad, poor devil. He worked like a beaver on the ram yesterday, which had stopped, and got it going. He knows no English, but she knows enough to interpret, and now I know the German for locust, pipe, ram, pressure, butterfat, bull-calves and lots else besides. Jos is in his element, but I do wish he wouldn't try to teach them farming, as it will be so difficult for them if we tell them opposite things.

The stream of uninvited guests continued unabated, almost as relentless and expensive as the convergence upon Ithaca of Penelope's suitors. Nellie must have longed for another Ulysses to drive at least some of them away. After her rewarding contacts with the Leakeys and Audrey Richards,* she was disposed to welcome anthropologists, but changed her mind when a much less congenial one arrived and stayed for weeks, resting from her labours. On top of all this, Nellie got a septic hand from a dog-bite and had to go to hospital to be treated with the drug 693.

7 April 1939 Got back from hospital to a cheerful reception with a terrific locust invasion and a grass fire and still no sign of rain; the heat and dust and dryness are foul beyond words. It is absurd the way 693 pulls you down, I feel as if I'd been weeks in hospital with several major ops, but doubtless this will pass.

18 May 1939 Kenya is preparing. Several of the minor telephone exchanges have been told to stay open till 8 pm instead of 5 pm so that the Kenya Regiment can be collected. Someone has started the idea, I'm glad to say, that pyrethrum is an essential industry. Delousing in the last war cost £8 million plus great loss of efficiency, now they hope to do it more cheaply if the gallant little band of pyrethrum growers in Kenya will stick to their posts and Carry On. I shall try. At the Hospital Board meeting yesterday we considered the behaviour of the Hospital in air-raids, and made arrangements for operations to be done, and babies to be born, by safari lamps and candles. We can do no more.

* Then Senior Lecturer in Social Anthropology at the London School of Economics, later to become Director of the East African Institute of Social Research at Makerere College in Uganda, and then Director of the Centre for African Studies at Cambridge. She was President of the Royal Anthropological Institute from 1959 to 1961, and published a number of distinguished studies of African tribal structures and customs, notably of the Bemba tribe in the present Zambia.

24 May 1939   The girl-Jew has one parrot cry for everything you try to tell or show her: 'We have that also in Germany.' Yesterday evening there was a perfectly lovely partial eclipse of the moon, the cloud effects were marvellous. I called her from her room on to the lawn to see it. Her only reaction was: 'We have that also in Germany.'... On Sunday I went to the old Von Turques, the Germans at Njoro. He is a marvellous vegetable gardener. It was a sad evening. More and more aged and decrepit Germans kept appearing from bedrooms at the back until the house was quite quite full of them. My sundowner was a glass of the most heavenly Château Yquem, thirty-six years old. There's an Austrian refugee there, a boy of eighteen who has no idea of what has happened to both parents. Wasn't it a pathetic evening?

Sympathy for the plight of the Jewish refugees did not, despite every effort, prevent them from getting on Nellie's nerves. The girl started a baby, a place was found for the man on another farm, and they departed. A personal sorrow at this time was the death of Gillie, her favourite brother, whom she had scarcely seen for many years. The drought continued.

29 June 1939   Last Saturday Fish, Hans, Pat and I went off to camp for one night at the south end of Lake Nakuru. There is a cliff from which you look down over about two thousand acres of plain, enormous thorn trees to fringe it, and then the lake, now all white soda dust, a heavenly spot. The two lads went off to hunt and got a good impala. On Sunday morning more hunting; they saw lots of game and also a fight on the cliff between an eagle and a young baboon. The baboon got away. After breakfast we set off to make history by becoming the first living people to cross the lake on foot, but soon got ankle-deep in mud. There's no water at all in the lake now, and marvellous sea-like effects are produced by shifting waves of soda being blown about. If we'd had skis, or a boat on rollers, we could have gone anywhere on foot, as it was we gave up and climbed back to beer and lunch and then came on home.

7 July 1939   The road to Nakuru is practically all hoppers now, and the cattle people are desperate for lack of grazing.... There are two huge puff-adders on the boundary – such a worry because of the dogs, also one ox has already died from being bitten. Porcupines are eating my spuds.

30 August 1939   My war work to date has consisted entirely in offering to house one dachshund of the Von Turques, as, poor old things, they'll be popped inside if the worst happens. Beyond that, I have a great hope that I may be taken on at the plant-breeding station here. Robert Ball has asked his department to apply for me. The Red Cross are sending wool and told me to knit ten pairs of socks and Ingrid is going to stitch ten shirts. We shall do so, though I think Mrs Desai and Mrs Njeroge would do it much better.

War was declared on 3rd September.

10 September 1939   The old Von Turques were decreed too old, too anti-Nazi and too ill to be disturbed, so they are left provided they don't stir off their ten-acre plot. We returned their beloved dachs to them so my war work has been taken away from me.... The damned locusts come every day now, not a sign of rain either.

15 September 1939   Had about a hundred Kikuyu in the sitting-room today to listen to the weekly broadcast. They certainly enjoy it. Govt. is starting a Swahili paper from tomorrow called *Baraza*. I've been studying Swahili quite earnestly, instead of crosswords. It's a lovely language, and I like it. Can read and write fairly well, but do want speaking practice with a real coast Swahili. The Secretariat burnt itself to ashes Tuesday night and all the early records were lost.

17 October 1939   We're in the throes of the worst drought since '18, and some say worse than '18. Production is sinking like a stone, we shall presumably have to import food to feed the swarms of militaires, and not a whisper of any plan to keep production going at all, let alone increase it. Truly a strange, strange war. Personally, I'm going all out for things on four legs and boldly buying cows – on terms – and have ordered six gilts in pig from the Kinangop.

135

Ingrid is just like Boadicea these days, and might at any minute spring into an ox-cart and dash off to war with two old oxen.

24 October 1939   There has been a plague of puff-adders, advancing up the farm in waves, never seen before. I give Sh 1/- each and cut off their tails. Eight have been brought in in three days, mostly by small children staggering under their weight. The last enormous one, full of eggs, was slain in the garage. It is the drought, of course, which continues to rage unabated.

15 December 1939   I have contacted Sir Howard Elphinstone, the Resident Magistrate in Nakuru and a great Swahili expert. He is full of his new teaching method, and guarantees to get one through the Higher Standard in six months. He has written out all his notes. I've also got Taylor's aphorisms, or 'Saws from Swahililand'. There are 746 saws. I try to learn one every day in the aunt. If I go every day, as one should, I shall know them all in two years and a fortnight, provided I haven't forgotten the early ones by then. Have been rather discouraged by number 3, *Adhabu ya kaburi ajua maiti* – only the dead know the horrors of the grave. Not the best jiggery-pokery at all.

The War Years 1940 – 5

Kenya's role in the war was clearly to grow food, and yet more food, for the armies of the Middle East and North Africa, and for the troops stationed in the Colony itself, which became a launching-pad for the Ethiopian campaign. Progress was inhibited partly by the call-up of able-bodied Europeans from the farms, even more by the apparent inability of the Colonial Government to make the necessary plans to increase production, and take the practical steps to carry through such half-hearted plans as did exist. So there was, at first, a mood of uncertainty and frustration among the farming community. Nellie found the inability to know what best to do, and the lack of a sensible overall plan, extremely irksome. And, of course, she felt 'cut off', as so many British people overseas did, from the centre of events where she might have been taking her share of the dangers and discomforts experienced by her family and nation – perils that always seem worse when you hear about them from a distance, than they do when you are on the spot.

However, her search for useful war work was rewarded when, early in 1940, a neighbour who had started a vegetable canning factory at Njoro was called up. Nellie took over the factory from its owner at a week's notice, despite a total ignorance of canning techniques. The Lindstroms lent their young pupil, Hans Stjernswärd, to help.

9 May 1940 We are working two shifts now, Hans in the mornings, me from 2 to 10 pm. It gets a bit gloomy towards the end, so if I can arrange the work accordingly I slip off to the St Maurs' to get the 8.45 news, which, of course, invariably makes one gloomier still. The Italian war has come here very much lately. Blackouts are imposed in all towns, and you can't even go to Njoro without proper lamp arrangements. My household take the blackout very seriously; the house is festooned with all sorts of queer things which operate excellently in the day-time.

16 May 1940   There is a twenty-five per cent cut in petrol, so joy-riding is finished. East Coast Fever has broken out again in the Rift, Rose has lost three more very good cows, and leopards have started on her calves. Two nights ago she had to listen to awful screams while one calf was killed and another maimed. This is the third time. Ken Balfour (neighbour) tried a gun trap which first shot his sweet Alsatian dog, and second shot a cow of Rose's. They have now put down strychnine.

9 June 1940   The factory is really busy now, half a ton of cans a day, and I hope up to one ton per day this week, all going off to the military. Frightful crisis, as awful trouble with tanks (rainwater not military). Hans and I and about twenty boys wrestled with the main two-thousand-gallon one perched about twenty feet up. It came down like a parachutist, and altered the shape of its top, which unfortunately is visible from the road.

Hans Stjernswärd, her young assistant, recalls memories of those hectic days:

For over a year I was with her in the canning factory. Her generosity and patience was always there, coupled with an extraordinary sense of humour. Lilian Graham lived very near, and having nothing to do used to call in at the factory very often. Two more totally different characters one can hardly imagine, and her visits were not always appreciated. The office was not built in the most solid way. Lilian came to call at, for her, a suitable time for a cup of tea, and parked her car on the slope without securing the brakes. I was in the factory, heard a crash, came out and found the two ladies in the office drinking their tea as if nothing had happened, with the very damaged front half of a car half-way into the office. Lilian's only remark had apparently been: 'Oh dear'. Nellie's response was an icy silence, only suggesting that should Lilian call again, it might be in everybody's interest if she walked – a thing she would never do. We were canning a lot of carrots for the army. The year's crop had been good, and the carrots were the size of swedes. The labour force was supposed to cut them up in slices to go into the tins. Quite naturally they got bored and I discovered that they had been ramming whole large carrots into the tins, one carrot to a tin. Hundreds had already been done, and I wasn't going to waste them, or tell Nellie. A few months later I met a friend who was serving on special patrols in the Northern Frontier District, living very rough and entirely out of tins. When I asked him what the food was like he said it was pretty rough, and the bastards who had supplied tinned carrots without a corkscrew, he would like to meet. I owned up, we had a good laugh and Nellie nearly died of laughing when I told her. Eventually the machinery wore out, spares were unobtainable, resulting in blown cans, not properly sealed. One morning Nellie arrived in her battered car, I on my horse, to a scene of disaster. Thousands of cans gone, and the stink awful. The day was spent clearing up the mess, it was a blow to both of us. I can remember Nellie's set jaw and clenched teeth and not a word did we exchange that day. Finally the canning factory closed down, we could get no spare parts and the army moved on.... Apart from that, Nellie was always the centre of everything and the moving spirit in all conversation, be it serious or otherwise. She stands out for me as a shining light – one always had to be on one's mettle when talking to her, if not you were quickly put in your place, but never unkindly. In a country that was very farmery and dull, she was intellectually head and shoulders above almost everyone else.

18 July 1940 Am kept at it hard at the factory, as Hans has been called up. Have engaged a venerable African to replace him.

Jos, meanwhile, had been no less frustrated than Nellie – perhaps more so – at having, as he put it, 'to sit out the war'. (He was sixty-six.) So he was delighted to be offered a job on one of the tea plantations, replacing a younger man, and went off to Kericho, leaving Nellie alone on the farm.

22 October 1940 I do this farm now before 9 am and after 4 pm, and the canning in between. I have discovered the secret of a carefree life, as far as housekeeping is concerned. This is a diet, worked out by Dr Anderson, with everything necessary to perfect health. It is: five glasses of milk, five oranges and five slices of Vita-wheat per day. You can substitute tomatoes and lettuces for some oranges, and up to two ounces of cheese to replace some of the milk. I make tea furiously, and haven't had an alcoholic drink for a fortnight. The joy of never organizing any food, or having a grocer's bill, is marvellous.

14 November 1940   Have you ever toyed with the idea of how utterly and completely the whole economic structure of the world would alter if, at a stroke of the pen, everyone took to my diet? Try to work it out and write a book about it, just to show what a really fragile little world it is, and how ridiculous most of our cast-iron institutions are.

21 November 1940   You could have knocked me over with a fevver yesterday, for I got a letter from HE asking me if I would accept a seat on the Council of Makerere if he nominated me as one of the two Kenya members, a vacancy having arisen. I've said I would agree. Actually it would be extremely interesting, especially at this stage of the world's madness, to have a finger in the pie of fitting the African into a post-war culture, and really attractive to have a job connected with construction, and not unending destruction. And one would meet people like Mrs Trowell.* So I hope he doesn't lose his nerve over it.... God bless you, and take the very greatest care of yourselves. Oh, that you were out here.

28 November 1940   Would it be an awful sweat and bother to find out if there really is a shortage of medicinal herbs in England, and if one could do anything about it here? It is a side-line I would love to try, and one might work it up into a post-war industry of value.

6 December 1940   Moore has nominated me as one of Kenya's two members of the Makerere Council.† It is really a bluff. What do I know about any education? But if the Govt. do try to give non-

---

* Makerere College near Kampala, in Uganda, had been started to provide higher education for students from Uganda, Kenya, Tanganyika and Zanzibar. It was intended to become a University to serve the four countries and offer professional training to their diverse peoples. Mrs Trowell was in charge of the art department.

† Sir Henry Monck-Mason Moore (1887–1964) was Governor of Kenya from 1939 to 1944. Subsequently he became Governor of Ceylon.

officials a chance of helping over native affairs, would it not be gauche to reject the little gesture? Anyway, I want a trip to Uganda.

12 January 1941 There was a gymkhana in Nakuru on Saturday, attendance ninety-nine per cent military. I took to wheels in the ladies' bicycle race and came last, but that was because I was all dolled up in my best blue and white frock, so had to bribe a small girl to hire me her very minute bicycle, as I couldn't get on to a man's machine in that kit. So I'm not unduly discouraged.... I went to see poor Ken Balfour in hospital who had his arm shattered by an anti-tank bullet. Modern surgery seems too brutal. They put the arm in plaster of paris up at the front and it was left for a month. It went terribly septic, he was dreadfully ill and lived on 693. They opened it up without an anaesthetic, and the dressing had grown into the wound. They now repeat this every fortnight and say that in four months it will have cleared itself. Meanwhile the dressings are agony and the arm stinks to Heaven. They say the idea came from the Spanish war – I think they must mean the Peninsula War.... I had two convalescents for a week, they did in my wireless by putting through six volts instead of two. All five valves were done in and cannot be got in the country, anyway they cost £1 each. I am selling all my donkeys which should exactly realize the cost of a new set.

30 January 1941 The great sensation locally has been the murder of poor Joss Erroll. It is indeed ironic that the Ngong road should have proved more dangerous than Tobruk.*

2 February 1941 The Standing Committee on Education seems to have been most casual about the salary of the first African graduate teacher. He is a graduate of Yale. It is terrifically important, because he is the first-ever graduate appointment and they have put his salary away below that of Europeans *and* of Achimota in the Gold Coast. My view is that they ought to keep the standard of admittance to such posts extremely high, but that all who do attain it should be on equal terms. If education sinks into mediocrity, God help

* He was found in his car, shot through the head, just outside Nairobi, on the road to Ngong.

Africa.... Seventy South African FANYS [First Aid Nursing Yeomanry girls] have returned to the Union pregnant; they came up as ambulance drivers and have returned as troop-carriers.

3 March 1941   The most lovely photo album I have ever seen has come, of Woodfolds. What a lovely place it is, and what lovely people in it. Oh, dear, how crude Njoro seems after all those lovely pictures of Woodfolds. I don't see how you can ever love any other place.

Woodfolds was the seventeenth-century farmhouse in north Wiltshire which Gervas and I had been fortunate enough to buy at auction in June 1938. Modernization was completed just before the outbreak of war, and it was to remain our home for thirty-two years, although during the war we could go there only at weekends. Gervas, after a visit to the United States and Canada in 1939–40 to put his tea campaign on a care and maintenance basis, worked for the duration at the Ministry of Information, and I for the BBC until the birth of our son in 1944.

24 March 1941   The house has been full of South African nurses from Mombasa, really splendid women, terrifically keen, and it is no fun nursing in Mombasa with the heat and blackout. They were all tired out, having just had the first Mogadishu casualties down in a hospital ship.... I have decided, rightly or wrongly, to let Donald Seth-Smith buy three hundred acres at the top of the farm. I hate letting it go, but think the time has come to set one's house in order. I feel now I shall never have enough capital to develop the farm really well. Pyrethrum, everyone thinks, will soon be off the map as a rewarding crop. Donald will give me £6 10s an acre, and I shall be able to get clear of the Land Bank, Piggery Nook, etc. It is, of course, the part of the farm I like best, but it is silly to mind that. Donald will care for the land, which is one thing....

25 April 1941   I left Nakuru Monday night for the Makerere Council meeting. It was very exciting stepping into a train, and lovely to get away.... The outstanding personality at the Council is, of course, George Turner, the Principal. He would be outstanding anywhere, a marvellous man, a practical idealist – almost a saint? If anyone can start the College off on the right lines, he will. His whole aim is to counteract the crass materialism of everything, and to impress on the students that when they leave, they are only *beginning*. They have, of course, got the idea that on leaving Makerere they should at once get the most stupendous salaries.

16 May 1941 The pigs are doing well, but a leopard scared two sows the other night so they farrowed at once all over the place, all piglets dead, a sad loss. He also took two piglets the other night. The new crop, perennial sorghum, has all germinated.

12 June 1941 I've got a really good Seychelles clerk at the factory now, a godsend. He has been living in a very bad stable built by Hans, with a wife and three small children, he seldom complains except when the snakes squeak loudly at night. . . . The Erroll murder case is nearing its end. It has got terribly boring and technical, all about bullets. I can't see myself how the jury could convict on the evidence. Popular opinion is very much against the Bart.* I hope to God they will all be kicked out of the country for ever, it has done an infinity of harm, and has all been nauseating. . . . The countryside has never looked more lovely, nor the crops more like they should. If only one could sit back in a happy world and drink it all in.

18 June 1941 The Arts and Crafts Exhibition at Nakuru was a very good little show, I think. Peggy Trowell sent down a selection of her students' work from Makerere, at my suggestion. They all sold, and I think people were interested, but can you believe it, when Powys Cobb brought down his wife's paintings to exhibit, he told the secretary he wouldn't allow them to be shown if 'native paintings' were included in the exhibition. Can you beat it – from an 'educated' man too? The secretary, after a great deal of trouble, persuaded him that it was all right.

---

* The Bart was Sir Delves Broughton. His beautiful wife Diana was alleged by the prosecution to be having an affair with the the Earl of Erroll. A protracted trial, which even in wartime attracted great attention, ended in Broughton's acquittal. Subsequently he committed suicide in a Liverpool hotel.

2 July 1941 I've been put on the local Production Sub-Committee which is supposed to tell everyone what to grow. The 'patriotic' things are wheat, flax, potatoes, butterfat, pigs and beans. Pyrethrum is no longer patriotic. Butterfat, pigs and spuds for me.

12 July 1941 All the ineptitude makes one sick. *Surely* we need an agricultural policy? *Surely* the masses of stuff we could produce is wanted? Everything go-as-you-please. The Italian prisoners of war are said to go complaining because they are given too much butter!... The next war has got to be against Bureaucracy, and the sooner it starts the better.

31 July 1941 The great thing is to have a job. Much as one hates work, one realizes that it does hold at bay the awful monster that is lurking just beyond, which is Thinking About the War.... I went to Kericho to see Jos last Saturday. He has got a very adequate little house, and tidier than you might think, very comfy beds, a lovely fridge and a nice view with a corner of the Kavirondo Gulf visible. We had a gentle game of golf on the Sunday morning and a walk-round in the evening.

10 August 1941 The military contracts for canned veg. have ceased, owing to the new veg. drying factory at Karatina and also because the army has moved on. I feel in a quandary, and don't know what to do.

Nellie had not had a holiday since the war began, and this seemed a good moment to take one. She arranged to drive with Jos, Rose Cartwright and her daughter Tobina, a Danish family called Middle-boe, Karanja and Rose's personal servant Mbugwa (not to be confused with Nellie's of the same name) to Lamu on the Coast, an old Arab sea-port. They set forth in two cars but ran into trouble from the start. First a wheel of Nellie's car came off and the brakes seized, and the sound car had to return to base for repair equipment. They reached Garissa, on the river Tana, to be told that unseasonable rain had made the Lamu road, or track, impassable, or nearly so.

14 September 1941 We decided to go on as far as we could, and camped at Burra, about fifty miles south-east of Garissa, a waterless camp. Next morning we proceeded very cautiously through dense bush country, wonderful birds, a good deal of game. . . . About four miles on we came to an awful stretch of swamp, and alas I stuck irretrievably. Rose didn't, but our rope wasn't long enough to reach her. So we had to camp then and there in that awful swamp, no *kuni* [firewood], and billions of mosquitoes. It was a hellish night. Also we'd seen fresh lion spoor, and signs of buffalo and elephant. However if they did roar, moo and trumpet, mosquito noises drowned it all. We were almost eaten alive. I had a little spirit stove so we were able to have hard-boiled eggs and tea, but next morning Mbugwa monkeyed about with it and blew it up, and set his trousers alight. He was very badly burnt, poor devil. I had cod-liver oil ointment with me and dressed his burns as best I could. Eventually a huge PWD lorry arrived and they had to get me out before they could proceed. Eventually I got towed and lifted out, and joined Rose's party back at Garsen. By that time we'd had to decide to give up Lamu, and came on here to Malindi, determined to camp somewhere on the beach. After various negotiations we got in at a deserted military camp right on the sea-shore, and have two *bandas* a few yards from the sea. We got Mbugwa into hospital, where he still is, rather bad. On Monday when we really thought we'd have a bit of a holiday, Ulrich Middleboe got a temperature of 105°, malaria, so poor Ulla has had to nurse him all the week. . . . The safari was largely a matter of hauling loads on and off lorries and cars, so we all had a change if not a rest.

21 September 1941   We found *the* perfect place for a Coast refuge, near Ngomeni, a tiny fishing hamlet of Swahili fisherfolk. In spirit it strikes one as akin to the fishing hamlets on the west coast of Scotland. We chartered a dug-out, and were paddled along the shore to the southern headland, Ras Ngomeni, and this is the place. There are about five acres perhaps of sandy land jutting into the sea from some low cliffs. Millions of the most beautiful shells and, on a spit, hundreds of sandling terns and dotterels feeding, and an old pelican. There is a well of marvellously sweet, clear water sunk last year by an Arab, and elephant spoor all over the place, they come down on the 'kusi', or south-west monsoon. A sand reef keeps the sharks outside. The sand was hot underfoot but a cool breeze blows all the time. The Indian Ocean in September is heaven and Ngomeni a place to dream about. The road was plastered with Carmine Bee-eaters, the most lovely birds imaginable.

26 September 1941 Your little dachs sound adorable. *Now* you know what dogs mean, and what an unbiased welcome is, and how heavenly it is to talk to someone who doesn't know all about the International Situation.

1 October 1941 The opening of Peggy Trowell's African Art Exhibition at Makerere was a real occasion. I was deposited next to the Governor, an unbelievable man. He says 'aw' very often. Our meeting was quite an encounter. *He* (on introduction): 'Aw. Are you in the Education Department?' *Me*: 'No, I live at Njoro. I'm just a settler.' *He*: Aw. I didn't know there were any.' Pause. Mrs Turner arrives: 'Mrs Grant's daughter has just given us her books, sir. We appreciate her gift very much.' *He*: 'Aw, is it your daughter who helps us on Our Domestic Side?' *Me*: 'I'm afraid not. My daughter is a good cook, but she is in another situation at present.' End of encounter. Mrs Governor is equally unbelievable. She announced there were *ladies* in Entebbe, *women* in Kampala. That took the minds of the Kampala women right off the war in an instant, so presumably was good for morale.... Uganda never stops raising huge sums for war charities, and everything is devoted to that end, even unto the effort of a local hen which laid an egg with a large 'V' on it (it really did, I saw it on show).... Uganda is, on the whole, in one continuous state of gentle sozzle, and will probably remain so. How far anyone will get, who knows?

Nellie's twice-yearly visits to Kampala made a welcome break from war-time farming routine. Often she stayed with Dr Hugh Trowell, a consultant at the local hospital, and his wife Peggy, the art teacher at Makerere.

My happiest picture of Nellie [Mrs Trowell recalled] will always be of her seated in a first-class railway carriage on her return to Kenya from a meeting of the Council. Quite unconcerned by the glances of two supercilious young Government officials who shared her carriage, she strummed happily on a musical instrument she had just bought by the roadside. On the seat beside her in a very rickety home-made cage scuffled half a dozen white mice, while overhead a lidded basket containing anatta, a local plant from which a brilliant scarlet dye can be extracted, was already beginning to drip great gouts of gore on to the seat below. She had lost her heart to my children's white mice, bought half a dozen of them for a fabulous sum, searched the town for wire netting for the cage and bought it at black market price in an Indian *duka* – the sale of such material was supposed to be strictly controlled – and was setting out on a career of mouse breeding for experiments in hospitals and research stations.

Nellie lost no time in making an arrangement with the Government laboratories near Nairobi whose scientific staff were delighted to take all the mice she could supply. A new farm industry was launched. It thrived for a while, but the mice took to cannibalism. Experiments with diet failed to check the habit and eventually, disgusted with the mice, Nellie released the survivors in the forest.

The Erroll murder case had been the swan-song of the Happy Valley band whose goings-on had scandalized and entertained gossip-column readers between the wars. Wartime realities scattered or extinguished the survivors, sometimes in tragic ways.

23 October 1941   Alice de Trafford shot herself the other day – with surer aim, poor thing, than she applied to Raymond at the Gare du Nord. [She had shot her former husband in the stomach as he was getting into a train: he survived.] She was very miserable, did about one mile to the gallon on gin, and had had a major op. and lost her beloved little dachshund.

31 October 1941   The canning has come to an end. It is all very unsettling, and I am profoundly dissatisfied with my war effort. My only real war crop now is spuds.... Women are said to be much needed and Sydney Farrar is recruiting again for the FANYS but it is pretty much of a circus, apart from the ambulance side, as the girls drive elderly generals from the Muthaiga Club to the New Stanley for pink gins or to have their grey hairs cut, which Africans could do just as well.

11 December 1941　The whole production situation is heartbreaking, everyone is longing to go flat out, and yet no one can get the Govt. to budge one inch in getting a move on for the '42 crop. Thousands of acres of cereals are being lost every week now through inaction over organization of harvesting machinery, manpower and so on.

18 December 1941　There is a great movement afoot to save shipping and do two things – to produce really good yarn to replace Australian supplies for the Red Cross etc., and to teach African women to hand spin their own low-grade wool and make their own blankets, sweaters, etc. I unearthed my spinning wheel which I brought out in '28. I've got two grade Romney rams to put on the squatters' sheep, and have ordered three high-grade pregnant Romney ewes. If these live, I shall get a few ewes when people cull next March, and try to work up a small flock for a home spinning industry.

Jos had grown restless on his tea plantation and, despite his age, yearned for a more combatant job. He applied to the Occupied Enemy Territory Administration, which, following the defeat of Italy, had taken over Italian Somaliland (now Somalia) with headquarters at Mogadishu and, to his delight, was appointed to the Intelligence section.

8 January 1942　Jos has been offered his job, passed his medical and we went to N'bi on Sunday. He is frightfully bucked at getting the job and of course, being Jos, it has to be the most important in the world. He went off by lorry in a convoy of three, one of them a dilapidated object labelled 'Somalia Mail', like the contraption that goes to market in remote country districts and the passengers have straw at their feet. It should take five days at this time of year.

6 March 1942　Great spinning and weaving activity. The weavers spent last weekend here and were very helpful. They are a little couple who have been all their lives in a Lancashire mill. Saturday morning's weaving was interrupted by Lathbury ringing up to say there was a leopard in Thorpe's garden and would Fish go and help shoot it, which he did, and returned here with a huge carcase. Each weaver insisted on being photographed, rifle in hand and foot on leopard, obviously to show the Lancastrians how difficult weaving is in Kenya. Despite all the struggles, unemployment, etc., at home they say they would gladly leave their Government job here (good pay, free house, etc.) to go back to Lancashire, as they are so lonely. They live in a little row of houses just outside Nakuru, but there is no one there from Lancashire.... Wheat, wheat, wheat is all the cry. The local sub-committees have had the inspection etc. pushed on to them. I do the twelve farms between here and Njoro. Petrol is allowed but the tyre situation is very tricky indeed. But I can get around on the pony.... Had a delectable morning yesterday dosing and treating the feet of my fourteen sheep. My lovely ram we sheared on Saturday, his fleece weighed eleven pounds.... I wonder if there are any second-hand copies to be found of *The Place of Animals in Human Thought* by Cesaresco Martinengo?

5 May 1942   Jos had got a new job which is very pleasing. He went through in the train last week and I saw him for about five minutes. He was looking very well, thinner and younger. This new job entails a lot of travelling and parley-voo-ing.

The job, in a division of the army called Movement Control, consisted of taking drafts of army recruits by lorry from Tanganyika, Nyasaland and Northern Rhodesia through Uganda and Sudan to Egypt, and also acting as Liaison with the Belgians in the Congo. It entailed travelling thousands of miles over the roughest of tracks through bush and desert in most unhealthy country, and would have been a strenuous task even for a much younger man; for one of nearly sixty-eight it was punishing. So it was not surprising that a few weeks later he was admitted to hospital at Tabora in Tanganyika, suffering from what was at first diagnosed as a coronary thrombosis, but which proved to be a combination of influenza and malaria. He was soon back on the job, with no convalescent leave.

2 June 1942   Karanja is sending you some fudge and lemon curd. His other name is now Robinson, so look out for K. Robinson on the parcel.

26 June 1942   Have got in forty extra acres of pyrethrum this year and am just planting out the heavy tobacco. Its nicotine extract should replace the present cattle-dip which is difficult now to get.... Could you possibly find out the best book on basket making? Ingrid and I are anxious to work up a small industry as we have the raw material.

7 September 1942   Met twenty hyenas on the farm after tea yesterday and there is a leopard on the forest boundary and wild pigs are eating the mazie.

27 September 1942   Have enough sheep now to make a collie a necessity, just a small one, so have booked a puppy from a Cretan miniature sheepdog which was evacuated from Crete and has flown everywhere and has its own parachute.... Am doing the most interesting rabbit-feed trials and trying to segregate out a line of lovely black-skinned ones with silver points. Please get me two books, *Home Dressing of Furs* and *Fur Breeding Rabbits.*

27 October 1942   Last night four petty officers rang up from the Stag's Head to ask for lodging; that is N'bi's latest cunning trick when they are swamped under. I went to the station frothing and concocting a fierce letter of resignation from the Naval Hospitality scheme, but found the most charming and sweet and appreciative people needing their leave so badly, so of course have melted.

15 November 1942   This farm is *too* mixed now, yesterday a sow ate two heavenly girl-twins of a ewe, as the herd put them in the wrong paddock. I am heartbroken.

29 November 1942   At long last I have heard from Jos. He is in a very unhealthy place full of malaria [in the Belgian Congo] and expects to be relieved soon and get some leave. It looks as if he might be here for Xmas. The Middleboe family want to spend their leave here then, they might overlap with some sailors, and I am sprouting barley in Jos's bedroom.

14th February 1943   The drought is foul; never has there been a nastier hot season, now over five months long, so everyone is very

Jos Grant in 1902, shortly before his engagement to Nellie

Nellie and Elspeth in 1908

Motcombe House, Dorset, Nellie's childhood home

Government Road, Nairobi, in 1914

Nellie, Jos and Elspeth outside their new house, Kitimuru, in 1922

Thika in 1929: the road to Ol Donyo Sabuk. Getting stuck in a muddy pothole was a common occurrence

Group at Gilgil farm in 1924.
LEFT TO RIGHT: Josslyn Hay
(later Lord Erroll), Bobbie
Roberts, Jos Grant, Lady
Idina Hay, Cockie Birkbeck,
Princess Philippe de Bourbon
and Nellie

HRH the Prince of Wales
(future Edward VIII and Duke
of Windsor) with Cockie,
whose husband, Baron Bror
von Blixen-Finecke, was one of
his white hunters

Nellie (SECOND FROM LEFT), Lady Grigg and a group of local farmers in the
Kipipiri district – the so-called 'Happy Valley' – after slaying a pride of lions
that had been killing cattle. Nellie didn't shoot any. 1928

Ingrid Lindstrom, Nellie's neighbour at
Njoro

Nellie with dachshund, circa 1938

(*Left*) Picnic near Njoro, 1930. FROM LEFT TO RIGHT: Judith Denman, Trudie Denman, Nellie, Jos, Evelyn Waugh

(*Right*) Elspeth talking to Kikuyu women at Njoro, circa 1936

The first Imperial Airways aircraft on the London to Cape Town route, opened in 1933. London to Nairobi took six days, landing for night-stops en route

Masai *moran* (warriors), employed as cattle-herds on a ranch in the Rift
Valley, playing a game of *bao*: beans are dropped into shallow holes in a
board, or in the ground

Nellie with wives of her 'squatters' at Njoro. The leather bands around their
foreheads were used to support heavy loads carried on the back

Nellie's household staff:
Mbugwa (LEFT) and Karanja

Muchoka, headman, in the
pyrethrum shamba, circa 1950

snappy. Very busy on the farm breaking new land, and have applied for the water-boring unit to come.

Italian prisoners of war were proving generally useful; many were skilled tradesmen and some were loaned to farmers as mechanics, masons, carpenters and so on. Nellie took advantage of this opportunity.

21 February 1943   I've applied for an Italian stone-cutter, shall sell stone to Donald Seth-Smith and take the royalty in cut stone, so we should build up a little reserve. Have borrowed an Itye grammar and can now say Yo Ho, which I could before really, but feel I am getting on. . . . My veg. garden is really good, and I start on the Govt. seed production scheme's bed tomorrow. . . . This famine and endless controls means a devil of a lot of work for Production Sub-Committee and if I have to go and tell my neighbours to put down all their pigs, I am not likely to survive.

20 April 1943   Letter from Jos at long last, from N'bi hospital where he is having a complete rest and overhaul. He is very sad at his job coming to an end. [He was invalided out of the army.] Of course he is too old for anything so strenuous but hates to admit it. He has been very gallant to do what he has done, and must be content that he has done all he could. Drought raging here. . . .

21 May 1943   The view from this house is one large smoke-screen, owing to grass fires – the Aberdares have been burning for weeks. The damage to the poor forest is fantastic.

7 October 1943   Would you believe it? Njoro settlers Assn. are asking Bishop Beecher to address a meeting and bring an educated African with him. This was my suggestion, I pointed out that we had really better know a bit more about the modern African than we do, and that the best way would be to meet a real one. Fixing the time of the meeting led to much talk – it couldn't be in the club house at 6 pm as usual because it wouldn't do for the educated African to see European ladies in the bar (really because one of the members thought he might get landed in the position of having to

151

offer a 'bloody nigger' a drink). I longed to ask why an educated African couldn't see this, as a long succession of uneducated African bartenders had survived the spectacle, but thought the company had had about as much as they could stand for one day, so sweetly said what about an afternoon meeting, and that was agreed. Leonard Beecher is very good value indeed. Louis Leakey's brother-in-law, a cultured, wide-minded chap first, and a missionary in orders after.*
... The Ities work away. The old gardener is good value, but the clerk a ridiculous creature, very conceited, and incapable of increasing his English beyond about four words, two of which are 'perfect correct'. I have tried hard to increase his knowledge of the sex life of cows, but 'heifers in calf' remains beyond him; they have to be 'cows waiting for sons'.

15 May 1944   Have gone utterly and completely compost-mad since Nell Cole came to stay the other day and lent me her sister's book, *The Living Soil*. She also lent me Lord Portsmouth's book, *Alternative to Death*; both thrilled me. I have schemes to get everyone in Kenya worked up to make the Dept. of Agriculture start experiments like the Haughley Research Trust, and am instituting a Farm Compost Service of my own. Of course I used to make compost with all the right incantations and moon-portents, but this slightly more prosaic method may do the *shamba* more good. Before I forget, will you please see that Lord Portsmouth is sent as Kenya's next Governor? I told Francis to get busy with the idea. It will take some time to sink in but the seed is sown. There *does* seem to be a swing-over to the agriculturalist, and if Lord Portsmouth gets busy about the dying soil, all may yet be a better world, what is left of it.

22 May 1944   The great excitement on the farm is a brick and tiles works. The German genius architect Mr May has reported on our murram clay as beating all records for pisé work.† I had the idea of burning it, and it makes grand bricks and, even better, roofing

---

* The Most Reverend Leonard Beecher, of the Church Missionary Society, Archdeacon 1945–53, Bishop of Mombasa 1953–64, and Archbishop of East Africa from 1960 until his retirement in 1970. His wife Gladys was Louis Leakey's sister.

† Stiff clay or earth kneaded, or mixed with gravel, used for building cottages, walls, etc., by being rammed between boards, which are removed as it hardens.

and floor tiles. So now there is a grand Estate Housing Scheme on the tapis and about time too.... Mr May has also invented a marvellous 'grass shingle' but it wants long grass which I haven't got, so have put in eight acres of rye-grass to harvest by hand, and preserve the straw for thatching on the farm.... Jos has gone to Kericho to run old Brayne's tea plantation for a month while they go to the Coast. It sounds hard work but he is very glad to go, I think.... Hope shortly to send off a peacock-blue pram set for Charles, dyed with Pea Green dye from canning factory days. God knows how many tons of peas I dyed peacock-blue. I go by books for the measurements and they seem to me most odd, but you can always give the garments away to some deformed infant.

28 June 1944 Jos got really bad at Kericho with bronchitis and flu, got so that he could hardly breathe at all. He came down and went into Nakuru Hospital till he went off on a train to Malindi. He really is miserable with breathlessness. It isn't his heart, but something called emphysema, which means that your lungs lose their elasticity and get all crackly like cattle with quarter evil.* Dr Tennant says it's a condition that will never clear up, but that living at a low altitude in damp air will make for less discomfort than living elsewhere. If he comes back here it will 'shorten his life considerably'. He is a desperately bad patient and won't realize that he is just on seventy.... He is toying with a scheme to go in with Rex Fawcus over fish, but I really do hope he won't, as he is not fit for any sort of scheme.

Nellie had been asking for photographs of her grandson; some now arrived.

24 July 1944 I think the snaps are entrancing. I shall now enter Speke's grocery with head erect and flashing eye, facing my cronies with confidence. Have been so much put to shame by always hearing 'What? No snaps *yet*?' I first showed them at the PO to the Seychellois postmaster, also a proud parent recently. He exclaimed: 'Intelligence personified!' Candidly I think Charles looks rather drunk in

---

* Also known as blackleg, this is an infectious disease characterized by swellings in the shoulders, neck, thighs and quarters. The swellings become puffed up with gas and, if pressed, crackle as if filled with tissue paper. It is almost always fatal.

some of them.... A parcel is about to go off with my first sample of home weaving – i.e. two cot blankets. The warp is my Corriedale ram, the weft mainly merino but partly my angora bunnies. They were woven by a deaf and dumb boy.... There is now tethered on the lawn, and sometimes strolling into the house, what must be the most uneconomic sheep in the world. He's a high grade merino ram bought to shear every eighteen months or so to get a really long staple, destined entirely for Charles's pants. The ram is called Aries, and can't possibly live long enough to shear very often, but the wool should be marvellous.

11 September 1944 Talking to people like Audrey Richards makes one realize how deep-felt is the point of view that Africans are happier without white settlers. I have a profound admiration for her psychological wisdom so think she is right, but in this wicked world is it to be expected that any one people, e.g. Kikuyu, can be singled out for perfect lives, and won't it be good enough if they get a fair deal on European capitalistic lines, or should we really hand everything over to them? It makes for depression to feel we've all been so mistaken....

1 October 1944 I had a turn-up with an old ex-squatter, a really bad old man who was trying to run donkeys and potatoes across this farm from the forest. This unauthorized running goes on continually and one can't allow it because of disease, theft, etc. There were fourteen donkeys, four men and two women, and they wouldn't listen to my words at all. The wicked one drew a knife at me while I was standing on the bridge shooing the donkeys back while everyone else was beating them on. When I saw the knife waving at me I retired with dignity saying I would telephone the police, which I did, and they rounded up the party running away in the forest and they now await trial. It is too much really if a respectable old girl can't walk around her farm in the early morning without having knives waved at her.

11 October 1944 It is unjust of Audrey Richards to say that Aries eats my knitting patterns – he only eats carbon papers when in the house so far as I know.

16 October 1944 I attended the swearing-in at Leg. Co. of the first African member, Eliud Mathu. He has written a foolish letter, or so I think, to *Baraza* saying that Africans should put up no longer with small *shambas* and growing food, they should have vast coffee and tea estates. They will be damned fools if they are led away from food crops to supposed cash crops. I think the whole country is set for riots after the war through food shortages.

5 November 1944 The Seed Production people came last week on one of their periodic inspections, accompanied by five thousand cabbage plants to put in the irrigation *shamba*. They said all was well. I am harvesting cauliflower seed at the moment.... My Basic English classes are horribly popular. I think Basic Intelligence tests are really more needed. E.g. yesterday: 'Mwaua, how many legs has the table?' 'The table has four legs.' 'Kupanya, how many ears has the table?' 'The table has four ears.'

20 November 1944 Spinning and weaving trainees, sent by Govt, are flocking in. I have coming the wives of a railway guard and of a Health Dept. clerk, Kikuyu wives of a schoolmaster and of a RM court clerk, and so on. It is taking hold among the women, but goodness knows if they will ever learn to set up a warp by themselves.... Oh, you asked, does the farm pay. The answer is yes, but you wouldn't notice it, as everything has always gone back into the farm, as is the case with so many.

Jos's future was a cause of worry to them both. A low altitude was a necessity and he was temporarily at Mombasa, but had turned against the Coast. The farm provided a livelihood for both of them and Nellie could not abandon it altogether to live elsewhere and look after Jos. In December she went to join him at Diani, near Mombasa.

26 December 1944 The worrying thing is that two months of the Coast don't seem to have done Jos any good at all. He can walk very little and is thoroughly depressed about himself. I really am in a flap as to what to do.... Came back via Kilima Kiu, which has never looked more beautiful, in fact it was incredibly beautiful all the way up – brilliant green after rain at last, lush grass, and thorns in flower smelling like English may trees, damn them.... Spinnery and weavery opens on the 8th with a posse of [African] intelligentsia females.

2 February 1945 My irrigation is ticking over with a harvest coming off for seed of beetroot and cabbage, plus a thousand pounds a week of fresh stuff for the OCTU [Officer Cadet Training Unit], for a four-months' contract at hot weather prices. And hot weather it *is*.

11 March 1945 Alas, the irrigation has been out of action for a month. Someone dropped six-inch nails down the borehole and one got mixed up with the foot valve. I am afraid it is sabotage and one cannot but suspect the Italians, as they alone have access to my six-inch nails. I am in despair about my veg. contract as of course a thousand pounds of veges have dried off.

30 March 1945 The irrigation is going again at long last but the lapse was disastrous for the veges. Oh, how I wish it would rain and the wind drop. Rivers, streams, springs all disappearing and people carting water for miles and miles for their cattle.

Despite his failing health, Jos was offered a small job supervising building operations at Mac's Inn, a wayside halting-place half-way between Nairobi and Mombasa, and at a half-way altitude. Nellie was settling him in there when news came that peace was about to be declared.

9 May 1945 Had a hectic journey by train back from Mtito Ndei where I left Jos at midnight on Saturday, as everybody in the train seemed to pick up news out of the bush. Half Nakuru was on holiday and half wasn't. The dear Lindstroms asked me over for the evening meal and we heard the King and all about the royal family till 11 pm.... What a year this is being – never before has there been such an absolute and complete failure of the March/April rains. There isn't a chance of collecting a penny from anywhere so far as one can see. Heavens, what problems there are in every direction....

23 June 1945 I am going to have a short (very) course at the Vet. Labs on rabbit-skin curing, as I've got the pelts good, but not perfect, and there's still an Italian expert there. It is a very good industry here in conjunction with the vegetable *shamba*, as so much green stuff is available all the year round, and much more fun than pigs.

1 July 1945   I worked furiously at the Vet. Labs on bunny tanning. There is a tremendous expert there on all kinds of leather work, an Italian Doctor of Science. We carried on in bad French on both sides and he couldn't have been kinder in showing me it all. Between operations he liked talking about Italy's future, and his own, and invariably burst into tears. He cried a great deal on Wednesday but not so much on Thursday and was able, between sobs, to do some snappy work in de-hairing a bunny skin in thirty-five minutes to make a superb leather glove. They are doing the most heavenly book-binding in a back shed at the labs out of skins of goats used for the rinderpest vaccine, complete waste material, really beautiful work, and all this man's idea. He implored me to return to continue my studies and bring him monkeys, crocodiles, lizards and all. I shall send him some moles.

23 July 1945   This farm is one of the three Rural Industry Centres. I am part-time supervisor and take £10 a month. I have a permanent staff of four spinners and weavers. Pupils swarm in; I can't take more than ten at a time. I myself supervise, which means a lot of instruction too. I am a poor spinner, but quite a good weaver. I like the craft, and feel there is a lot to be done with it in combining materials and patterns. Magdeleine de Reffye, who really does know about clothes, says my pattern tweeds are good enough for any Parisian sports outfits, but I don't suppose they would be for long.

19 August 1945   Mitchell* made a very good speech on Peace Day, very good indeed, but did say that we must have no idle rich and no idle poor – I had so much looked forward to being idle poor, but perhaps he didn't mean the idle and useless and worn-out.

---

* Sir Philip Mitchell, MC, 1890–1964, formerly of the Tanganyika Administration, Governor of Uganda 1933–1940. In the war he acted as Chief Political Officer to the GOC East Africa Command. In 1944 he was appointed Governor of Kenya until his retirement in 1952.

1945-9

In October 1945 I flew to Kenya via Northern Nigeria, at Sir Philip Mitchell's request and at the expense of the Government, to draw up a scheme for the provision of reading matter in simple English, Swahili and the main vernacular languages for Africans who were leaving school in rapidly increasing numbers, but few of whom had, as yet, reached an advanced stage of literacy. This became the basis of the East African Literature Bureau, set up jointly by the three East African Governments soon afterwards. The enquiry involved visits to Uganda and Tanganyika and work in Nairobi, so I could not spend much time on the farm, but reported to Gervas its attractions after England's wartime austerities.

You would love the garden. There is a big honeysuckle hedge dripping with blossom, clambering roses all over the house and other creepers like streptosolon and bignonia. You should see the antirrhinums, about three feet high, and enormous blooms. The borders are a mass of colour.... Lots and lots of rabbits for wool and fur, some lovely angora goats, a busy hive of industry with people spinning and weaving, and some nice looking mainly Guernsey cows. I wish I could send you some of the sunshine and crispness, not to mention the cream, strawberries, mutton, soft cheeses and luscious fruit.... I've seen several of the old retainers, Njombo, Machoka and others. Machoka insisted on being photographed with his three wives and flock of children, and has given me a present of a chicken.

There were, of course, problems: Jos's health and Nellie's uncertainties. She had sold off about half the land and was proposing to sell more.

She means to do very little farming, but to continue with the vegetables and seed production, and with spinning and weaving and with the goats, bunnies and sheep [I reported]. She is over sixty and feels

158

she can't go on for ever, and has only been keeping on the farm to hand over to us. Personally I hate the idea of everything going completely and having nothing here, but I don't feel I can urge her to keep it indefinitely without being able to give her some sort of assurance that we will relieve her of it one day. She is rather depressed about the future, I fear, and is getting much older, as of course is poor Jos.

But Nellie never succumbed for long to depression, and did not allow her worries to cast a shadow over Christmas festivities. On the principle, no doubt, of 'put out more flags', she issued invitations to 166 adults and 77 children to a monster party on Boxing Day. Trestle tables and benches were knocked together and placed near the irrigation tank, which also did duty as a swimming-pool; a paddling-trough was made for the tots; cases of beer arrived; clues were invented for a treasure hunt; piles of sandwiches, cold meats, green salads, fruit salads, were assembled. The day dawned cold and cloudy and remained so, most unusual for the time of year. But the treasure hunt warmed people up, followed by a donkey derby. Despite the cold all the children plunged into the tank, as well as many adults, and everyone appeared to enjoy the party. A few days later I left for Nairobi, and thence for England.

During 1946 Jos's health continued to decline. Sadly Nellie sold or leased off most of her remaining land, sold the flocks and herds she had built up with such enthusiasm, and worried about the future of her Kikuyu families. Post-war unrest and dissatisfaction was beginning to sour race relations; and Kenya seemed to lack leadership and a sense of direction. Nellie drew up a scheme, which she called Maswali Matatu ('Three Questions'), to start small study groups throughout the 'settled area' with the idea of bringing together Europeans and the new generation of educated Africans. Officials with whom she discussed the scheme were enthusiastic, but it got bogged down in the bureaucratic machine. She made her own personal gesture by inviting two Makerere students to stay.

4 February 1946   The two Makerere lads duly arrived; they are very nice, and self-sufficient. One is an ardent biologist and found a protozoa in the duck-pool yesterday which Dr Edney [the biology lecturer at Makerere] says is probably a new species. We looked at it through my microscope and it had cilia which were lashing in a fury such as has never been seen before, said Dr Edney. He (Edney) has a good theory about the next civilization after ours is atom-bombed out of existence. He says that after a suitable interval it will be an insect species who will rule the world, on highly fascist lines. A few humans may crawl out of caves, mines, etc. when they come to, but the dominant insect will use them as egg-receptacles.

12 March 1946 All the animals on the farm are going off in various directions. The Harrieses came today and took twelve bull calves. Donkeys and sheep start going tomorrow. The buyer of the land swore he would take my labour over on the same terms as I have had them on, and I told him all along I wouldn't do a deal unless he did. Today he tells them they are too expensive, and can't have a one-acre *shamba* as well as *posho*. Most of the old chaps I wouldn't have turned off for anything are going to be let down. And how *can* a family live off one acre, I ask you? Damn and blast.

13 March 1946 The squatters are more or less divided up and a good many have gone. Old Njombo has pushed off, which makes me very sad, and old Manvi wants to go as his wives don't want to break new land for their *shambas*. I do hate signing off people taken on in 1924. So far I find that with a smaller acreage you have to be on it just as much, and instead of wanting to know the land by the acre, you want to know it by the square yard, and to see that the few workers you have got really do get round. So I've done more *neapara* [overseeing] work than I've done for years.... Maswali Matatu is all but accepted and the Sollys in Kiambu and I are each to start one as trial trips.

7 April 1946 Makerere Council sat at Entebbe. It was horribly hot and stuffy, all windows firmly shut against a thick black swarm of lake flies which got into your eyes, throat, mouth, nose, ears, and the files wherever possible. I can well understand why the Uganda secretariat isn't the most active in the world.... There is something very wrong with both the quality and quantity of students coming up to Makerere, and we must know why if we are to consider more and ever more 'schools' which people clamour for – this time it was law and engineering. There will soon be only one student in the Veterinary School! Everyone is fed up with the frightful standard of English, both pronunciation and knowledge.... A most brisk American lady is in charge of the women's hostel which swells and swells – the girls haven't yet, thank goodness.

In the hopes of easing Jos's increasing discomforts, he and Nellie went to the Coast where they had been lent a cottage at Likoni.

5 May 1946 It is all a vast problem. Jos has never been so gloomy, so querulous, so crotchety as he has since we have been here, and I never know whether he is like that because he is feeling ill, or whether it is psychological trouble. I think he is extra annoyed because I have set myself up with something to do. I've got a highly educated Arab to come and give me Swahili lessons, which is fun. The little dogs, especially Daisy, make violent love to the proud Moslem; he says he can change his sect for a couple of hours daily and then it won't matter their touching him, anyway in his sect it's only the dog's snout that matters.... I am, I hope, going on expeditions with Hassan the vet to find Arabs who will sell me milch goats, which should be grand foundation stock for my future flock, if only we can find coloured ones. They are mostly white, and the black British Alpines have a most definite anti-white colour bar mating tradition. A lesson to us all.

19 May 1946 Have read every word of Trevelyan's *Social History* and adored it. Jos has been put off because a pheasant is mentioned as being in England in the fourteenth century and Jos says it couldn't have been. He isn't, alas, a bit better, in fact I think he's deteriorated since we've been down here.

The Kenya government, aided by the British Treasury, had started a post-war settlement scheme to enable ex-Service men and their families to acquire farms in the 'white highlands', either as assisted owners or as tenants. Land already in European ownership was bought up or sub-divided to provide the farms. The tenancy scheme was designed to run for forty-four years, and it was assumed by all that Kenya would remain a British Colony and that the land earmarked for white settlement would be reserved for Europeans. Intending settlers were selected in London from a great many applicants. In Kenya, a Settlement Board was set up, with Michael Blundell in charge, to allocate farms and supervise the new settlers, who went immediately to the Egerton Farm School at Njoro, and their wives to a hostel in Nakuru. Nellie was appointed a member of the Settlement Board and was closely involved with the newcomers' problems at Njoro and Nakuru.

10 June 1946 We interviewed them all individually from 10.30 am to 6.30 pm, twenty-seven of them. Some are grand stuff, most all right, and I should guess two complete duds. The hostel has fourteen wives now and is ticking over.

16 June 1946 On Wednesday twenty-four new settlers arrived ex HMS *Fencer*, all in the last stages of disgruntlement, as apparently they had been told by the London office that they would live with their wives in cottages at the Egerton School. God knows who told them that, there was never the least idea that they should live together at the School, and no cottages.... A sour woman at the hostel set about me because I said hostel dwellers really couldn't have personal boys – fancy forty personal boys there besides a perfectly adequate hostel staff! I wouldn't have thought new arrivals from home these days would have been like that, but we've just been running through a bad patch all round.... Very little rain here so no pyrethrum coming off. So no money coming in from the remnant of the farm and just a wage bill. It doesn't pay unless I am here and able to reduce the wage bill, so if I am to be with Jos elsewhere I must sell off the rabbits, goats, etc., and all livestock and close down the weaving.

14 July 1946 The Settlement Scheme men were so disgruntled at the family separation that we've now arranged for men with wives and no children to live at the Egerton School, those with wives and children to live at the hostel and go daily to the school by bus.... I had two interesting men to stay last weekend, new settlers. One had been all through the Spanish war in the International Brigade and then in the Palestine police, the other was the gentlest little mouse-like man, very democratic and very sweet, a wing commander with two of everything – DSO, DFC each with bars. I think the ex-Palestine policeman will be able to take on any future trouble single-handed – give him a bridge and a *rungu* and leave him to it.

6 September 1946   I cannot tell you how thrilled I am by the book on *Education Through Art*. It has a tremendous philosophy and needs much thought. The link-up between art and natural science is just the stuff that might save the world, and it is so thrilling when he says that all nature works towards a goal of perfection through the laws of physics, like honeycombs and water-lily leaves – strains and stresses – and when perfection is achieved, all is well until a new set of conditions arrive and everyone starts again. It might just be that man, having practically reached perfection in his weapons and methods of self-destruction, might suddenly find everything altered by a new social order. Otherwise the whole world and future are just too awful to contemplate.

13 October 1946   Have got that foul pyrethrum poisoning on my face again only worse this time, so am looking like a beetroot which isn't fun. Am having a combat with the Scott Labs [the government agricultural laboratories] over the import of Russian comfrey [a fodder plant].

27 October 1946   It is the spinning and weaving that entails such a lot of detailed work, as the trainees pinch the raw wool so frightfully unless there is constant issuing, weighing, etc. I really don't know if I can go on with it, but have thirteen trainees now including four ex-*askaris*, it would be letting them down to close this centre now as there is no way of replacing it. Such a lot of women have come to be trained on their own this year.... I was at Makerere Council last week. Every single lecturer I spoke to told of the extreme difficulty of lecturing to these lads whose general education is absolutely nil in the secondary schools. Peggy Trowell's art training has done more than people will ever realize to 'integrate' the African student.... My face which went to Uganda as beetroot has returned the brightest lobster and really is inconvenient as it affects the eyes.... Am planting out millions of sweet williams for seed.

163

24 November 1946   Hutchinson, the information officer, came to address the incipient Maswali Matatu League about Education. They had appeared mad keen on it and fixed their own day and hour and – not one single English-speaking person turned up. The school-master here who should have got the school ready and been on tap just went off in the morning leaving no message or anything. I suppose someone has nobbled them about its being a government show and they are boycotting it. There were about thirty others, mostly illiterate, and Hutch was very good about talking to them.... He showed me his plan in outline. Countering subversive propaganda is the order of the day, and – he may get £18,000 for everything! His output in literature is to be three booklets and six leaflets per annum. The whole situation is grim, and our efforts too puny for words.... I think I shall wind up the spinnery and weavery.

Early in 1947 Jos grew worse, and I flew on the last service of the flying-boats that had plied between Alexandria and Lake Victoria to Kisumu, where Nellie met me in her dilapidated car. At the end of January we drove by easy stages with Jos and a nurse to Malindi on the Coast, where, in the doctors' opinion, Jos's life might be prolonged. But he had reached the point of no return, and at the end of March we went back to Njoro. He died on 7 April in Nakuru Hospital. Nellie returned, worn out, to the farm. Years later, she told me that she slept badly and, in her dreams, Jos had appeared with empty sockets where there should have been eyes; and she wrote:

Poor Jos, things never went right for him. He longed to get into the Indian cavalry – Bengal Lancers – but a bee stung him in the eye and impaired his vision. Then came the Boer War, and dysentery which really impaired his health for keeps. He adored his mother, hated his step-mother, and was frightened of his father. Robin always stole the thunder, he was much easier and far better at 'personal relations'. Jos really was a soldier at heart, and a dyed-in-the-wool Highlander.

Once a year, Jos had donned his kilt and its accoutrements to preside at the Caledonian Society's annual dinner in Nakuru. I remember him

164

as a gentle, humorous, dreamy person whose dreams never came true.
In July, Nellie's letters were resumed.

14 July 1947   Do you know about Hydroponics and have you ever
had a Hydroponicum? Am studying the question.... I had a show-
down with Karanja a few days ago; the drinking really has got
beyond anything. One night I saw the lights on in the kitchen long
after they should have been, so dashed out and found Karanja moon-
ing about aimlessly, obviously quite tight, and unable to make sense
about anything. He had a large bowl of water in his hands and looked
such a fool and so inane that I seized it and poured it over his head
and shooed him off. Next morning he said I'd hit him – quite untrue
– and he must go at once as he hadn't been drinking and it was all
most unfair. However that evening we agreed to forget the incident.
It may have been undignified but I couldn't resist it. I don't mind
their having their glass of beer but this unceasing sozzledness can't
make them realize when they're giving away information to
strangers, and that's what I resent. The policeman called one day,
he says there have been twenty-three houses broken into round
Njoro.

28 July 1947   I appeal to you in the name of humanity, plus that
of a mother, to do something about the music as laid on by the BBC
via N'bi. Sat. evening at 8.30 pm surely ought to have something
cheerful? The announcer said it would be Dido who, having ordered
the building of her funeral pyre, was bidding farewell to her devoted
attendant. Dido then shrieked: 'Farewell Belinda, farewell Belinda',
about two dozen times. I wish we could have heard Belinda's re-
actions, which I feel would have been: 'Thank Gawd the old girl
has gone and set 'erself alight.' When Dido had incinerated herself
beyond power of being able to shriek any longer to Belinda, we had
a Fugue from King Arthur, which was gloom personified and completely lacking in charm. I gave up then; tried again yesterday when
a sonata of Chopin's sounded promising; it turned out to be a
Funeral March played by Sergius Rachmaninoff.

18 August 1947   Would you believe it, old Njombo has fetched up
asking to stay here to end his days. I feel much warmed by this.

Newcomers were continuing to arrive under the Settlement Scheme, and Nellie volunteered to have two families to stay because the hostel was full up.

11 August 1947 The Boorers have arrived. I think he is grand stuff, a real handyman and a very pleasant personality. She is a rather emotional cockney, very much a fish out of water about not doing things for herself. But very natural, thank God, and a worker. Doesn't like sausage flies in the tooth-water yet, and says that the rats they catch in their room are as large as small cats, but she is very content and a 'walk in the woods' (Mau forest) fills her with joy. I've fixed her up with some rabbits of her own, as she really does want a job. The household is fairly equable, but it is really a bit too much to have a pack of seven here, and the two children mean separate meals and no one ever goes out for a single meal.

The other family was much less congenial:

He has adenoids and talks like a stage colonel, wau-wau-wau. I cannot think how he was ever admitted into the scheme, he is work-shy, takes no interest in anything beyond his food, and has obviously never done a hand's turn of real work in his life. She *may* be good with cows, I hope so, as she is going over to the Seth-Smiths to lend a hand in their dairy. I've advised Donald to keep her firmly in the cowshed, where perhaps she'll be AI'd.

5 October 1947 On Sunday we had quite an Old Kenya day. Lunch with Cecil Hoey in the new house he has built at the foot of the Cherangani hills, having sold their lovely place to the Duke of Manchester. All over the Uasin Gishu plateau now are signposts 'Manchester' – gives the Plateau quite an industrial tang. After tea we went up to the Manchester abode. It is quite fantastic. The Duchess has fifty-three dresses still not unpacked – she simply hasn't time between gins. They are importing a silver mantelpiece weighing five tons, and eight thousand books – not that they have time for reading. Her drawing-room is virginal white, with tables all glass or silver chrome. Beautiful flower arrangements, straight Constance Spry, everything defoliated so that even quite heavy sprays of honeysuckle look slender. There is a small boy with a double chin, rolls of fat and curly locks; the tutor took to drink so no one has any education. We had a nasty trip back as we ran into a terrific storm and stuck miles from anywhere; sent an SOS to the nearest farmer whose car died on him, coming to rescue us. Staggered in soaked and hungry at 11 pm.

16 November 1947 The Boorers have had their first taste of real difficulties when the nightwatchman pulled him out of bed to say *siafu* were in the poultry pens. He reacted well, plunged into the fray with a torch, attended to the wounded, and moved the lot into another ark. The damned *siafu* had already killed one of my lovely Rhode Island Red pullets, but that was better than the imported Light Sussex next door. Poor Ingrid had her chicken life wrecked at Xmas too, an incubator went up in flames and about a hundred and fifty of the most expensive eggs she ever bought, with all the chickens just hatching, were roasted.

Nellie had always been a hen-wife at heart, and on her shrunken farm returned to her first love, poultry. E. W. Bovill, senior partner in the trading firm of Bovill Mathieson and a scholar as well as a businessman (he had published Caravans of the Old Sahara, *a classic history of the Western Sudan) readily agreed to bring with him by air from England two dozen hatching eggs of pedigree Light Sussex, Nellie's favourite breed.*

15 February 1948 I'm sure you'll want to hear all about the eggs and it is indeed a thrilling story. On the strength of a wire from Bovill Mathieson I went early to N'bi in good time to check about permits etc. with Import Control. The York got in about 2 pm and there was Mr Bovill all smiles – and the eggs. He was sweet about the eggs and wouldn't let me pay a thing. I sprang into the car and came back here. My best broody hen went broody on Monday and she was laid on under lock and key, and two incubators had been ticking over for a week, so if Ginger the broody deserts, or one incubator goes bats, there are still resources. I popped ten eggs under Ginger that night, and the rest into one of the incubators. One was cracked so I ate it for lunch. Everything is now in the lap of the gods, and the incubators. Ginger always sits on the second storey of a rabbit hutch. We've dug a ditch all round and filled it with ashes, and made a ladder which is removed directly she has retired after her daily time off, so it should be *siafu*-proof.

15 March 1948   The final hatching was six, four out of the incubator and two under Ginger. Ginger had four more absolutely formed chicks which failed to get out of the shell. If they had, I should have had nearly a fifty per cent hatch, which is wonderful. As it is, twenty-five per cent, which is all one can count on or expect. They are all under Ginger. If they grow up it will be *more* than worth while. Have just under five hundred head of poultry on the last count, but that includes a few turkeys and ducks.

The constant flow of uninvited guests continued, and Nellie was too generous, or perhaps weak-minded, to turn them away.

4 April 1948   I do wish the hotel business would open up more, all these people are self-invited and do make it difficult to do the chicks as I should. Have a family here now, very County and true-blue, obviously the Flight from Moscow and they breathe a 1919 spirit. They have brought the most odious and repulsive three-year-old son. Never did it do one thing it was told and it yelled and screamed. Was never made to sit at table but wandered about spitting. Its mother pursued it after meals with bits of food and popped them into its mouth when she thought it wasn't looking and of course it spat them out. It fondled its private parts ceaselessly. Its mother I don't think has ever thought of anything but herself and has no intention of doing so. They like the country less and less and I expect being here has helped that all right. . . . This popping in business so often gets me right down that I've wondered whether I might not clear out and look for something with real privacy about it. . . . Bui [a dog] went off hunting and when she didn't come back I went to hunt for her, and with great difficulty, just as it was getting dark, found her tied up in a snare. Owing to this, I got back after dark and found the Bells had been, wanting to see the poultry. That night Dr Stanner rang up from Kisumu wanting to pop in on Sat., so he came to lunch. The whole Gourley family, four of them, turned up about noon so they came to lunch too, and Hans Middleboe came to stay that night.

25 April 1948 I hope I've made a good *shauri* [agreement] with Ntiro, the super artist who is now assistant art teacher at Makerere. I've asked him to stay here for the short vac. and will pay his fare and get paid in paintings. At last I hope to see the Rift Valley painted by an African – and *what* an African.

2 May 1948 Fish is looking terribly ill and old and has been living for weeks on penicillin and M & B, and neither of them will contemplate going home without the other. A group of Swedish friends are so convinced of the urgent necessity of getting them home that they have hatched a plot. Koren, a very rich Swede, is throwing a party for their wedding anniversary, and when they are all completely alcoholic and brimming with emotion and tears streaming down, an envelope containing two return air passages is to be pressed into Ingrid's hand as an anniversary gift. I do wonder if it will work. It is supposed to be a deep, dark secret, and Nils and Harriet are quite exhausted with the secrecy of it all, but I wonder if it *is* such a secret, as one day this week Fish and Ingrid went together to Nakuru and came back with Fish's hair cut – this is for Europe, he said – and Ingrid's hair permed – this is for Europe, she said – and Ingrid bought a skirt down to her ankles – this is for Europe, she said. It will be interesting to see if the psychology works.

6 May 1948 The Fish home trip went absolutely according to plan. Koren gave a party for his grandson's christening so over flocked the Fishes, Viveka and Hans, the Fjasteds, etc. There was no end of a party, and after the sun went down Koren made the perfect speech, and as Ingrid dissolved into howls an envelope was pressed into her hand with a Banker's Order. Fish of course heard nothing, so there was quite a bit of trouble with him next day, but all is now well, and he already looks ten years younger.

In one of her poultry magazines Nellie read of a new strain of 'rain-worms' being bred in California. She immediately followed this up.

9 May 1948 I got an answer from the S. African poultry paper to say that rainworms are earthworms. The famous breeder Dr George Oliver Sheffield of La Canada, California, has produced a special strain for poultry feeding. They are hermaphrodites, so at least shouldn't suffer from sterility diseases.... I supported a meeting at the club on Friday when Grogan spoke for an hour and a half on 'The gnats dance in the beams of the setting sun'. His thesis was that calamity would overtake Kenya unless we all voted for Francis Scott next Wednesday.

Lord Francis was defeated at the poll by Michael Blundell.

13 June 1948 I had to have Sunny put down last week. He suddenly got worse and started to die, so I got the vet to come and shoot him. There will never again be more utterly faithful companionship. The other dogs don't mean a thing to me now, except, possibly, a little bit of old Buibui.

29 June 1948 Had a *lovely* letter from Colorado to say that Dr Oliver has been dead for some years, but the Colorado Earthworm Hatcheries are carrying on the good work, and could easily send me twenty thousand capsules by air. I've applied for an import permit for a very few, not twenty thousand, to keep as pets.

The import permit was refused, but Nellie, not to be defeated, arranged for a consignment of 'capsules' to reach Woodfolds in the luggage of an American visitor. They were released in a garden frame, and on her next visit Nellie spent some time digging up worms in the frame, pronouncing them to be bigger and fatter than the non-pedigree worms to be found in other parts of the garden.

25 August 1948 A quick visit to the Boorers on their new Settlement Board farm near Lugari. They have 1,300 acres and already 230 cattle with maize, etc. Boorer is a born landsman and so is his cockney wife. My brakes packed up forty miles before I got there and it is very unnerving to drive with none at all, so was glad to see they had a quite solid brick house against which I could come to rest at the end of the journey.

24 October 1948   Show week in Nakuru has ended and it was hectic. Really an excellent Show, bigger and better than anything yet. My Light Sussex were defeated by a lovely pen of birds imported by air by Brigadier Baines, but mine came second to his. I showed twenty-eight varieties of vegetables. Had eight in all staying, laid on picnic lunches at the Show and had twenty mouths eating on Friday, so it took a bit of planning, but the household kept sober and coped very well. . . . Went over to the Ellvers at Elburgon to collect a mass of foxgloves she had given me. I got leave from the forest officer to plant them along the edge of the forest and along the fishing paths, which should provide the dappled shade they like, and they should look lovely there. The Ellvers are fairly new from India, he made a real fortune in the timber trade and lived for years in Kashmir. He turns out to be a son of the Motcombe parson of my youth who didn't have a bean, he was so poor his coat was green – and here we both are now.

28 December 1948   Christmas was quiet here, even the weather. I laid on the usual Lucky Dip, despite breaking it up in fury last Xmas owing to excessive cheating and thieving, and *no* peace and goodwill anywhere. Crime was less rife this year, due entirely, I fear, to improved police-like methods and not to moral regeneration. No. I ticket was an elderly sheep; this was drawn by Muchoka, which seems odd, but I don't see how he *can* have cheated; but his brother Manvi got the best prize last year. The objects – 119 in number, so that every man, woman and child got something – were mostly my old rags and some of Jos's, interlarded with parcels of tea, sugar and fat, with a few rather good prizes, such as a kettle, *pangas* and *jembes*. One tiny girl won a *jembe*, and burst into bitter howls and tears; the shadow of Things to Come was too much for her. At the end a scramble for sweets among the tots. I got a few cheerful moments out of it as I had to stitch up small bags for the sugar out of oddments, which enabled me to have a blissful session with my beloved sewing machine. I had some lovely presents. To my amazement, and I must say shame, the Purvii [Purveses] trundled over the most lovely and expensive wheelbarrow with a pneumatic tyre for its wheel. And I had sent her a dozen garden labels! What can I do? Harriet sent over a large muscovy drake with a red ruffle round its neck; I hope it will live for many years in the irrigation.

Nellie paid a short visit to a farm called Kapsiliat, belonging to Mervyn Ridley, whose pack of hounds she had looked after at Makuyu in the First World War.

11 February 1949   It is ten years since I was here, and the wealth and development is terrific. Two thousand head of cattle, thousands of bags of wheat, three European managers, dams galore, paddocking, tractors, etc. It really is staggering, and so, so rich. All this wealth staggers and indeed depresses me. What a hellish misfit one has always been, but it's too late now to do anything about it, except try not to be a nuisance for the rest of one's life.

21 February 1949   The very silly party I planned ages ago occurred last night. It was really meant to be for the Fish family, as the whole lot are together here after all these years. Then, it was twenty-five years since I came to Njoro, and the only way of limiting numbers was to say it was only for those who were already here when I came, and still are. One or two were away or ran out so we were fourteen, and quite enough too. Kate Petrie presented me with a really wonderful cake, all iced, with an effigy of me standing on top with a lot of reins in my hand which led to segments of the cake with the dates on them, and all my 'activities' supposed to be represented – polo, almonds, silkworms, cattle, white mice, angora rabbits, pyrethrum, poultry, spinning, hospitality to the navy, etc., and twenty-five little candles. It really was a noble effort.

6 March 1949   The Trowells arrived last night to stay. Her account of the meeting between the Makerere staff and the Senate of London University is too gloomy; it seems that Makerere is to be pegged a hundred per cent to the academic sausage machine, so will undoubtedly lose its soul for scraps of paper. Art is never to be a degree subject, so the Dept. of Art may have to go. Turner is writing most strongly about it all; it is a complete negation of all that he has worked for. It is a sad moment to be leaving the Council, but one couldn't do anything.

12 March 1949 I was driven out of my bed by *siafu* at 2 am one morning and that should mean rain within twenty-four hours, but it didn't. It is blazing hot and nothing but dust and wind. In '41 a bee stung me on the right eyelid during a Production Sub-Committee meeting and there grew a wart. In '42 I was being fitted for glasses and the oculist said the wart must be removed or it would 'turn into something nasty', so he burnt it off, causing me great pain and giving me an eye like a poached egg, and the wart grew again in a month. Now Dr Tennent says I must go immediately to an eye specialist. The wart has grown a lot lately and is weakening my right eye, or I would not bother.... I had something like a major forest fire here the other evening. Columns of smoke curled up to the very skies: it was the great burning of all my files. Nine years of Makerere and whatnot. The more I think about it the more tragic it is that Makerere is now handed over to the London sausage machine and all hope of a really African college and soul are gone. The Africans will take no interest whatsoever in the social studies and art courses when they are the only ones not tagged on to a London degree.

Nellie had not been to Britain, or had a real holiday, for twelve years, and agreed to take a break as soon as she could find someone to look after the dogs and farm. In due course an elderly Scottish couple, looking round for somewhere to retire to, were installed, and Nellie flew to England in April, taking twenty-three pounds of food presents – Britain was still on short commons. Her intention was to stay for a year, in order to see whether, after living so long in the tropics, she could stand the winter climate and adjust to life in England. Sadly, she had accepted the fact that Gervas and I would never take over at Njoro, and the possibility of her retirement to Wiltshire had been discussed. She bought a small Bedford van which was to soldier on gallantly in Kenya for many years, and in it she and I embarked on a tour of Scotland. We started with a week at the Edinburgh Festival, a very great treat for Nellie, so long deprived of the enjoyment of music and the arts, good architecture and ancient buildings. Remarking, in a restaurant, on the hum of conversation, a gentle kind of buzz, she said: 'That is the sound of civilization, to those of us who don't live in it.' We went on to stay with a cousin of Jos's, a correct and conventional retired general with an eccentric wife, thus described by Nellie:

16 September 1949   She weighs I should think eighteen stone, and a large moon-white face flashes out from a cloud of chiffon draped round a sort of jockey cap and tied under her chin, skilfully concealing swollen glands and double chins. Her hair is dyed a bright terracotta shade and she wears a red linen coat and white plimsolls and talks incessantly, mainly about spirits (ghostly not Scotch) whom she calls the Higher Command. Communication with them came at first through spirit writing, but now she dispenses with this and just allows them to speak direct to her mind. One of the High Command offered to put her directly in touch with God, but she modestly declined, preferring to have an intermediary. She is very rich (her mother was a Rothschild) and I think as a tax-dodging device has a large lorry in which she always sleeps when away from her various homes, and in which there also lives a carpenter who makes horrible objects to sell to shops called 'signs and designs', little model animals and things; her table-mats, of the cheapest possible cork, have printed on them: 'Hungry horse? Clean manger'.* Little else, I'm glad to say, strikes this note of austerity; there are six servants, including a Polish butler and an Italian maid.... I got some salmon fishing, but although huge things leapt all about me, nothing thank goodness attached itself to my fly, or hook, so I had all the fun and none of the responsibility.

Not to be a nuisance in the houses of a Britain now practically devoid of servants (except, it seemed, in parts of Inverness-shire) was one of Nellie's most determined resolutions. She had always been a good cook, and had taught Karanja all he knew, but decided to bring herself up to date in all branches of domestic economy by enrolling in a 'Brides' Course' run by the Good Housekeeping Institute.

15 October 1949   My course has very lady-like hours, 9.30 am to 3.30 pm, and is great fun. My chief companion in the cooking class

---

* This unusual character was Lady Sybil Grant, daughter of the 5th Earl of Rosebery, a former Prime Minister, and Hannah, only daughter and heiress of Baron Mayer Anschel de Rothschild. She had married in 1903 Lt-General Sir Charles Grant, Coldstream Guards, and had one son. She died in 1955.

is a large, round, very jolly Jamaican lady with five children, so her bridal status is no better than mine. We have long cracks about things like yams and sweet potatoes and feel we could teach the instructors a thing or two, which is good for morale. The cooking side, actually, is easy, but with washing woollens and scouring pans my touch is less sure.

Gervas and I were, at this time, launching out into a small farm (too small, as it turned out), starting off with some pigs and poultry and a land girl, Vera. Nellie was in her element tending day-old chicks, working out rations, washing eggs and helping generally; this did not seem much like a holiday, but I think she enjoyed it, and was glad to find her Bedford van of use in transporting bales and sacks, and sometimes gilts on nuptial visits to a neighbouring boar. The sight of Nellie driving through the village with a pig peering over her shoulder, both front trotters resting on the seat-back and its black head nestling up to her white one, is remembered to this day by older inhabitants.

Her sister Blanchie, now a widow, was living temporarily not far away in Berkshire near her brother Hughie, who, too old to hunt a pack of fox-hounds, had a farm and kept his race-horses. After fourteen years' separation, Nellie was looking forward to a reunion. But the once gay, amusing, warm-hearted Blanchie had become a sad and soured old woman. 'The devil jealousy', Nellie commented, 'has entered in and I'm afraid the even worse devil of remorse. And the wounds of disillusionment never healed.' A date was made, and Nellie went off determined to make the fortnight's visit a success. That evening a subdued voice on the telephone enquired: 'Please may I come back tomorrow morning?' The question of who was to wash up and who to dry the tea-cups had unleashed a thunderstorm, followed by a severance of communications which could last a week. Nellie came home dejectedly next day.

There was more sorrow to come. Her brother Hughie died on Christmas Eve at his farm near Lambourn, and on a wet December day we went sadly to his funeral in Motcombe churchyard where his parents and his old grandmother lay.

Nellie's year in England came to an end without any definite decision having been reached about the future. If she returned to Kenya for the rest of her days she would see her family, what little there was of it, only at infrequent intervals, and her only grand-child would grow up a stranger. But she had commitments, most of all to her Kikuyu families, which she did not feel she could repudiate; and, she could not afford it. Little would be left from the sale, if it could be sold, of her shrunken farm after loans had been repaid. She had no pension, annuity, or anything of that nature. No African or other nationalist could have set greater store than she did on independence. As it became, with age, more difficult to achieve, it became almost a ruling passion. There was no way in which she could have lived in England without some sacrifice of personal uhuru. *To live without a garden and growing things around her would have been a misery, but she was too stiff in the joints and arthritic to work out of doors without help. So, when the year was up, there was a great packing and sorting. She had taken several courses in the winter, accumulated a lot of pamphlets, done a lot of needlework, and invested in a set of long-playing records of classical music, having arranged with friends who were returning to Kenya by sea to take them in their baggage. But the friends changed their plans, no one else could be found and the freight was too expensive, so the records languished in the loft until Woodfolds was sold. Early in 1950, she returned to Njoro, and to a boisterous welcome from the dogs.*

Mau Mau 1952 – 4

A gap now occurs in Nellie's letters, or rather in their preservation, for she continued to write. When they were resumed the Mau Mau revolt was under way and a State of Emergency about to be declared. For several years, those living in the two provinces that were affected – it was never a Colony-wide affair – had felt it coming. The symptoms were increasing lawlessness, sullen looks, attacks on white farmers and their livestock, mysterious secret meetings in huts at night, and then rumours, and eventually facts, about the oathing ceremonies which formed the core of Mau Mau. This is not the place to analyse its causes. It may be said, however, that the revolt was virtually confined to the Kikuyu; that its aim was to drive Europeans from their farms; that the Independent Schools Association had been its hotbed; that Jomo Kenyatta was universally regarded as its author and begetter; that recruitment was carried out by means of secret oathing ceremonies of increasing obscenity as time went on, until the details were considered to be unprintable; that intimidation was widespread; that the Christian missions and their adherents opposed it root and branch; that most of the chiefs and headmen remained loyal to the government and refused to join; that a great many murders were committed, and a great many cattle slaughtered and mutilated; and that the united efforts, lasting for over three years, of the Colony's police force and police reserve, the KAR, the Kenya Regiment, a home guard formed from Kikuyu who had refused to take the oath, and several units of the British army, were needed before peace was restored. There are, of course, many points of view about Mau Mau, from that which regarded it as a savage retrogression to the darkest side of tribalism in face of pressures from the West to force the pace too quickly and break up the familiar patterns of people's lives, to that which proclaimed it as a struggle for liberation from colonialism, and its leaders as freedom-fighters against imperialist oppressors, while those Kikuyu who refused to join, called loyalists by Europeans, were traitors deserving of the nasty deaths meted out to them. As with most political movements, there is no doubt

177

some truth in both concepts and absolute truth in neither. Whatever the judgement of history (if there is such a thing) may be, this was an unpleasant period to live through for both black and white. Europeans went armed day and night in constant readiness against attack, and Kikuyu, unless they were themselves members of Mau Mau gangs, lived in constant fear of visitations, generally at night, by Mau Mau activists bent on forcing them to submit to oaths that bound them to commit murder and slaughter livestock when told to do so. Thousands of Kikuyu men and women who resisted these demands were murdered, generally in most unpleasant ways. Throughout the Emergency, Nellie lived alone on her farm and among her Kikuyu families. The next series of her letters starts less than a fortnight before the State of Emergency was declared by the newly arrived governor, Sir Evelyn Baring, on 20 October 1952.

9 October 1952 Kenya is in a very poor way at the moment; whenever the powers that be announce that the situation is contained, improved or in hand, something worse than ever quickly happens. On Tuesday poor old Chief Waruhiu was murdered and that *has* created a row. Last week it was one headman per day for three days, and another European woman stabbed to death, making the second in a fortnight. And the Bindloss family at Kiambu nearly wiped out by Africans arriving in their sitting-room while they were listening to the wireless. One fired point blank at Mrs Bindloss and missed her by tripping on the carpet; Bindloss rushed at the man and got a bullet in his collar-bone and a slash on the neck; a visitor closed on the knife man and got a bit of his clothing, which led to his arrest through police dogs.... They had a monster raid up here last weekend, a company of KAR, police and police reserve, but I'm afraid the army blew the gaff and they hardly got anyone – only about forty – in the forest behind here; Elburgon's bag was over four hundred but mostly minor offenders, not Mau Mau.

I was away Friday and Saturday and when I got back found the maize store had been broken into and two bags stolen, and the electric light in my bedroom tampered with. John Adams fixed it next day and said it had definitely been wrenched out. So now I'm taking the firearm situation seriously and going to the police to be told how to load my revolver. I'm told I must keep it loaded and

I shall live at the far end of the house from it; how I hate firearms. Eight headless bodies were found in a forest glade near Thomson's Falls – loyal Africans – and lots of Christians near Nyeri have been locked in their huts and the huts set on fire.

20 October 1952. It is most dear of you and Constance [a niece] to be perturbed about the Trouble. No one can possibly pretend that it is nice in any way, but at the same time, here we are, in it, and I do honestly think it is utterly impossible to visualize doing a bolt. Apart from anything else, what happens to the animals, crops, etc.? Some people are bolting from the Nyeri district to the coast, presumably having arranged for their dogs, etc., but it probably means that when they go their headmen and staff will be done in.... I trust my aged Tiriki* nightwatchman isn't asleep *all* the time, and doesn't wander round the farm too much, but I don't like to ask him. Neither do I ever discuss Mau Mau with the staff; you'd only get lies anyway, and it's better to take up the attitude that it's all *shauri ya Serkali* [the government's business] and leave it at that.... Bishop Beecher preached at Nell Cole's church at Gilgil on Sunday and said that what the wretched Christians had suffered and still were suffering round Nyeri was indescribable; early martyrs had nothing on them.

General opinion seems to be that on farms it is practically certain all Kikuyus have taken the oath, but some at least hope fervently they will never be called on to do anything drastic about it. But of course if the terrorism does go on, they can't help themselves. Edward Windley [provincial commissioner of the Central Province] has been 'threatened' and it was one of his dogs found headless on the Timau road.... Very hectic week at the Nakuru Flower Show on Friday; was dogsbody as usual and had fourteen exhibits of my own to cope with. I retained the cup for most points in veg. section but was beaten in every direction in flowers and quite justly too.... Rose and Rebecca and lots of farmers took their headmen to Waruhiu's funeral, there were at least four hundred Europeans, one Asian and terribly few Africans. All frightened of course. The dear little school-children are singing hymns substituting Jomo's name for God. They

* A small non-Kikuyu tribe, not involved in Mau Mau.

will get their little bottoms smacked here by me personally if I hear them.

26 October 1952 The Kenya Police Reserve are marvellous – wretched settlers like John Adams with all their own work patrolling every single night round the farms. I have two sets of visitors here, John with an *askari* about 10 pm and one of the plant breeders about 7 am. All the telephones have been taken over, all messages screened and only English ones allowed. Sucks to the telephone clerks who are all Kikuyus and practically all Mau Mau, as they now work with a stalwart Britisher with a revolver *very* close to their heads.... I'm told that low-flying aircraft come over the farms, and just before you are chopped up you put out two sheets in the form of a cross and light a smudge fire close by, and then they rescue you. Haven't seen any yet. There is a special relay of police news every morning at 9 am from Nakuru for the Rift Valley. It mostly runs like this: 'There is no truth in the rumour that the Kikuyu are massing in strength on Menengai nor that African children have been chopped into little bits at Lessos'.... I went to judge at Molo Flower Show yesterday. Sharpie was my only co-judge as Rose had to stay on her farm to help screening telephones, and Mrs Cooper's son-in-law has been called up so she has to do his job.... I am going to N'bi again tomorrow, must go to a Jeanes School Conference and meet my day-old chicks from Pretoria next day.

1 November 1952 Locusts have come over the Northern Frontier District border in strength, to join Jomo* at Wajir, no doubt; hope they stay with him. Absolutely no sign of November rains anywhere.... Kenya's National Theatre was opened last night with a grand broadcast and Sir Ralph Richardson gave the opening oration with *The Hunting of the Snark*. Sir Evelyn Baring sounded in rattling form and made a cheerful, carefree, funny speech. I shouldn't wonder if they hadn't had a jolly good dinner at G.H.... Poor Ingrid was in rather a flap about the Bouyer murder and being herself murdered in her bath, so I suggested she should have her bath in the mornings, and that seemed to clear up the whole situation....

* Jomo Kenyatta had been arrested with 167 other suspected Mau Mau leaders on the night of 20 October and imprisoned at Wajir in the Northern Frontier District. on the night of 20 October

I see the first murdered European woman was *not* by Mau Mau but merely by her husband, which has happened before. Kenya really has nothing on Lady Derby who was attacked having her supper in the smoking-room, with a butler, valet and chef in close proximity.

17 November 1952 There are the most desperate problems ahead, e.g. the govt. have most rightly closed thirty-four Kikuyu Independent Schools, hotbeds of sedition, which should never have been allowed to exist at all; that throws twenty-one thousand children out of school, which will cause the most frightful discontent until they are accommodated in govt. schools, which can't be until teaching staff – already goodness knows Mau Mau enough – are available. Things this last week have taken on the pattern that I foresaw – a marauding sort of turn, as bands have come out of the Aberdares and raided farms, burnt down European houses etc.... Police yesterday killed one of the killers who have been trying to get the last remaining chief, Eluid, when they shot at him for the fourth time. He had a bodyguard of three hundred spearmen – quite a party to meet in a country lane. Mau Mau did a horrid murder in the forest just up at the back here last week – a poor timber contractor, an honest Kikuyu, also a police informer; the regular routine, strangled dog and a threat, the man's disappearance a few days later, and a mutilated corpse found a few days after that.... I fear the police informers may be rather too naïve, judging by what happened yesterday. I am trying to supplement my very indifferent nightwatchman with two Dorobo with bows and arrows. They have become extremely fashionable and very hard to get. Two appeared in company with another Dorobo who said he would like to show me his chits, and produced one, which said: 'Bearer is a Police Informer. Please give him all the help you can in case of need'.... I hope I have secured two Dorobo; Fish has six bow-and-arrow men on his farm.... Saturday I went to a wedding at Upper Gilgil. I think it is a mistake to be social these days, as when you are alone the last thing you talk to yourself about is Mau Mau, but from the crowd you hear all the horror stories, and lovely dogs and cattle poisoned etc.... Have had an entrancing morning, as the provincial agricultural officer and the head of Soil Conservation Service spent it here to plan my farm for me on a beef-maize proposition.... When

181

organized, the plan will be to turn off forty steers a year fed on oat hay, lucerne (grown in the irrigation), maize silage and Kikuyu grass. It means buying fifteen more cows and improving the pastures at the rate of knots.... My day-old chicks are now three weeks old and looking fine, touch wood.

25 November 1952 The situation deteriorated shockingly over this last weekend. There is a murderous gang round Thomson's Falls which seems to be doing just what it likes by night and day. The poor Meiklejohn couple were horribly caught out; he died, poor man, and she is critically ill from awful *panga* wounds. I'm afraid it was just because he had his shot-gun unassembled in its case, and she her revolver in a handbag out of reach, when the gang burst in. She had always done wonderful work as a doctor among the Africans so may have thought she was secure, but all that has gone by the board. The daily murders of loyal headmen go on in a crescendo.... Of course those Europeans who leave their firearms unlocked should be strafed no end, but it is indeed a discipline trying to remember where you've hidden all the oddments; if it's keys, I ask Mbugwa, but don't like to do it with the .256 bolt and ammunition. The revolver generally comes with me and I try not to hide it somewhere and forget. Am thrilled by the farm plan which Sandy Storrar made for me last week. I've got an electric fence and the most attractive little 'Porto Pylons' which save all stake work....

26 November 1952 I've made the intended increases to my bodyguard. With great difficulty, Fish secured two Dorobo for me. They arrived, after many days of not coming, for an interview, so I went out of the office to see them. Saw no Dorobo but heard a little rustle at the very top of the tree outside the office. This was the bodyguard, frightened of the dogs. However they came down complete with bows and arrows and parked themselves just out at the back; they are a great moral support; the nightwatchman sleeps much better for their being here, and so do I.

2 December 1952 Tom Askwith was here yesterday about women's clubs in the Rift Valley; he was extraordinarily interesting about the growth of Mau Mau, saw all this coming and reported it two years ago. He painted an appallingly gloomy picture of the Kikuyu young men who, of course, are the murderers, not the older ones. He says they are desperadoes with nothing else to live for and nothing to care about except murder and theft. They *must* be exterminated or controlled before anything can be done. They have grown up like this as a result of frustration after the war, and of course don't stop to think that anyone else had frustrations and difficulties. It then all clicked with Jomo and the criminal neglect of Govt. to do anything about the Independent Schools, Intelligence, etc.

We were all so sad on this farm today as poor old Njombo died in Nakuru Hospital yesterday. He came to us at Thika in '13 and has never worked for anyone else. Mbugwa [his son] has never worked for anyone else either and *his* son is just leaving the school here. Njombo was a grand old man; hasn't worked of course, for years, but was always about. Mbugwa is much distressed and has gone into Nakuru; I expect they hate him dying in hospital. What a difference between that generation and this!

9 December 1952   I have an incident from the home front to report of which I couldn't be more ashamed, just can't get over it. On Friday night, instead of taking my little revolver in with me to my simple evening meal, I left it wherever I had left it, which is usually either behind the radio or stuffed down the side of the sofa nearest me while I listen to the news after dinner. Just before the 9 pm news the Tiriki nightwatchman popped his head in through the door to say he was very ill. This struck me as odd, because I know so well by now the signs of his having the jitters, and was sure it was jitters not illness, so told him he'd get some medicine in the morning.

After the news, started to collect things to take to bed, such as glasses, etc. Could I find the revolver? *No.* Hunted absolutely everywhere. Finally most reluctantly, because you have to, rang up the police to report loss. About half an hour later Toft arrived and again we hunted everywhere. Then he had his men round up the household and poor Mbugwa and the under-lad Waweru were allowed to stage *their* hunt, round the house. Finally about midnight Toft departed with Karanja, Mbugwa, Waweru and the Tiriki, leaving an armed *askari* in their place. About seven next morning the party came back, this time in charge of the African sub-inspector Marcellus. I didn't hear them arrive, as was making my bed at the back, but very soon went into the sitting-room to find Karanja grinning from ear to ear handing Marcellus the revolver, which he, Karanja, said he had found in the side of the small armchair. Both Toft and I had hunted to the limit in that chair. I am quite convinced that Waweru caught sight of the revolver while I was eating next door and passed it to Karanja in the kitchen, and the watchman, seeing trouble ahead, went sick or tried to at that moment. Then somehow, next morning, Karanja passed it back into the sitting-room and 'discovered' it in the armchair. My goodness, I was relieved to see it. Since that shameful incident, an emergency law has been published saying anyone leaving any firearm in any place not absolutely safe will get six months *and* a £100 fine. That isn't specially because of me, but people have been so frightful about it, and the Kikuyus have so many arms now, far more it would seem than the KPR [Kenya Police Reserve], who mostly have batons.... The Cole family have had it badly. David at Solio had about sixteen cattle slashed and either killed or having to be destroyed, and Tobina's lovely little cream Welsh pony stallion was poisoned. That can't be proved but the night before four donkeys and thirty-two cows on the farm just above them were found dead in the same way and a post mortem found them full of maize, sugar and arsenic.... On the farm where Ingrid's brother is, near Punda Milia, a poor Indian storekeeper was brutally murdered on Tuesday by an armed gang of forty.... My goodness, what *awful* weather you have had, really awful. Today's paper says two hundred deaths due to fog.

28 December 1952 It was a gloomy Xmas really, as all KPR and home guard were working overtime to keep things quiet. We had a low-flying aircraft around all Xmas Eve evening; I think this was because Osborne's sawmills went up the night of 23rd. Awful horrors in the Nyeri district, eleven murders in one night, all Church of Scotland Christians who are the 'spearhead of the resistance'. Another chief attacked, his tribal retainer hacked to pieces with *pangas*, another loyal Nairobi chap shot; they do seem to have got a lot of firearms these days.... Oh please, this is important. I am out of knitting which is so boring, don't you think Charles ought to have a summer cricket sweater – very conventional – white cable-stitch and school colours in the band? I do hope he can stand still for long enough to be measured.... I'm told that of all the savage hatred shown against settlers in Kenya the most savage is from Canada. Why do they hate a white man so much? What harm have we done them?

Mau Mau was the fourth war in Nellie's lifetime and the one in which she was personally the most deeply involved. All through 1953 it continued unabated; farming, gardening and good works continued too with added difficulties.

1 January 1953   Everyone is after one's Kikuyu houseboys now as they have been in every single mess-up lately. People have been asked to lock them all out of the house from 6 pm, if they won't sack them out of hand. In lots of houses you can't even boil a kettle inside your house, so surely stumbling about outside in the dark would be lovely for Mau Mau, who would then pounce out of every corner without having to bother to enter the house? It really is a worry to know what to do about Karanja; there is no doubt that the return of my revolver was a frame-up, but it can't be proved. It would just be making bandits out of him and his like to turn them off, as no one would employ them, and they would starve and have nowhere to lay their heads, and would know every chink of one's house and habits, the better to lead bandits to.

It is a horrible tragedy about the Bingley boy who was murdered; his father has had so many tragedies, lost his first wife aged about nineteen having a baby, and his second wife died of some unnecessary form of poisoning before M & B days. Lately he has spent a lot of money and a tremendous lot of personal service working for the model community centre at Dundori, quoted everywhere as a shining example of race relations. Very bitter. And, latest, govt. never bothered to give the poor Kiambu chief a bodyguard (bet the DC had one) and he was murdered in his private ward in Kiambu hospital.... Am just off to an EAWL meeting at Njoro to urge the starting of women's clubs – not a very bright moment for it. Karanja's wife Arieti has just come back from her Jeanes School homecraft course with a good report. Betty Roche is coming next Sat. to help start a club here.

185

17 January 1953   I went for two nights to N'bi to judge at the Flower Show which was excellent. Also showed veges and was put to shame by winning all the prizes and collecting three large cups.... Sat. morning started the women's club here which should be a great event though barely recognizable as such at the time. Arieti, Karanja's wife, is going to be really good, I think, full of drive and a good little soul. It seems to me absolutely vital to make contact with the women and bring them along friendly-like. People are getting a bit hysterical and thinking in terms of one tribe only and one section of that tribe. No wonder.

25 January 1953   Horrible murder of the Ruck family last night and lots of arson of wheat up at Molo and God knows what in the reserves.*... This was interrupted by Dorothy Thornton, EAWL district vice president, ringing up to say could she come to see me as she was sure all the women in the world would be at her tomorrow to demand a meeting over this Ruck murder. I expect they will. I counselled no meeting, they really get you nowhere.... The weather is quite bestial, blazing hot days with blasting wind and last week two nights of hard frost which has never happened here before; the bird bath was frozen quite solid – you should have seen the little tropical birds' faces. We are in no mood to brook such behaviour from the weather and none of the million Emergency regulations help at all.... Re next summer, would there be any chance of a real holiday all together, possibly a trippery trip abroad? Such fun if it were. There are luscious trips on yachts on the Seine, including Paris – would that widen Charles' mind without your being seasick? Or bus trips to Austrian Tyrol? Or something called 'friendship tours' – you make nice new friends?

12 February 1953   Terrific movement of Kikuyu going on – a thousand lifted from Elburgon yesterday. I'm sure it isn't the answer, but I suppose they [the government] can't think up anything better at the moment. Transit camp a shambles, I believe. Meanwhile a most odd migration of women and children going on, on their own, no one knows why. Thousands from Ol Kalau, and now it seems

* Roger Ruck and his wife were *panga*'d to death in their farmhouse and their six-year-old son murdered in his bed.

to have begun here – from the Fishes at the moment. Said to be 'something brewing'. No European is to have more than one firearm per head; it is because farmers have been so careless and had so many stolen; two farmers have lately been fined £75 for having guns stolen. Sabukia seems to be full of armed gangs. . . . A holiday on the Continent where no one had ever heard of Mau Mau would be heaven.

1 March 1953 Quite suddenly Gailey & Roberts have imported some small sirens which work off the main, and the Drummonds secured one for me on the spot. I have erected it on the lawn and John Adams is going to fix it for me; he has the very good idea of running all the flex which has to be outside through half-inch piping so that no one can cut it. And will fix switches in every room to work it. . . . Hugh Coltart had a store with a thousand bags of barley burnt down last night. . . . Did I tell you I now have a huge 'G–R–A–N–T' in whitewashed bricks on the lawn (croquet of course gone west for the duration)? It is to help the airwing KPR know where they are when fire-hunting. Everyone was 'asked' to do it – why weren't we told? Anyway the aeroplanes come to admire it; it was fun to do. We are now zoned into 'maximum danger', 'danger' and just 'special' areas. Maximum danger is N. and S. Kinangop, Thomson's Falls, Laikipia and Sabukia; 'Danger' Naivasha, Gilgil, here, Solai and Elburgon. This is only for Rift Valley of course. We have the curfew, which worries Mbugwa a lot about getting back to his hut after dark; he is being very correct about it; Karanja seems more than calm.

8 March 1953 Awoke rather early, as my Dorobo bodyguard (2), who now sleep very handy in the dog-room, seemed to be chattering and gurking more than usual. Always a cosy sound, except when anyone is staying, when I feel guilty about it. Read *George V*, very fascinating book, but shattering to find that in 1920, in Ireland, we had sixty thousand regular troops and fifteen thousand regular police, and they failed to cope with three thousand guerrillas. Here we have six hundred Lancashire Fusiliers, possibly two thousand KAR, police and police reserve, and about a million and a half potential guerrillas. However these are not so well armed as the Shinners.

At 10 am a split pin jumped out of the hammer-mill, so gristing today a washout, and was in the middle of a Seth-Smith order; never mind.... Njoro station is a sad, refugee-like sight; streams of Forestry Kikuyu taking themselves off to the reserve, no one knows why. Chickens, *totos*, sordid little possessions, are waiting about for hours and hours, very sad-making really, as what are they going to do? Talked to some of the women, but all very clam-like ... Aircraft have been circling round for three days now trying to locate bad hats known to be in the forest behind; please will all farmers mark their names in letters ten feet long painted white. We agreed that Feathers might have to buy more land, but all right for Prettejohn as he has twenty-seven thousand acres. I think I can just do it on the lawn.... Have been suitably shadowed by my bodyguard; in due course they attend me to the aunt and thence to bath and bed (they do stay outside). One most important security measure is never to do anything at the same time every day, i.e. one day you have your bath before dinner, next day in the morning, next day no bath at all.... Charming christening party at Hans and Viveka's, went there for lunch, first time since Boxing Day 1948. Am working furiously at Charles's white sweater....

The normal Kikuyu custom was to live in separate family homesteads, each one surrounded by bush or cultivation, rather than in clusters or villages. As the Emergency worsened, a policy was adopted of concentrating the people into so-called villages, either on suitable hill-tops in the Kikuyu land units, or in one village for each farm in the Rift Valley. Villages in Kikuyuland were stockaded and ringed by dry moats, on the lines of medieval castles. Mau Mau had by this time taken the form of separate gangs based in the forests, which were in the main devoid of roads, and offered almost impenetrable shelter. From these forests, gangs emerged to raid African shambas for food and European farms for food and firearms. After the detention of Jomo Kenyatta and other suspected leaders, the oaths forced upon recruits grew more and more debased, including gruesome sacrifices of goats and dogs, an eerie ritual derived from primitive witchcraft practices, and various sexual perversions involving parts of dead animals. Oath-administrators were crucial in the loose, amorphous yet effective organization of Mau Mau. The government endeavoured to identify and round them up and put them into camps where rehabilitation techniques were applied, which aimed at 'cleansing' them from the dehumanizing virulence of the oaths.

16 March 1953 The 'villagization' scheme has been suddenly and violently put into force to the utter disruption of all Kikuyu labour. The govt. made one scheme for farms of whatever size, which couldn't have been sillier. The result here was that all Kikuyu labour would have been squashed up like sardines.... My chaps all said that they would be photographed and finger-printed but that they would *not* live like sardines.... Personally I think the Kikuyus are so pushed about and harried and worried that they just listen to the last chap who comes along.... If *only* it would rain I believe they would settle down, as they would literally dig themselves in and couldn't bear to leave the sprouting maize if they could see it sprouting.... On the Hodges' farm in Sabukia the labour all went overnight, leaving their maize, turkeys, clothes and every single thing; the Hodges will be practically bust this year as all their maize and pyrethrum is lying out unpicked; no one has been kinder or better to their labour than they have.

1 April 1953 Lari massacre and Naivasha police station raid overshadow everything. Lari was indescribably appalling, for once worse than anything the press can say.* Rose Cartwright's beloved farm headman lost his wife and entire family there, ditto her carpenter.... Not a sign or smell of rain, couldn't be more catastrophic. Of all the years for this to happen! Had a hectic day on Monday as the truck for my maize arrived and it all had to be got off in a day. I sent off 150 bags, a very bad crop, but better than some people got, average 9.7 bags per acre.... Two cows I got from Hugh Coltart are in slight milk so am trying to rear four bull-calves; old Karanja Mukora [herd] adores them. Although he has no English he calls the calves 'darling' and the feeding times, especially the evening ones, are a joy, and it is generally a grim time as I am too cowardly to

---

* On 26 March, Mau Mau terrorists wiped out an entire Kikuyu village, slaughtering ninety-seven men, women and children and committing atrocities which shocked many of the Kikuyu as well as Europeans. Six months later, not one of the gangsters responsible had been arrested.

walk in the forest any more.... And, cheer up, one might not get bumped off by Mau Mau and go home and then be run over by a bus.

18 April 1953 I always panic – do you? – that seeds are never going to come up.... A quiet week on the whole, except for two killings nearby. An ex-student of Egerton Farm School, KPR, flushed ten armed chaps, ordered them to halt and they didn't, so he shot one dead; the others went off towards Ngongogeri, but later divided up and half came back this way. Police patrols were out next day hunting them and killed one just down the road on Tom Petrie's. I don't know what has happened to the rest – in the forest I expect. My lads, working near the boundary, heard the shots, so now there is a wild scuttle to move huts 'nearer in' from the forest edge. A little gentle digging of *shambas* has begun which is a comforting thought.... John Adams saw an *enormous* leopard on the road here on night patrol, as if we hadn't enough worries already.

4 May 1953 There has been much activity re Mau Mau in this forest lately; they say they've 'liquidated' a gang of thirty-five, some just above here, and some about fifteen miles up a new 'security' road. My labour got terrifically jittery when the Mau Mau murdered four people – two Dorobo, one Luo, one Kikuyu – of Beeston's at a new sawmill just above here, and instead of refusing to be 'villagized' they have now all rushed to move nearer in, even Mbugwa.

27 May 1953 Gangs round again at the back; poor Ingrid got a whole lot of very valuable laying pullets stolen on Sat. night; all the corpses were found neatly stacked along the forest tracks – obviously food for a gang. Behind Phyl Lewin's farm they had a 'do' last week: seven were killed and five captured out of fourteen, but some Kikuyu guards* were killed too, and Pip Beverley, KPR, shot in mouth and lung, but is going to be all right. The papers never give the loyalist casualties these days which are sometimes more than killed terror-

---

* Loyal Kikuyu were by now organized into a home guard partly modelled on Britain's during the war, armed mainly with spears and *rungus*, though shot-guns were issued as time went on.

ists. No sign of its really letting up, and no one feels in the least more secure. The gangs are so large now and so well armed that they are much more unpleasant when they do materialize, though of course should be easier for the police to hear about.

7 June 1953 On Coronation Day I gave out sweets, medals, etc., to tots about 9 am, then listened to the wireless for a bit. The service in N'bi sounded really lovely, wish I could have been at it. Then the march-past outside the cathedral with men from HMS *Newfoundland*, Lancashire Fusiliers, Buffs, Devons, KAR, and NZ jet fighters screaming past. About ten very dirty and weary Kenya Regiment lads quite rightly got all the cheering there was.... Went to the Egerton College African sports and was jumped into giving away the prizes; the winning team got a fat sheep, second ditto a thin one. I hope not to have to give away prizes again with a KPR sten-gun in the small of my back and arms galore everywhere. Also not to have to attend another royal garden party with a revolver in handbag.... The party was fun really. European manners were shocking; I saw someone snatch a chair away from under an African, and others were clicking cameras at any decorative African they could see. Hundreds of those were there, as the idea was to make a fuss of all loyal Kikuyu, but they can't have enjoyed it much, as no one looked after them very much, and the racial segregation was terrific.... The Mau Mau gangs are evidently getting hungry and raids accordingly increasing in every direction. But possibly the Kikuyus are out to help a bit more.... My little bull came today, a nice little Boran, nearly red in colour, polled, and the quietest thing. Only £40 as against goodness knows what for a pedigree Red Poll. I hope he will like his red wives.

22 June 1953 I have actually been away for four days, as got a sitter-in here; was due to judge at the Eldoret Flower Show and the Cecil Hoeys asked me to stay so gladly went. It was all marvellously pre- and non-Emergency and made one realize what a silly life it is in the troubled areas. Wonderful to be revolver-free, no bars on windows, no curfew, etc. And wonderful to be in a comfortable house and to see a fully developed ten-thousand-acre farm ticking over. All done in six years too, because they had to sell their place in the

Cherangi hills owing to Cecil's heart, and the altitude. His is a really high-powered success story. He came out in 1904....

8 July 1953 Weather continues to be catastrophic here, some look for a ninety-five per cent failure of crops in this district, and people who have had to plough in their maize haven't been able to plant wheat.... The last two nights I've had about four acres of maize done in by frost. I don't see how, at most, I can get more than five or six bags per acre, and I hand-planted everything to make sure of a fifteen-bag crop instead of my average ten.... There was an awful raid on one of the Bastard farms last week, a Seychelles *fundi*, wife and three young children burnt alive, all the dogs and farm guards shot, house looted and then burnt. Family away at the coast. The hearts of the so-called loyal Kikuyu just aren't in the game.... I forgot to tell you that I suddenly received a Coronation medal along with most of the rest of Kenya's population; presumably because I've been too long on the Hospital Board. The one I got in '35 unfortunately got pinched, or I could have worn one in front and one behind.

25 July 1953 Mau Mau seems to be boiling up more than ever.... Irene MacDougall's ex-husband has been slashed to death four miles outside Nyeri township, and gangs of a hundred are taking on the troops and getting away with it all over the reserve. We have two hundred Black Watch at Nakuru, straight from Korea. Plenty of gangery here this last week, there was a gang of about forty behind the Fishes'; it broke up and nine more were seen at John Adams and later at Egerton; the chaps who saw them never said a word for hours. That night they gouged out the eyes of a cow at Chauvain's and my chaps heard shots at 4 am. I reported it to the police who had a merry time up here all day but never a sign; of course they want eyes for oathing ceremonies. The drought is raging. The Fishes' maize, ninety acres, their whole crop, is lying flat on the ground and brown as paper.... I wonder if the home press got a good account of the large hideout the troops found last week; it captured my imagination; built to accommodate seven hundred, and a lot of neatly butchered elephant meat all ready for cooking on a grand scale. Makes barons of beef sound like *filets mignons*.... Am having fun with mud ovens in preparation for my great Summer School.... One project approved of even by Karanja is the 'Boer Meal' – you boil *posho* tightly packed in a bag for five hours and it comes out like a ball which is predigested and very good for delicate infants and the very old.

2 August 1953 I went to see Toft, the Njoro policeman; he is a really decent and excellent chap. It was a depressing interview as for the first time he was really down about Mau Mau. He said the moment he thought he knew a bit about it, or was getting somewhere, something happened to show him that the whole thing was as hot as ever. They got four oath administrators on Dick Prettejohn's farm this week, and Dick is the No. 1 KPR and has worked harder and knows more than anyone except possibly Toft himself. Toft frankly saw no end to it and said he just hated it all, whereas his previous wars and rebellions he had thoroughly enjoyed. Perhaps he was just over-tired; they never stop raiding from here to the Masai border.

16 August 1953 Last week I stood the farm labour their annual outing and took them all to the Coronation film, the long coloured one, in Mary Wright's large Bedford truck. Muchoka said he'd never seen finer mules or mules better trained to do their job; these proved to be the proud Windsor Greys. Old Kariuki said the dogs were magnificent; he'd never seen better, and the way they sat all the time without moving and their mouths open was superb. These were the gargoyles on the coach. Everyone was full of admiration for the weather; it was wonderful to have all that rain and a good omen.... The Summer School went with a flick and was exhausting, but proved how the women loved it and how accessible it makes them, but what of the follow-up? Goodness knows.

13 September 1953 Everything on the farm sadly depressing as the maize has definitely gone now; it is a question of making as much as one can into silage, an almost impossible task with no mechanization.... Very horrid things happening, such as the poor Symonds near Eldoret have had their eldest son killed by a grenade accident; they adored him and he should have been just leaving Egerton to go and help run their huge farm, only of course got caught up in the Kenya Regiment. Such waste and misery.... Have just finished making nine different sorts of marmalade for the Njoro stand at the Royal Show, none up to Show standard I fear but the stall has to be filled.

In October I flew to Kenya for two months. All my visits had to be, in modern parlance, self-financing, by means of newspaper articles and sometimes a book to follow.* This meant that I could be on the farm only for brief intervals between material-gathering forays, which was disappointing for Nellie, so sometimes she came with me, providing the car. To gather first-hand impressions we visited Fort Hall, Nyeri and two of the missions that were so strong a focus of resistance to Mau Mau in the Central Province. This was hardly a holiday for Nellie, but it did for a short while relieve her of the never-ending, nerve-wearing responsibility for the safety of her Kikuyu families as well as her own and that of the dogs. During this period Nellie's letters of course ceased, but the story may be carried on by extracts from my own to Gervas.

At Njoro The farm seems much as ever and quite normal in spite of the Emergency. Karanja and Mbugwa wreathed in smiles and all the farm people rushed up and enquired after you and Charles; no sullen faces and it is hard to believe in all that is going on beneath the surface. I'm sure they only want to be left alone; the trouble arises when the hard-core gangsters come in from the forest and start oath-taking and general nastiness. Not one of Nellie's Kikuyu has left. It is terribly dry and the maize a disaster. In spite of that, the garden is full of colour, and such variety. Just for interest I took down the names of shrubs and flowers actually in bloom – there are sixty-five names, and of course others not in flower as well. It is very gay.... Yesterday the police came and took away four of the Purveses' Kikuyu whom they (Purveses) had looked on as absolutely reliable, including two milkers, which makes farming difficult.... The police arrest these people on the word of informers, and goodness knows how many are guilty and how many are not. All sorts of home guards and screening teams are about and no one knows, or can know, what goes on in the way of bribes and intimidation.

*In this case A Thing to Love, a novel with a Mau Mau background.

At Weithaga, Church of Scotland Mission   There's an early Christian atmosphere here even down to the persecution, as Christians are favourite targets for Mau Mau and many have been killed, and still are being; only last week, two Christian women were strangled nearby. There are upwards of a hundred refugees living here who have come in to avoid being killed, mostly with large families. Last night, some of the Brethren came to a meeting. After hymns, prayers and a Bible reading, three or four Brethren gave their witness as to when and how they had been saved, and are now washed with the Blood of the Lamb and walk with the Lord Jesus. . . . They are completely sincere, and seem altogether happy, and it *is* an answer I suppose.

At Fort Hall   There are Kikuyu guard posts – stockades – all over the place, manned by unpaid guards mostly armed with shot-guns, and tribal police with rifles. They have killed and are killing a lot of gangsters, but murders still go on. It is, of course, a civil war. On the surface, it looks peaceful enough and everyone goes about his business normally except that markets are closed. There will be a terrible legacy of feuds and hatreds when it's over. A chief who was ambushed and murdered here a few weeks ago was betrayed by his own sister, and so on.

At Nyeri   Yesterday we started off at 9 am with the DC in his jeep. A mile or so beyond one of the home guard posts we met a lorry full of excited passengers who said there were many Mau Maus near the road and a battle was in progress. So we returned to the home guard post to alert them, the warriors assembled and tied strips of pink cloth round their heads to identify them, and advanced into the *shambas* in the direction of the battle. The country is heavily cultivated and all ridges and valleys, so you can never see far ahead. We proceeded to the top of a ridge overlooking the valley where Mau Maus had been seen. It was too thick to see much but we heard shots quite close and then bursts of sten-gun fire. Then the local chief appeared in a lorry full of home guards, a large, stout man brandishing a revolver. Then an RC priest came along and stopped for a chat, we sat in the sun and I got rather sunburnt. Two lorryloads of police arrived and also vanished into the *shambas*. We proceeded in our

195

jeep and found the valley crawling with home guards. We halted to talk to some of them, and one very enthusiastic warrior started to tell the DC how bravely he had shot a gangster the week before. As he approached the climax of his tale, he flung himself down to show how he'd aimed his gun, pressed the trigger and – bang, the chief dropped like a stone and a loud hissing came from a tyre. The gun was loaded with SSG and shot the jeep in the foot and grazed the chief's arm. Everyone roared with laughter for about five minutes except the poor home guard, who was overcome with shame and confusion.

After changing the tyre we proceeded to the top of the opposite hillside and saw much activity below. Two of the gang had just been shot while trying to cross the river, and two more captured. It was all just like a buffalo hunt, or even more a grouse drive, with beaters advancing in line and whacking the bushes. One of the captives was led up, a lad of seventeen or eighteen in tattered clothing with long, matted hair (a sign he'd come from the forest) and a very grim, depraved look, like a caged animal – they call it the Mau Mau look, and it really does exist, a look of complete thuggishness. He had some ammunition on him which is now a capital offence. It's an extraordinary sort of war – vast quantities of troops with their red-tabbed generals and armoured cars, lorries and jeeps, huge camps, engineers, aircraft, modern guns and heaven knows what, ranged against gangs of thugs armed either with *pangas* or home-made rifles made out of lead piping and fired with a door-bolt or a nail and elastic. It makes fools of us really. They are still murdering fellow Kikuyu almost daily, and stealing cattle, and maiming them, from Europeans. The gangs are hunted now like rabbits if they emerge from the forest, and in the forest they are very short of food. . . . Later we heard the result of 'our' battle. The gang was thirteen strong and of these eleven were killed and two captured – so gangs in daytime now seem to get pretty thoroughly blotted out.

In Nairobi Spent the morning at the Athi River camp for Mau Mau detainees run by Moral Re-armament, who are very sincere and devoted, but everyone else is sceptical as to how far they really do change the black hearts of the detainees, who are the hard-core ones, not 'greys'. There are about 1,200 of them in this camp and they are not obliged to do any work. Those who wish to 'cooperate' volunteer for work and thereafter do a little gentle gardening, there are about 250 of these. The rest sit around in compounds and do absolutely nothing all day. Until recently they even had convicts to empty their latrines. They wear their 'Jomo beards' and are fed on a Geneva ration scale for POW's about four times as heavy as the normal Kikuyu diet, so are as fat as aldermen, and have nothing to do all day but plot further Mau Mau activities. The MRA give them pep talks at intervals on their sins, and call them to God. There are no statistics as to how many answer.

At Njoro Just back from two days in Sabukia and Solai where there are some wonderful farms. We ended up at Bruce Mackenzie's, the Friesian king,* who has a thousand acres, all bush six years ago, now paddocked and down to leys with the country's best herd of 180 pedigree Friesians and about seventy Aberdeen Angus. The post-war settlers seem to have done exceedingly well almost to a man, and seem mostly a hard-working and desirable type. The change in all that country is remarkable. Sabukia is almost a paradise.... I think it has done Nellie a lot of good to get about a bit, as I gather lately she has been very much of a recluse. This is the first time for years she has been to the Hodges', although they are among the few people she really likes.

I flew back to England in mid-December and Nellie's letters were resumed.
   During 1954 the Mau Mau Emergency, far from being contained, grew worse. Forest gangs under the command of 'generals' such as Kago and China, had hide-outs stocked with food which was brought to designated spots by Kikuyu women, while constant raids on European-owned livestock kept them supplied with meat. The government had instituted a system of screening teams, each consisting of loyal Kikuyu with a European in charge, which questioned every man and woman detained as a Mau Mau suspect, with the object of getting each

* A South African, and wartime airforce pilot, he became Minister of Agriculture and the only white minister in Jomo Kenyatta's cabinet after Independence. He was killed when an aircraft in which he was travelling from Kampala to Nairobi mysteriously blew up in the air.

individual to confess his implication and then to repudiate the oaths. Once the screeners were satisfied that he was 'cleansed', he was released – in some cases, sceptics thought, to make straight for the nearest oath-administrator for re-oathing. Those who refused to 'come clean' were sent to special camps for detainees where rehabilitation was attempted. Those against whom offences could be proved came before the courts and received long sentences, or the death sentence in the case of murderers. At times, Nellie felt herself threatened almost as much by the goodies who might at any moment remove her entire labour force for questioning, and thus bring to a halt her farming activities, as by the baddies who might at any moment descend upon her from the forest to slaughter her cattle, set fire to the premises and probably kill her too.

3 January 1954 Wednesday, about midnight, John Adams on patrol knocked me up to say that all Kikuyu labour was to be ready for inspection at 7 am next day. This was because of the very disappointing oathing ceremony near Njoro on Andy's farm. The oath administrator had thought up a plan of branding all takers on the back with a red-hot *panga*; no one can understand why, as it gives more information to the enemy, us, than help to Mau Mau? There were thirty branded people in Njoro police station, one in a very bad way from septic burns. I did not attend the inspection, my people were quite bewildered, or pretended to be. I don't think any branded people were found on these farms, but it is very disappointing that it is going on more than ever.

Nellie attended a conference at the Jeanes School near Nairobi, an adult education centre for Africans where emphasis was laid on social welfare, and on the training of women, whose education still lagged much behind the men's. The women's clubs which Nellie had pioneered at Njoro were spreading and developing into a movement called Maendeleo, whose aim was to raise the standard of living and broaden the education of African women.

12 January 1954 At the last Jeanes conference there was a most remarkable girl, tremendously bright, called Elizabeth. She had been made the first African policewoman and was highly publicized, made to broadcast, etc. Absolutely the best type. She shortly afterwards married a police *askari*; I asked after her this time – she and her husband had deserted from the police and gone over to Mau Mau. It is really shattering, the power they have; that girl had everything to gain by being loyal; her mission education should have minimized the terrorism, yet she went.... Terrific boost at the conference for Maendeleo; there are 250 clubs now and over a thousand members.... I did a little mad shopping – mad as to haste – and popped into the US Information Centre to get a book on square dancing; Kit Henn swears by it and says it is quite easy to get it going among Africans. I do hope we can get it started somehow.... I sent some old hens to the Cold Storage Co., they always pay by return; heard nothing, couldn't think why – the poor office manager was more than half slashed in his office in broad daylight; everyone got away.

19 January 1954   Sunday was a great day on the farm as there was a circumcision for two girls, old Nganga (gardener)'s débutante, and a very much younger sister of Mbugwa's. Nganga had repeatedly asked me to ask Dick Prettejohn for the loan of a skilled operator in his employment. I was naturally reluctant to countenance the ceremony, but in fact one has no legal right to prohibit it, and Dick agreed that it would be a very bad plan to drive it underground just now, especially as it has so often lately been used as a cloak to oath-taking.... I did not attend, but the songs, beer-drinking, etc., all seemed to be in order, and Mbugwa said it was all nice and traditional, and no squeaks. The aged lady asked me to remit her fee to Dick – Sh 55/- for the two girls. Quite a career, think I shall take it up.... I have taken to making the most succulent soup out of lucerne – excellent.

21 February 1954   Pip Beverley, who has taken on Intelligence for KPR, was here yesterday and most pessimistic.... He says my only course in case of attack would be to tell the labour to scatter and flee myself, because of the house being so wooden; destination of the flee unspecified. The Barkers at Molo saved themselves through the 'flee plan' – they hid in a silage pit.... The nightmare about these raids, besides the risk of fire, is that even if the raid is anything up to ten miles away, the police will whisk off *all* your Kikuyu labour willy-nilly and so wreck your farming programme. They had two thousand taken away within twenty-four hours of the Barker raid, from all the surrounding Molo farms – into detention of course; there are six thousand in the Rift Valley camps now. It really is a strain all the time thinking of it.... Went to a Stockowners' Conference in Nakuru, *very* interesting – Gilbert Colville very good on meat marketing. Altogether a nice farmery day.

28 February 1954 Betty Roche brought her Mexican journalist to lunch, she is smart beyond words. She produced for Betty a most heavenly dish from an old hen with a glass of brandy and a lump of butter, fennel and thyme pushed into its innards, and then the bird tightly wrapped in *parchment* paper and boiled slowly for three hours. Could you possibly send me a sheet or two of parchment paper by air mail?... The journalist produced the seventh and eighth Mau Mau oaths, they are just pure (sic) obscenity, would you like them? All about copulating with a dog and then killing the dog and putting its penis into a virgin and so on for hours. So pretty.... She says she wants to get all the obscenity put across; actually I wonder if people really take in what it means. Would the village of Oaksey be stirred to the core by knowing that oath administrators have to have sexual relations with a virgin ewe? The Australian army gave Hughie's polo ponies vd near Warminster in the Kaiser's war and no one worried much.... I went to a lovely farm sale on Thursday and got a heavenly instrument, a 'clod crusher' only three feet wide, exactly what is needed for rolling in Rhodes grass and other pasture seeds, also a pet of an Ox Hay Sweep for £1, so came away with my tail up.

6 March 1954 I lost my ammunition – nineteen rounds – for five days and felt quite physically sick the whole time with worry. It happened thus: owing to police going on about it, I took to carrying the gun and ammunition when I left the farm. On Sat. when I got in, I found the bullets untidy and loose so said to myself I would make them a little bag. Thought it all out, the material etc., but never got around to making the little bag. On Tues. went to its hidey-hole to get it out – all gone. Terrific hunt, no avail. It was just appalling to find it gone. Then I thought, if they've taken the ammunition they will come for the gun, and/or set the house alight to cover their tracks. Also here I am with five bullets in the world, what yarn can I make up to get a permit for more? And so on. Really it was no fun, and the horror of wondering who really did it. Then on Thurs. pm I had to park the gun somewhere before bringing it to the wireless table for the evening, and went to a very special hidey-hole – and there was the ammunition in its untidy handkerchief! I had absolutely and completely forgotten putting it there, though had searched all the other hidey-holes. You can imagine the relief. I think in future it would be safer to give everything to Mbugwa to look after while I'm out.

21 March 1954   Just after my last letter we had the Bruxnor Randall murder which really was the most horrible thing. Poor old harmless things; do you remember them at Thika? She had a lovely collection of Waterford glass, very unusual in the early colonial period; I wonder whether that got slashed to death with *pangas* too.... Still lovely blue skies when you can see them for a smoke pall; frightful forest fire raging for ten days now behind here.... I've got a silly right hand which has developed an allergy; Jean Scott [the local doctor] says it must be due to something I grasp firmly in my right palm but can't think what it can be. Possibly a plastic knitting needle or a glass, but have done that all my life.

4 April 1954   Great news! *There has been rain!* It is incredibly wonderful, and it crept upon us almost unawares. Entirely from the wrong direction, i.e. from the west, came an all-night gentle drizzle; next morning, instead of the flaming, very beautiful but maddening sunrise of gold, orange, red, cerise, etc., from my bedroom window I saw the Rift with blue-grey, smoke-grey and brown-grey clouds and lights, and best of all, soft clouds sitting in the valley – to me a sure sign of rain within twenty-four hours. Next night we had 1.11 inches so planting of all sorts started madly. The relief and comfort are tremendous.... Now it is fun watching the faint green tints appear, and in a few days all will be green and mushrooms will be here.... This last and most horrible murder of a four-and-a-half year old child at Kiambu is most disquieting. What more can parents do than let a child ride its tricycle within a few yards of the back veranda, with a Luo houseboy just inside the house, at 8 am, and both parents in the house?... Started planting yellow maize yesterday with the Planet Junior, to be intercropped with field peas. Lots of oats broadcast with a fiddle and rolled in with my clod crusher which works like a dream. I've got about ten thousand cuttings of White Rocks Napier grass stuck into the furrows; they should do about two acres. Have to get masses more lucerne in too, and have the Guinea grass coming any minute. Must go and prune roses and citrus; the poor garden is having no look-in at all, all hands flat out on the farm....

16 May 1954   The cattle industry has been very exciting all this week. First of all the first Boran calf was born, such a pet and strong beyond belief. A heifer, father's colouring and his broad intellectual forehead, otherwise a Red Poll.... I wonder if you would like a recipe for a very lazy way of making marmalade?

23 May 1954   On Sunday went to lunch at Egerton to meet the twenty-two delegates to the International Federation of Agricultural Producers. The party proved to be fourteen very wet Scandinavians who arrived at 1 pm and had to leave at 3 pm to do a lightning tour of farms in their bus; it poured with rain and they never left the bus. The Scandinavians gave a very grey effect all round.... Collected my party to stay the night consisting of three Jugoslavs. One, a professor from Sarajevo, wasn't too bad and could talk bad French and lots of German; the other two were complete wets, lumps of one hundred per cent unattractive clay; am sure they were Russian. A strange thing happened; at one time in my life, only I cannot think when, I must have spoken quite good German, as under this awful strain it all came back, and by 10 pm I was telling the professor all about race relations, the true causes of Mau Mau etc. in a quite passable German accent, and next morning told the rather startled Mbugwa to bring the *Frühstück*.... The daily heavy rain and sudden lush growth has brought on an epidemic of bloat. On Friday I got back from a hospital meeting to be told that eight of my yearling steers in paddock near house had blown and two had died before they could be got around to with doses of paraffin. Karanja (cook) heard their awful groans and rushed with Mbugwa and got all the school *totos* on to it, but they just couldn't do more than save six out of eight; they really were splendid to cope as they did.

30 May 1954 On Empire Day we did our school tree planting. We planted a Cape chestnut, our most beautiful tree, for our most beautiful Queen, a *mweri* for the Duke of Edinburgh, a strong upright *podo* for Prince Charles and a sweet-smelling mauve affair in the drive for Princess Anne.

6 June 1954 Preston (from Egerton) came up one day for a walk round. He estimates my food potential on this farm according to my present planning as enough for four hundred head of stock, but says where would I sell steers in that quantity? However I have no intention of aiming at more than fifty steers a year well fed but home fed, and see how it works out.

11 July 1954 What I think of Capricorn* is, that it is mad to lay the emphasis, as they are doing, on the *vote* and only the vote. Of course Africans will take this to mean racial equality, as they did with Christianity, and what a frustration that was. In you go together through the church door, out you come together, and then is it 'Come on chaps, all to lunch together at Muthaiga'? No, it is 'Good-bye till church next Sunday', and so it will be with the vote.... The household were rather sweet about the Horticultural Show. Two horrible *totos* stole all the carrots I was keeping specially for it. Karanja produced some perfect carrots asking me to take them instead. And the old gardener, Nganga, brought me some priceless spuds to show, of a special sort which I'd been looking for for two years – they mature in six weeks. I did show them, hadn't the heart to refuse, but only in a class where I was the only entry, so couldn't do anyone down.... Many congratulations to Charles on the excellent results of Sports Day. It is good to know he is bitten with the sports and games bug, as I'm sure it keeps young minds in good trim and off more difficult issues, and the competitive spirit does mean a terrific lot of fun in life.

* The Capricorn Africa Society, started by Colonel David Stirling and others to foster multi-racialism in all the east and central African territories.

25 July 1954   Jock Webster (KPR) said I had an oath administrator on the farm. I met him (Webster) on the road and was allowed a peep at his secret little book and there, alas and alas, is written: Mrs Grant's farm – Karanja Kineku, clerk; Wakahiu, oath administrator. He said he wasn't going to do anything 'at the moment', I said how long is a moment, he laughed and wouldn't say, but did say that once he pulled them in I should never see them again. I *must* find out two things from him: how to trace *fitinas* [quarrels, feuds], and if a chap was in it say up to a year ago, and then pulled out, is he still put away for fifteen years or so? Personally I think that is what Karanja has done, but of course may be wrong. He has stuck like a leech to the farm, nothing is too much trouble, and he's had so many opportunities of doing me and my property in, and so on. Wakahiu is my only decent ox-driver so quite unreplaceable, and what will happen about cultivation I simply can't think. It is quite horrible chatting to a chap daily knowing he may shortly be hung by the neck; also I ought to sack him, which means he would be screened and pulled in immediately. I must go very gently with Jock Webster; a word amiss might start an avalanche of woe.... Simply can't resist a treat for the veg. garden to try, little black beets the size of small eggs, a new lettuce half cos, half cabbage, a tiny cucumber, etc., and a hybrid sweetcorn. It is a long time since I have given the veg. garden a treat. The flower garden is all flat but the Cape chestnuts are divine and visible from where I eat. And a big bowl of same is on dining-room table arranged by Mbugwa.

5 September 1954   Friday I went to the 5.30 matinée of the Kontiki film to which John Adams had invited Fish, Nils and self. I did enjoy the film. It was a harassing afternoon, as took my knitting-bag and so had two bags in the hand to which I am not accustomed. Went to sit for half an hour in the Stag's Head veranda to do a crossword as it was raining; when I left, and got as far as the post office, found I had only the knitting-bag and not the gun-containing handbag. Hared back to the Stag's, not a sign of it where I'd been sitting, thought I might have left it at Hari Singh's while stuffing a gin-bottle with difficulty into the knitting-bag, hared there, and there it was, intact; but if an energetic young policeman had chanced to come in and see it, even in Hari Singh's tender care, oh dear, oh dear.

Next day   Jock Webster has come and gone; the farm is apparently stiff with Mau Mau but no actual ceremonies held lately. Karanja is said to have very important books in his possession, and I am to tell him that if he stops lying and really wants to come clean, this is his chance, otherwise he is for it. Muchoka who obviously knows the whole thing also lied and lied and was shivering with fear. So for the present Karanja is still available for cookery.

7 September 1954   I must say Jock Webster couldn't have been nicer about the whole thing. He spent hours here yesterday, and finally took away Wakahiu the ox-driver and oath administrator, for screening at the camp. He and his screeners implored Karanja to come clean; he was definitely promised a clean chit if he said where the books were. On Jock's advice, I pleaded with him after they had gone, all I knew, but he was stubborn as hell. He did say he had lied to Jock in the morning, as he then said he had only taken one oath, and admitted to me that he had taken one at Petrie's in June '50 and another in '51 on Fish's, but this may be more lies. Jock was back at 8 am today having got a story from Wakahiu who admits to administering oaths on Adams's farm, but still not on this farm, which I think is a sure sign he *has* worked on this farm. Karanja is the clerk, he says, for all this district, and has all the books, Wakahiu said, in his spare hut, but the search produced nothing. He must have got them away somewhere. He *had* to go off to the camp so that is that. He bought it absolutely, and more I cannot do. They must be frightened by someone higher up. Wakahiu of course is deep in it and Jock isn't at all sure that Muchoka isn't in it too. The whole place seems to be lousy with it, and Njoro one of the worst places in the whole Rift Valley Province. Mbugwa owned to taking the first oath in N'bi in '52, and probably has had the second. Wakahiu owns to the third, which is the real gangster-killing one. Of course at the moment everything is chaotic in the back premises, but shall doubtless get it sorted out in time – but where is the time? I never attempted to combine the two systems, mine and Karanja's, and haven't a clue as to where lots of things are. Also the fridge has packed up.

14 September 1954   A poor wretched KPR boy called Major has been murdered in a forest village between here and Elburgon. He often looked in on his walks for a squash or a cuppa; such a nice lad; was here a short time ago and so bucked because he was the only European now in all the forest and everything under control. Such a tragedy. All patrols re-installed etc.... Another wretched KPR killed on Sat. at Kiambu ... a twenty-one-year-old Kenya lad, it is all so horrid, and seems worse than ever. It is all very near home nowadays, and most most depressing to realize how deep and hopelessly strong it all is.... Really this has been a week – ram packing up, fridge, Karanja, Wakahiu, three bitches on heat and a lunch party of ten! And the rain.

21 September 1954 When I got back on Sunday, who should greet me with a sheepish air but Karanja – no report, no discharge statement, nothing; it is monstrous that screeners should return people direct to farms, they should go the police who would find out whether the employer was willing to receive them. I sent him straight to his hut to stay there till I got a police report and refused to speak to him – after all, he is a Mau Mau officer. Dick Prettejohn advised me strongly not to have Karanja back, but if I did to be 'very, very careful' and never allow him near the house after dark and all that rot, and not to trust him an inch....

10 October 1954 I thought Lennox-Boyd talked absolute tripe at his press conference: said he never met anyone of any race who wanted the British to go. He can't have met many; at least it shows that he hasn't consorted with Mau Mau. And on what terms does he think the British will want to stay?... Would it be a terrible nuisance to find out about this said-to-be-wonderful strawberry Climax?

17 October 1954 Sorry I left Karanja in his hut as far as you are concerned. I got hold of Dick Prettejohn who fixed for him to go for screening to Krueger at Dundori, who I believe is terribly good. So I delivered him up to the Njoro police and heard no more for a fortnight, when I got a letter from the DC, to say that Krueger considered Karanja fit for re-employment, as he thought he had given up Mau Mau, and would I come and talk about it? So I went to see the DC, who showed me Krueger's report on Karanja. He acknowledged three oaths. They think that, generally, the third oath is really taking the second one again, because of not having been active enough. The second oath is the one which makes you take a strangling rope, knife, etc., about with you and binds you to kill on demand. Karanja was obviously very deep in it in '50. I said nothing would induce me to reinstate him unless I had absolute *proof* that he had given it up, and suggested to the DC that he should hold an oath-renouncing ceremony on my farm, and make Karanja take an Oath of Allegiance in front of everyone, including the DC and me. I said if Karanja did this, I would have him back. Dowson [the DC] said that Karanja would have to be warned that taking this oath might well lead to his being bumped off; I said I wanted him to be committed to loyalty up to the hilt.... Dowson had Karanja brought along after our interview; he was looking relaxed, fat and clean, evidently the camp is a good holiday resort. I thought and thought about what to do and can only hope all this is wise. It is sad but true that we are doing very well without Karanja now that I've had a real tidy and re-organization. Mbugwa I feel won't welcome Karanja back all that. Have got the cooking, such as it is, taped all right; the only time I can do it in comfort is in the afternoon when Mbugwa is having his beauty sleep, or attending oathing ceremonies, or whatever he does do from 1.30 to 4.30 pm. If I try to cook when he is about he will try to help, sniffs loudly all round the stove and *stirs my concoctions* which is unforgivable.... The horrible news of the Leakey murder overshadows all else. The poor old man disappearing – to what sort of end? And the daughter hearing her mother being strangled just below her attic. Gray Leakey* would not carry a gun. His daughter's husband was killed in an aircraft crash and this girl, the widow, had just gone to stay with her people to take her children out for half-term.

23 October 1954   Went over to the Fishes' this morning; Ingrid is in a very poor way. The neuralgia is absolute agony and nearly sends her mad; it is really a nervous breakdown all round. She has ghastly nightmares, can't concentrate and is deeply depressed. She is really

---

* An elderly cousin of Louis Leakey's, who had lived all his life among the Kikuyu and, like his cousin, spoke the language fluently and had been accepted as a member of the appropriate age-grade.

a Mau Mau casualty, I think; she took all the labour defections terribly to heart, also had the responsibility when they were threatening
to kill Ivor [a grandson]; crop failure last year, poultry no longer
even beginning to pay, and so on: just too much.... Humble, KPR,
arrived with his screening team which includes Bethel, brother-in-
law of my teacher Philip. Karanja made a very fine speech denounc-
ing Mau Mau and telling everyone to do likewise; everyone was
there; more than this one cannot do? Humble removed for screening, as a first instalment, a son of Karanja (herd) and wife of Karanja
(cook); he means to take three at a time.... The oath administrator
Wakahiu got five years, let off lightly because of his age.... Karanja
cook is very mealy mouthed but obviously very irritated to see the
results of Operation Hygiene in his domain, on which I insist, and
also I now know where everything is, which he abhors.

26 October 1954   The wireless said last night that Gray Leakey had
been buried alive, because the terrorists had come under the influence
of a prophet who said it was necessary to the wellbeing of Mau Mau
that all Europeans should be buried alive. Near N'bi a gang of thirty-
two was wiped out and near Ruiru an African was found wandering
with both eyes shot out, then he was turned loose to wander.

14 November 1954   Back we came [from a meeting in Nakuru] to
a late lunch, just sat down to it when in dashed a young policeman,
eyes all shining with excitement, to use the telephone. Had just had
a most creditable battle with four gangsters, three of them armed
with rifles, had chased them here with bullets flying in all directions,
and killed one on the *vlei* below this house just before we got back.
Said two others badly wounded and escaped. No police transport
available for him, so I joined the KPR for the afternoon and took
them all back, including the corpse which was on the road a hundred
yards my side of Seth-Smith gate. The corpse was very bloody and
an escaped convict from Kiambu. The policeman was a charming
young man, one of the UK recruits and quite diffident about using
the van for a corpse. His patrol was two seasoned police *askaris*,
one young Dorobo in a uniform and one old one in a smell. On
the way to Njoro, all this party burst into a lovely song like the
Wakamba porters used to sing going back to camp after a buffalo

kill, paeans of praise, and the young policeman's eyes got shinier and shinier and I got so excited myself. After tea Ruth Eaden and I took the dogs to try to find the wounded ones. They really did pick up the line and hunted across the *vlei* to the forest's edge; then they lost the line so we came back thwarted.... Meanwhile at the PO on Friday morning I tripped over some rough stones, had my arms full of papers so fell flat on my nose. Jean Scott tidied me up as best she could but my nose poured all through Central Urban District Council meeting where I am in the chair so *most* humiliating. My nose is five times too large and skinless and both eyes have gone black; too silly.

21 November 1954   The latest Kenya romance is that Tom Delamere is going to marry Diana Colville. [Sir Delves Broughton's widow, who had subsequently married a cattle-rancher, Gilbert Colville.] Did you ever? Apparently Tom took a great liking to the Colville house, formerly the Erroll mansion, and moved in. It is said that Gilbert Colville moved out with joy to his old shepherd's hut; Lady D. is quickly divorcing Tom, and Gilbert, ditto Diana; and there we all are.

28 November 1954   The two of my labour who didn't get through the screening have copped it; Waweru, who I always thought was in the stealing of my gun, got four years for being an *askari* at Mau Mau meetings, and Karanja (herd)'s son who had stolen ammunition which he put down the *choo* [latrine], a year. There was another oath-taking ceremony at John Adams's a short while ago, some of the gang in the forest were invited to administer the oaths. The administrator was the one who got killed in the forest soon afterwards. So it goes on. Friday was a Hospital Board which went on and on too; I have resigned from it as from the end of this year.

9 December 1954   There was a *baraza* at the Njoro location yesterday, with Chief Ignatio from Fort Hall, under-secretary Waweru Wangitu and two locals, Bethel the screener and David Wangutu the Njoro contractor (he went to the USA to Bible-read for two years and came back after three months because a haircut cost him

Sh 8/-). They all spoke; I think it did absolutely no good whatever; the chaps – we had all taken a carload – remained completely stolid and are obviously not going to stir off the fence unless sten-gunned off it. The chiefs appealed to them so prettily – *asked* them not to feed Mau Mau, reminded them of what good chaps the white men are, building roads, schools, etc. Surely the days have gone by for that sort of appeal? I would have staged the whole thing differently. Would have had a gibbet with a corpse depending therefrom, preferably a local exhumed for the occasion (there are lots available) with bursts of sten-gun fire every five minutes *just* over the heads of the crowd, and condemned murderers on view in chains. Then the Chief would have said, 'You —s, we all know you are on the fence and unless you come off it good and quick this is what is coming to you'. Bang... bang. It is all so utterly hopeless, this velvet glove and save-your-souls business. I came back from the *baraza* very depressed.

12 December 1954   Mr Humble came up yesterday with Bethel his No. 1 screener and coped with Mbugwa all over again. Humble says they have got the blackest of things against Mbugwa through cross-checking – it seems till right into '53 he was allowing ceremonies to be held *in his hut* here and was deep in it; he *won't* come clean and Humble is still waiting for him to make up his mind. So am left completely in the air.... It is really heartbreaking about Mbugwa; I just don't speak to him any more except for orders.... Am scrapping the farm Xmas do's until the end of the Emergency.

20 December 1954   Went to the christening of Tobina's youngest, Hugh, at the Church of Goodwill at Gilgil. Afterwards Nell Cole threw a birthday party at Kekopey for her eldest grandson Berkeley with fifty-six children, sixty grown-ups and a magician; quite a tribute to people to turn out with all those brats, as the raiding all round there is terrific. I wore my new red alpaca for the christening and am going to like it very much.

26 December 1954   Like the author of *Return to Laughter*,* I have withdrawn from any attempt to foster friendship, understanding, etc., with the Africans after their defection to Mau Mau, but must

* By Elenore Smith Bowen, London 1954.

say came very near to it again when, on Xmas morning, Mbugwa staggered in with my morning cuppa and laid a huge box of potatoes on my bed tied up in (my) brilliant violet crepe paper. This is a very special sort of spud called 'Mweri Umwe' (=one month) which he knows I love and have looked for in vain for a long time now; he had got some, and grown it on specially for me. Disarming? Especially as this year I didn't give anyone a single thing for Xmas.... Rose's brief holiday came to an abrupt end when the security forces killed two out of four on her farm where they found five hide-outs along her river bank, so they proposed to arrest all her labour and she had to rush back. There was continuous bombing on Kipipiri for two days before Xmas, making the dogs bark here and shaking the windows in Nakuru; nothing was said as to whether any of the gangs were inconvenienced on Kipipiri itself or not.

1955−9

The year opened sadly with the death of two dogs. Mau Mau raids and hunts, police swoops and alerts went on as before. A scheme was introduced to post farm guards, non-Kikuyu men armed with shot-guns, on farms particularly vulnerable to Mau Mau raids. When laying the line for a paper-chase Nellie was arranging for a children's party, she discovered that the cave in which the Leakeys had made their finds had become a gangsters' hide-out, 'with curious things like oranges and peppermints stored there'.

27 February 1955   A horrid thing has happened here with these bestial farm guards who have been forced on me. One made a little chap called Mbugwa wa Thamburu [not Mbugwa the houseboy] go into their room to repair a bed – no right whatever to order farm labour about. The other guard was lying on his bed with his shot-gun in a corner. Somehow or other the gun went off and shot poor little Mbugwa in the leg. I was in Nakuru; everyone seems to have done all they could; Karanja rushed in from the kitchen, Philip heard the shot and telephoned the police who quickly came up and took Mbugwa to hospital but he died that night. Poor little Mbugwa was a bit weak in the head but everyone liked him, he adored the dogs and always played with them and had such a good laugh. Everyone here is furious with these damned guards and hates them. I'm afraid that if I hadn't been in Nakuru when the poor little chap got shot he might not have died, as it was loss of blood and he hadn't been tied up properly.

Nellie had now had no holiday for five years, and for the last two and a half had been living under a strain difficult to imagine by those who had not experienced it. After dark, night after night, she sat alone save for the dogs, her revolver beside her, unable to resist turning on the radio news which invariably told of Mau Mau raids and murders. Karanja and Mbugwa, whom she had trusted implicitly for so many

212

years, she now knew to be deeply involved and to have taken oaths to destroy her. In addition were all the normal worries caused by droughts, frequent in these years; breakdowns in machinery; tragedies among farm livestock and financial worries which never let up. All this was telling on her health – she was now seventy years old – and early in the year she agreed, after some resistance, to take a break in Europe. Her friends Francis and Jean Drummond, who lived in Nairobi, took her on a fortnight's tour in Italy, which she enjoyed enormously. In July she returned to Njoro to find no improvement in the general situation, and to be plunged immediately into the same troubles as before.

24 July 1955   The day after I got back, the Njoro policeman and a posse of Dorobo arrived from the forest and said they had tracked a gang who had slept in the blue gum plantation on my boundary, and there were tracks going to and coming from my Kikuyu village. Complete ignorance of course on the part of my home guard from Philip downwards. The police took off Karanja's two sons, another home guard and a woman. Of course they were feeding the gangs, and probably will again; Philip has no authority whatever over the others. The gangs are coming over from Gilgil for food. The policeman sent up my gun by special patrol last night so was obliged drearily to load the damned thing.... I am frankly very homesick but it is only a question of doing jobs and there are lots of jobs to do. Winkle and Lottie are most consoling.

19 August 1955   Kenya is full of 178 Moral Re-armers who have arrived in four Constellations, too awful. Nell invited me to a 'settlers' lunch' at the Norfolk to meet them all and a matinée of their awful play. No, no. Nell is losing a beast a night from cattle thefts and several headmen, not hers but nearby, have been murdered.

3 September 1955   The thrill of the week was the Meat Commission man coming to see my steers. He approved very highly of the five I have been trying to finish off in a little yard and says they are ready, and 'very nice', and will take them soon. I think they may all die or break their legs at any moment so go and stroke them many times

213

a day. It is marvellous to think the farm may really be coming into proper production. There are several others hot on their heels.

17 September 1955 This week was Horticultural Show at Nakuru; I got first for twenty kinds, HC for six kinds (a strong class), second in Herbs, second in Any Other Veg. I got the Cup again for most marks in Veg. section, not a very honourable or exciting win but I think my staging was quite good this year.

8 October 1955 High spot of the week was the report on the six steers I sent off. Two were first grade 'well finished', a comment which is highly pleasing, three were the usual standard, and the dear Boran third because his meat was black due to his having been a bull. He gave me such a hauntingly sad look as he led the party into the truck; he was always a leader; I do feel a brute, but he was v. difficult on the farm.

3 November 1955 The horribly sad thing this week is the murder at Lanet, residential suburb of Nakuru, of Mrs Milton and her eleven-year-old daughter. Milton is the sweet man who has managed Howse and McGeorge [the chemist's] for years, a really God-like man always doing good and very much a part of the day's shopping in Nakuru for everyone. He went home to lunch as usual, found doors locked, looked through a window to see his family lying murdered on the floor inside.... Amazing to get away with it in a closely housed suburb in the middle of the morning and just walk away.

11 November 1955 A boy cut off the top of a finger in the mower and brought it in hanging by a thread; I clapped it back, put on Cooper's Wound Powder and tied it up hoping some day it would stop bleeding; four days later Betty Roche (Red Cross) was here so we untied it and she said it was a wonderful job and it really does seem to be growing.... An ill-spared Special Branch chap John McNab was killed in action three miles from Naivasha on Wed. night; Kenya-born, aged twenty-seven, lived at Njoro; everyone very het up.... I had a sweet chit from Ingrid: 'And so it is Silver Jane and Idina both left their happy hunting grounds the same day,

5 November'. Poor Dina had had a desperate cancer for a long time.... Must go and listen to my guest who has verbal diarrhoea. She is busy on Xmas cards and is doing fifty, all the same elephant. Oh dear.

2 December 1955   One of the farm guards that have been foisted on me got quite ill and I telephoned daily for the screening camp people to take him to hospital – no response at all, and last night he informed me that he had a tapeworm. It really is the limit that they should send people out to farms without de-worming them; they are completely unsupervised, presumably never use a *choo*, and therefore jeopardize all the work and propaganda one has done on this subject.

17 December 1955   I came to Rose for breakfast yesterday to do a quick dash to N'bi to an arts & crafts exhibition; a nice comforting little event. Robin Anderson had the best – such clean, decisive gouaches.... Rose has a poisoner on her farm who has killed her two best cows, eight-galloners; she suspects a Kikuyu *toto*.... It is all a hideous reign of terror, one sees no bright future. The depressing thought is that not one shred of progress has been made in African ethics since our advent: rather, codes relaxed, and character deteriorated terribly. Same everywhere, I suppose.... The Foreseeable Future man says that *hands* are neglected so monkeys ought to be roped in to pick flowers and fruit. How I wish we could.

30 December 1955   Two days ago one of the oldest, *shenzi*-est, Kikuyu women approached me and said she wanted to take her son to hospital to be circumcised. I checked up on this with Muchoka and with the hospital, and, sure enough, the local lads flock to the outpatients' dept. to have it done; it takes a quarter of an hour and home they go. They don't mind whether the surgeon is a Kikuyu or not. All the glamour, toughness, ritual, etc., swept away! The reason given here is that all the circumcisers are in jail as Mau Mau, or hanged. There is still a local female circumciser and the girls on the farm are still being done in traditional style; the little boys know a better way. I should have thought it would be the last ritual to die, and so quickly too.... I had seven turkey chicks hatching, due Xmas

215

morning, and instead of Father Christmas came *siafu*, and killed the lot including the poor hen; all eggs were chipping, maddening.... I didn't make any Xmas food at all, but Charity, the Kikuyu wife of Hans Raj the Indian contractor at Njoro, sent me two pounds of wonderful apples, some fine bananas and an iced Xmas cake!

Mau Mau gangs were still active during 1956 and murders still frequent; nevertheless the tide had turned. By October 1955 the entire population of the Kikuyu, Meru and Embu land units, numbering over a million souls, had been concentrated into villages, each one stockaded and protected by a watchtower and armed guards. Gangs still operated from camps hidden in the forest, but they were on the defensive. Kikuyu who had denounced Mau Mau were cooperating with the security forces and joining 'pseudo-gangs' which penetrated into the forest and shot or captured the genuine gangsters. Overseas troops were gradually withdrawn, and in October 1956 the capture of the last and most elusive of the Mau Mau leaders, Dedan Kimathi, virtually brought active resistance to an end. Nellie revisited parts of Kikuyuland and found a calmer atmosphere.

17 February 1956 We went on Sunday to the district above Chief Njeri's, high up on the forest's edge, called Kigumo. The DO in charge, a remarkable man called Hopf, a German Jew, took us right up to Fort Worcester, one of the line of military 'forts' [wooden huts] at 8,500 feet, well inside the forest. In his office we saw the wallet he captured with Dedan's letters, one just written and about to be published. We had elevenses with Chief Njeri and saw the famous Union Jack which has never been pulled down. Govt. have built him a very good stone house absolutely surrounded by police huts, so he should be all right now.... Cecil Hoey died last week, and was buried off his launch at sea.

8 March 1956 Betty Roche is the most wonderful maker of tripe and onions; you can't think what a sumptuous dish. The very, very smartest party Jos and I ever went to in Madrid was given by the Duke of Alba for the King and Queen at the ever-so-smart Golf Club, and the only dish was tripe and onions, and the only music barrel-organs. It was a supper party and oh, so smart. Haven't eaten it since but now we have it here.

14 April 1956 There was a bridge-opening ceremony at Egerton on Monday. C-B* as president of the Board of Governors opened it, I cut the tape and he made a benign speech, mentioning my name as being, with Sandy Wright, the prime instigator of the college. All this sheer invention†.... However I made a pair of scissors out of it.

The failure of the rains to fall when they were due was the Kenya farmer's most frequent hazard, but sometimes his crops were ruined by their failure to stop. Then maize, wheat and other cereals rotted in the cob or ear and could not be satisfactorily harvested, especially by small-scale farmers such as Nellie who lacked expensive mechanical aids like dryers. 1956 was such a 'wet year'.

21 April 1956 The real snag about this farm's economics is that steer production has been slowed down by breeding troubles. So I have to go on with as much maize as possible for a cash crop; I simply cannot do this without mechanization, which I cannot afford. So it is a jam.

27 April 1956 My last – I hope – blow came when the KFA rang up to say my whole maize delivery – 270 bags despatched on Wed. after infinite sweat – had been rejected through mustiness. This means it will fetch whatever price they can get for it for pig-food, instead of £470. The rot must have begun in the ear, but Dick Henderson advised me that the only thing was to harvest and get the cobs out of their wet clothes. I built special little wire-netting cribs

---

* Sir Ferdinand Cavendish-Bentinck, a settler-politician and former Minister of Agriculture. He was speaker of the Legislative Council from 1955 to 1960, and subsequently became the Eighth Duke of Portland.

† It was not. The then Egerton Farm School, now Egerton College under Kenya's Ministry of Agriculture, grew out of Nellie's suggestion that money being raised for a memorial to Lord Delamere should be put towards a training centre for young European farmers. She drew up a scheme, with Sandy Wright's help, to establish it on the land at Njoro presented gratis by Lord Egerton of Tatton.

for the cobs so that the air could circulate, but of course all the air was damp. Finally it dried enough to shell, and I winnowed and sun-dried and did everything, but the harm was done in the standing crop. Inefficiency? So I shall sell the cows, *must* sell the cows, to pay off everything and carry on. I shall to try to lease the land but can't think anyone will want it as everyone has masses of feed.... Many and many a grower is in the same quandary at this altitude this year, but that doesn't help. What really bites is not being able to leave you a tickety-boo farm – that was the mainspring of existence, so to speak. There is no possible expansion of veg. trade; I jog along with my 'basket' trade but can't do much more than I do at present. But enough of these sorrows.

6 May 1956   Have advertised twenty-three of my best cows, good breeders, and will see if anyone wants them. After that, shall take steps to try and let off the land as a pyrethrum proposition, with labour force complete.... Ingrid's attitude to catastrophe is most commendable. The other day, a hundred day-old chicks disappeared; she thought a theft, and bought a hundred more. They too disappeared and she caught a *shenzi* dog in the act of swallowing the last one: 'Oh, Nellie, you have no idea how funny that dog looked when he had eaten a hundred day-old chicks!'

26 May 1956   A very nice couple from Sotik came on Thurs. to look at the cows. I turned them loose among the poor moos and he chose eighteen out of the lot. Prices quite good, £30 and £35 for most. It is very, very sad and I can hardly look old Karanja in the face. He will still have twenty-one cows and young stock at the moment. I don't know what the next move is, but this sale is to replace the maize crop that failed; it's no use waiting till the wolf is right up on the veranda. This was the only answer I got for the cows.... Masses of rain. Masses of couch.... Have evolved a Worry-to-end-Worry and embarked on a Shetland shawl. Eve got me the finest hand-spun wool in the world in Shetland and has lent me a book of traditional patterns. There's been a struggle: either I went not round any bend, but straight to the loony house, or else recovered some of my powers of concentration which, fifty years ago, weren't too bad. After ten false starts the concentration won and

I am quite enjoying it, provided no interruptions at all; it doesn't look a bit like the picture, but still.

Nakuru lay at the heart of the European farming area, and, at its annual Royal Show, a replica on a smaller scale of Britain's 'Royal', the best of Kenya's livestock and produce was displayed. Nellie became deeply involved in the horticultural section, responsible with others for mounting the exhibits and collecting and arranging the flowers, vegetables and home produce to be shown. This meant days of preparation, culminating in a twelve-hour day setting up the stands and arranging the exhibits. One of Nellie's gardening friends who stayed with her for the show was astonished by her energy.

There she was with a hammer and tacks fixing the stands – no job was beyond her. She must have been well over sixty but was absolutely tireless, with a terrific sense of humour and flashing wit. Her 'boys' loved her and worked for her all hours. When we returned to the farm she said: 'Now a bath, a drink and an early bed ready for tomorrow.' I fully expected literally a snack, but we had an excellent soup followed by a truly delicious artichoke soufflé which she made herself. Next morning she appeared at crack of dawn in my room carrying a bowl, and I thought: 'Good gracious, not porridge at this hour', but it turned out to be plaster of paris, which she proceeded to slosh on a leaking crack in the hand basin, saying: 'It will dry in five to ten minutes and then you can wash your face without getting your feet wet.'

It may have been on this occasion that one of the stewards who was helping Nellie to stage the exhibits incurred her displeasure by rearranging them at the last minute without consulting her. She wrote to a friend 'I hear that he [the steward] is keeping out of my way because he thinks I'll bite his head off if I see him. You can tell him from me that his head would make such a disgusting morsel that he need have no fears on that account.'

8 July 1956 I am making what I have always longed for – a tiny, tiny veg. garden all of my own. It is a very modest project and will keep me off the eighteenth-century urge, never far below the surface, to make acres of artificial lake and a double line of statuary from here to the river. My unit is the square yard. Each square yard has to produce a mass of food, manured at the rate of a hundred tons to the acre and full irrigation. The whole art lies in getting the water to the roots of every veg. You may think rainfall is the best watering, but it isn't. I have ideas of how to get the moisture to the root of the matter by putting diatomite at the bottom of the trenches; it has worked marvellously on a tiny experiment I've done, so we shall see. My garden is to be fourteen yards by twelve, and in due course my book 'The Story of my Garden' (illustrated by Grandma Moses) will become a best-seller and undoubtedly buy me a Peugeot pick-up.

23 July 1956   My party of yesterday was quite a success. I got the consultant baker to Unga Ltd to come out (free) and asked the ladies of the EAWL local branch to attend a Yeast Cookery demonstration at 10.30 am and stay on to a picnic lunch on the lawn. About thirty came to the demonstration and thirty-five to lunch plus five brats and two babies in cots. I said loftily we *wazungu* would do everything for ourselves, and I didn't want to see anyone about except to bring out coffee. Mbugwa without saying a word dug out all the old *kanzus* of past years and put every young chap on the farm into one, so it looked as if I had at least ten house-boys. The menu was stuffed avocado pears, stuffed eggs in different colour schemes, a platter of cold meats and a very good Russian salad; fruit salad, a rice cream pudding, cream cheese and oatcake. We made ourselves hot dogs on a little electric device on the lawn. Practically all the food was home grown and home made so it wasn't an extravagant party. I do like yeast, a most mysterious thing, and it smells so good.

In October I flew to Kenya on another self-financing visit, having been commissioned to write a history of the Kenya Farmers' Association. To a considerable extent this involved the history of white settlement, so was more interesting than it sounded. (It was published by the East African Standard *in 1957 as* No Easy Way.) *Nellie was in good spirits and looking no older, but the Bedford van was; it had almost shaken to bits. My visit coincided with that of Princess Margaret, and all the farm labour went down to Njoro to see her cavalcade go by on the way to lunch with a settler family at Mau Narok.*

To Gervas from E. H.   24 October 1956   Security officers scarcely leave the Masons [Princess Margaret's hosts] alone, and have insisted on putting a stronger bolt on the loo and expanded metal grilles on all their windows. Enormous sums have been spent on doing up the road, as she mustn't travel at less than 20 mph. Her personal staff numbers fourteen, and Daphne Mason has to provide lunch for fifty-two journalists. They go everywhere with her. We went down to the corner for about an hour; nothing to be seen but cars going by. Hers slowed up a bit and we got a wave and a smile. Old Karanja (herd), asked if he had enjoyed it, smiled and said '*mkono tu*' ('only a hand'). Four gangsters had been captured the day before on the Seth-Smith farm, very ragged and half starved, they had been hiding in the forest and stealing food, but it threw the police into a frenzy and the road was stiff with policemen in big cars, lorries and jeeps; some had come right down from the Northern Frontier District. The entourage looked like an army on the move. One of the women journalists was practically a nymphomaniac, it seems; the only thing she took any interest in was how many African mistresses the farmers had.... Nellie won first at the Royal Show for a beautifully knitted Shetland cape.

Nellie's letters were resumed at the end of the year.

28 December 1956   It is very unfair that the going away should be so full of misery and doesn't *seem* to balance – as of course it must really – the elation of your arrival.... Am busy mucking out the deep litter house and giving Niftin [a veterinary medicine] to the two surviving hens.... The sour milk cure is going well, I propose to do it on Sundays, Tuesdays and Fridays.

The average Kenya cuisine, in Nellie's opinion, lacked imagination and needed cheering up. Together with a few friends who shared this view, she started an informal Gourmets' Club, whose members foregathered on a Sunday bringing his or her own prepared dish for critical assessment by the other members.

16 February 1957   The Gourmets' Club is to have its first meeting on the 24th. Betty Roche has something up her sleeve for her menu;

for mine I suggested sucking-pig but she says porcupine is much better. There is a large family of same living just inside the forest here doing great harm to crops, so have told Asonga to trap one. In fact I should like to remove the whole family to a warren on the farm and sell the progeny at vast prices. Have written to Archie Ritchie to enquire about their love life etc. Please, when Julian [Huxley] next comes to stay with you, would you ask him? This is what I want to know: are they likely to breed in captivity, how many wees do they have, and how often? It might be fun to try to tame them, but I think they would be difficult to keep under control and might dig themselves out of their caverns.

16 February 1957 The Gourmets' Club lunch duly took place in Michael Levine's little house in Nakuru and went very well: sixteen people. Michael did a delicious fish in aspic with a superb sauce. Kate, mutton marinaded to taste like venison; Nils a lovely stuffed artichoke dish; wine was Bordeaux and there was a good apertif. Lunch worked out at six shillings a head; quite cheap?

The disaster of the 1956 harvest had put paid to Nellie's cherished plan to base her farm economy on raising beef steers, and to give up growing crops, save those needed to feed the animals. The fact was that in Kenya, as elsewhere, the small mixed farm was no longer viable owing to the high cost of mechanization and the lack of reserve to tide over bad years. This was the final blow to her farming hopes, after nearly thirty-five years of effort at Njoro. A lot of effort had also gone into the various shows staged by the Royal Kenya Horticultural Society, and it was perhaps some consolation that she was elected president in April of that year.

10 March 1957 I am going to try to keep the land between the road, bridge and forest which will work out at about fifty acres. Without mechanization I simply cannot do the cattle, cannot grow winter feed. So the remaining two hundred acres would be unproductive and might just as well be sold. A pity but there it is.... I was lucky in my sale of steers last week, two were first grade, the rest standard and good weights, and none condemned.

18 April 1957 Dolly went at long last, thank heaven, verbal diarrhoea until the end. She was just pushing off when I said 'For God's sake drive carefully, Dolly.' She said: 'I've left you £500 in my will to buy a new car.' I was so overcome I could think of nothing to say except 'In that case drive like hell.'

18 May 1957 Saw a really terrible sight this morning. A wood hoopoe sitting on the power line with a poor little *live* chameleon in its beak, the hoopoe trying to swallow it but taking ages. Karanja and I threw things at it trying to make it drop the chameleon but it flew off with the agonized little creature still in its beak. Horrid.

3 August 1957 Sunday was Gourmets' day at the Andersons. I thought the first dish was too rich, said to be *asperges en riz* but there was a very savoury rice bed, then a rich sauce over the asparagus and masses of shrimps, so bless me if I knew which the main ingredient was. Then a wonderful duck cooked in sour cream by Elsa, and really good *pêches flambées* by Jane. I want to guide the Gourmets into having really first-class plain roasts etc. We can all do the messed-up things more or less, but I want to know all there is to know about the preparation of simple, high-class English food.

10 November 1957 Wed. was standing committees of EAWL. I am on Inter-racial and African Affairs. They say they are getting on with what they call 'guide circles', i.e. get-togethers of all three races at a high intellectual level, most exemplary, but it just hasn't worked. The few reports given were a most pitiable record of failure. The chairman's remedy was to suggest a four-day summer school with cake-making competitions etc. Nothing could be more fatuous, so I really had to throw spanners into the works as best I could, much to the fury of other council members, but I am sure it is right to go ever so slow until Asians and Africans *say* what they want; they hate this reaching down to them, and I am sure the intellectuals would find cake-making competitions and patchwork quilts somewhat insulting?... The poor farm has nothing coming in and now the beef market has gone to blazes and people cannot get their steers taken by the Meat Commission. When I planned the steers, everyone said it was *impossible* that such a thing could happen. I have sold some immature ones and had hoped to get good prices for others when ready in about eight months' time; now I shan't. People are really shattered at this development.

16 November 1957 Great shemozzle in Njoro township where, apparently, drunkenness goes on non-stop because it is so important to make lots of money from the township's beer hall, whose profits go to Social Improvement. The police *askaris* are the best spenders, and yesterday one of them murdered a very nice lad, the Somali butcher's shop boy, terribly good at cutting up joints; such bad luck it should happen to him himself?... Old Nganga has gone mad and uprooted my *precious* seven germinated auriculas. I could weep.... Have been hot on the war-path, as got a notice from the county council saying I am only to have five squatters instead of six and must dismiss one immediately. Wigs on the green, and am told that at a meeting on Tuesday they agreed I might keep my six. Anything so absolutely fatuous as this interference by one's own community and to what end, what end? Said all this and a good deal more to the clerk of county council with a demand to know immediately to which higher bodies I might appeal, hinting at the House of Lords. Brutes, *brutes*.

In December, Gervas, Charles and I flew to Njoro for Christmas and spent the Christmas holiday in Kenya with Nellie on the farm and at the coast. I stayed on until the following March, when Nellie's letters were resumed.

28 March 1958 Would it bore you intensely to do this? Get six Easter eggs secretly and pretend you took them home from Les Delices in Nakuru. An egg each for the family and others for Cleggie, Dolly and Vera (farm). Just a surprise? I should so like to conjure up the Family Scene. PS It is hell your having gone.

13 April 1958 I long beyond words to find *something* to get the farm on to a less dreary footing than spend, spend, spend, and continue to rack brains. But everything absolutely stagnant, it seems.

20 April 1958 What a day! Early afternoon, an Indian greengrocer from Mombasa arrived wanting me to grow *huge* quantities of veg.

for him. Before he went, another car arrived – the Molo auctioneers with a client for the farm. Also a man from the horticultural station at Molo, to help him, I suppose. What a plethora all at once.

28 April 1958   I took up the references of the Indian which were very satisfactory and have offered to grow him a hundred pounds of cauliflowers a day, fifty pounds of Brussels sprouts, and some oddments; total takings would be about £5 a day with containers and freight taken off. Then the young man with the wrong sort of haircut and his buddy from the Molo horticultural station; he wants to do strawberries, asparagus and a few others things for export; I think he is mad; he talks about complete 'Europeanization' as being the only solution to Kenya farming. I'm afraid he would sack and turn off all the labour. The Indian arrived first by a matter of minutes. Everything fluid. Then on Sunday six enormous men from Turbo turned up to look at the three little bulls – they looked ever so much more virile than the bulls, who appeared to me to shrink every minute. I don't expect a deal; the bulls looked so very small for their age. . . . People are in despair about the Rift Valley candidates for this election: G. appalling, R. catastrophic and T. unspeakable. There's a movement afoot to persuade Sandy [Wright] to stand – he wouldn't contribute much to the 'body of moderate opinion' we are supposed to be building up, but he couldn't be quite as bad as the others.

4 May 1958   Such interruptions: first of all Kathleen [Seth-Smith] carrying a most beautiful bloom of *Magnolia grandiflora* as an olive branch after her cattle broke into my maize, messed up my seed-beds and cabbages, and one poor old girl's *shamba* completely done in. Also her cattle are in quarantine for lumpy skin disease and you must slaughter on sight if a case appears, maximum compensation £15 even for a pedigree bull. Kathleen is giving me twenty cabbages and a cartload of *kuni* and of course paying compensation for the *shambas* but am now in quarantine for lumpy skin disease so no chance of selling those little bulls. . . .

12 May 1958   Biggest news of the week is that the Mombasa Indian wired to confirm all my suggestions, saying 'Go ahead'. It is all very exciting, am sowing seeds madly and making plans. I love my little seedlings dearly but shall love them much more when they are about to be eaten. Difficult months ahead....

18 May 1958 I've been reading something by Naomi Jacob, who has the deplorable habit of writing about her mother, and she hasn't made all that of a job of it – mothers *aren't* good subjects, unless like Queen Victoria or Cleopatra.

25 May 1958 The first item of news this week is the so, so sad one that dear old Fish died on Friday. He had been getting weaker and weaker, and they never really found out the cause. It is so deeply upsetting to think what a sad life he had really; financial worries always, and his deafness; a mountain of debt and Ingrid struggling to save the farm now growing veg. with no irrigation and worn-out land. He had his happy moments long ago with the safaris and animals but not much else. The next bit of news is something terrific, I suddenly got a letter from Daisy [Balfour] enclosing a cheque for £250. She said she was doling out the legacies she had meant to leave to her personal friends and had decided to give them now, instead of waiting for her demise. I have settled to invest most of it in the supplementary ABC irrigation plant so as to ensure that I have really sufficient irrigation of the most economical kind to cope with this enormous veg. contract. I swear that I have thought of all the drawbacks of this venture, and if this effort flops, this is the last. Retirement and nothing else, except of course a general wind-up. I shall continue to try hard to sell off all the land except the irrigation and this side of the farm road.... Well, we are embarking on the veg. project and seed-boxes, growing in numbers daily.

I had at this point completed the manuscript of a semi-fictional account of my childhood, to be published as The Flame Trees of Thika, *which aimed at re-creating the atmosphere of the country in 1913–15 while not always sticking exactly to factual details. Nellie had helped me a great deal by recalling various incidents; but she disapproved of the whole idea.*

4 July 1958 If you really want suggestions, checking up etc. of course I will do it, but as you know I loathe anything like publicity etc. about myself. Anyway, it can't matter much, as nearly everyone of my time is dead or soon will be including myself.

8 July 1958   Have read two-thirds of the typescript and like it very much. I am *not* like Tilly. Very nostalgic, all the African part.... The most noticeable tree at Thika was the *Erythrina tomentosa*, the sealing-wax tree, with corky looking trunk and brilliant red flowers which happen when the leaves are off. They were wild all over the place. I had very good roses in the garden which came from a grower at Orleans in a huge crate – only three pence each! They came by sea, of course, and survived well. After the Kaiser's war I asked the same grower to supply some 'La France' bushes to have planted on my brother's grave in Flanders, and he fixed it all and wouldn't take a cent of payment as the life had been 'spent for France'.... I think you were ever so nice to the Africans in the book. I only remember one episode when any real gratitude was shown. An old man was brought in obviously with bad pneumonia, for which of course there was nothing in those days like M & B. So I made him comfortable in the bathroom of the old grass hut. We went to dine at Kichanga's and got back about 1 am when the old man appeared to be quite dying, so I gave him half a bottle of neat brandy. Next morning he was round the corner, and he brought me eggs as gifts for years.... Could you get for Betty to bring out a *very* thick pair of men's long woolly pants to the ankle? I want them as an Xmas present to old Manvi who gets perished with cold coping with the irrigation at night.

2 August 1958   I've read a twaddly thing by Lady Curzon, the sort of autobiography where the writer fails to give you any idea of anyone's personality – e.g. the only thing to say of her first husband was that he looked beautiful after death. I do wonder whether those frightful, pompous, rich people really kept the old Empire tottering on or brought about its demise.

10 August 1958   I will try to talk to old Karanja (herd) about old times but am very bad at that sort of chat; might ask him in for a drink but a young man at Ol Kalau who started evening drinks with his cook and houseboy got shot dead by one of them; quite a deterrent.... Betty Roche writes that an extremely heavy suitcase has arrived from UK. If the Customs get difficult, she is going to say it is the foundation stone for a church on my farm....

8 September 1958 Great veg. activities; deliveries amounting to £16 gross for the week; if we can treble that I shall feel we have got somewhere. At one stage in my career, can't remember when, Trudie and I had a craze for learning about factory methods, and how no one should walk fifteen yards if they could walk ten; it irritates me madly now to see someone carrying one small lettuce seventy yards, placing it if possible in full sunlight and returning for another. Everyone is now harnessed to trays; there are two old women about a thousand years old and four feet high who work like tigers, but put up a stiff resistance to any introduction of new methods; they screamed like parrots for two hours non-stop, when first harnessed to their trays; these trays are stretcher-like affairs of hessian and light poles and take up to twenty lettuces each.

9 November 1958 Had twenty-two African ladies to see the veg. and have tea on Thursday, and it did actually drizzle and spoil the garden trip, and we had to have tea indoors. Mbugwa was superb. A Kipsigis lady said to me 'How old are you?' I felt too weak to go into the matter of manners, leading questions, etc., so said simply 'Three hundred.' Mbugwa came in at that moment, so I said to him: 'You have known me for two hundred years, haven't you?' Without batting an eyelid he replied: 'I think slightly more, madam.' To my horror the lady took out a pen and started writing it all down. I suppose she was covering the outing for the *Kipsigis Daily Worker*. It took the rest of the afternoon to explain it was a *joke*.... Mbugwa has made great friends with Rosie [a highly-strung, rather standoffish dachshund], who greets him with my early morning tea by sitting up on the chair and offering him a paw to shake.

20 December 1958 Now a funny thing. I have bartered one rabbit every fortnight with Kate for six young Light Sussex capons, so thought I'd stand old Thickers [a rather dreary guest] a treat and have *coq au vin*. The recipe said mushrooms, twelve small ones. I said to myself no, no, at Sh 5/50 a tin. Then that very morning as

I was going down to the irrigation, there by the side of the path was a ring with twelve small mushrooms. *Never* have there been mushrooms in that spot before, and never have I picked a mushroom in December. Makes one believe in Providence? (But better really if Providence dealt more with cancer, polio, etc.)

26 December 1958   On Xmas Eve Ingrid and Nils came to an early tea and we went to Egerton Castle [Njoro residence, in baronial style, of Lord Egerton of Tatton] for the carol singing, quite pleasant. There was an odd-looking choir with locals dressed in ill-fitting grey housegowns; the clergyman gave the most awful sermon and said, *inter alia*, that he *knew* Christ simply adored wicked people; I saw a gleam of interest come into the faces of the many children as they obviously began making plans for next term. Had hoped my Xmas treat would be *not* to have to go to Njoro, but no – poor old Karanja (herd) was discharged from hospital and telephoned to say he would be at Njoro Xmas morning, so I went to look for him; no sign of him; however I returned there in the afternoon and he had come. So it was two trips to Njoro as a treat instead of none.

In January 1959 I flew again to Kenya to gather material for more articles and yet another book. I found Nellie rather depressed. The vegetable contract with the Mombasa greengrocer, on which she had built all her hopes, had collapsed. The greengrocer's cheque had bounced, and no amount of effort had sufficed to collect the debt. Yet the vegetables she was growing were superb; 'terrific cauliflowers', I reported to Gervas, and 'marvellous tomatoes grown by ring cultivation, an enormous crop'. As usual, I had to go off on a fact-gathering tour almost as soon as I arrived, and returned to find her far from well.

She does too much, all the worries of finding a market for the veg. have tired her, also she can never get away, as the veg. need constant attention. She has found two buyers in Nairobi who will take some, only small quantities and poor prices, but she has to take the orders to the station several times a week. While she was in bed, all her peaches – a heavy crop – were stolen, and mouse-birds got into the cage and ate the figs. She has to supervise everything. She badly needs help but I can think of no way to provide it.

On top of all this, Nellie's favourite dachshund, Winkle, died. In April I flew back to England, and Nellie's letters were resumed.

2 May 1959   Veg. markets despairing. The Ministry of Defence have turned down my offer to supply the Gilgil camp so really am defeated. And so what?

15 May 1959   Rain is the devil, just over three inches in April mostly in drizzles; crops all in jeopardy and no sign of more. Haven't been able to plant out any pyrethrum splits and only half the maize I had intended. The mushrooms came back in a half-hearted way but weren't a patch on those we picked that evening; were they really super mushrooms or did they seem so because it was such fun picking them with you?

If Nellie came up against a blank wall, sooner or later she found a chink through or a way round. She started up a correspondence with a pheasant-breeder in England, and in May a hundred chicks arrived by air. Her intention was to build up a stock and sell pheasants to hotels. As president of the Royal Kenya Horticultural Society, she launched the project of a National Rose Show. A new farming programme was drawn up.

26 July 1959   I have evolved a five-point plan, each of the following to produce £20 gross per month: veges; spuds; pyrethrum; poultry; rabbits. An average, that is; rabbits can't do more than £10. My Black Leghorn × Light Sussex capons are really astoundingly good: some are three pounds at nine weeks. My, they do eat.... The cantaloup melon was delicious; have put a little seed in a day-old chick coop with a 25-watt bulb which makes it just 60°F, supposed to be the germinating heat.

7 August 1959   I have got the great snake-catcher of Africa staying here, Ionides. He is a bit round the bend, I think; he eats practically nothing and not one single vitamin; looks about seventy although actually only fifty-eight; has a three-ton lorry and goes about collecting snakes etc. for museums with a retinue of seven tents full of Africans with their wives and children. He came Saturday about 11 am and asked for chameleons; before lunch he had four lusty males and eight females brought to him. I said at tea-time jocosely what were the chameleons having for tea, and they were all *dead*, going to St Helena. It made me feel sick. He is really after the Njoro horned viper, and has heard of one nearby, and is away after that now. I suppose he is a good naturalist in his line but a very narrow-minded man. He had a great argument with Mbugwa about a buzzard which he said wouldn't eat chickens, and Mbugwa said did; I looked it up in the bird book which says it only eats them occasionally; Mbugwa is the better authority. He (Ionides) is very deaf and boring, which is sad, as I thought his visit would be fun. Difficult to feed as he won't face up to anything except a tiny slice of meat at lunch; I asked him what he had at home; he said he sometimes shot a small hornbill which lasted him for days, otherwise iguanas, and he liked his meat high; he won't hear of a fridge, or newspapers or wireless.

20 September 1959   I counted chicks yesterday; of Indian Game I have thirty-four pullets and sixteen cockerels, total fifty, and of Light Sussex also fifty, all very handsome. I go to open the Orchid Show tomorrow week, taking forty-five capons for Muthaiga. Today was horrid as the capons had to be killed, it made me feel sick all morning, especially as unless I was there at frequent intervals, they wouldn't kill them in the right way.

18 October 1959   The White Paper on the release of land to Africans has been published. So far no one seems to have paid it much attention except Briggs and X who say if necessary they will *demand to see the Queen*. All I hope is she doesn't catch sight of X before her little son is born or we shall have a venomous toad for our next princeling.... Am very keen on my succulents; they are lovely pets and eat and drink practically nothing. Orchids are a bit more tricky but they live on air and die very easily from drink.... Thursday 8.15 am was the Nakuru send-off to the Barings at the royal train; I thought it polite to go, masses of people from all over the place, everyone very sad. She couldn't have been nicer, and persuaded me to step into the train and go with them to Rongai, having a hearty breakfast on the way; really very sweet of her; she had a matey chat with Mbugwa again on the platform in fluent Kikuyu to the rage and disgust of a millionaire-ish Asian couple waiting to get their say in. I breakfasted next to HE who had been going to give himself a month in Uganda with John Williams entirely on birds, and was so sad at having to give it up – the life-saving business.* He got a Sikh medal at Nakuru. They really are a wonderful couple and their like will not be seen again in most ways. Universal sadness at their era gone.

25 October 1959 Mbugwa was too sweet – when I got home, very weary after a twelve-hour day on the tables, etc. [setting up a flower show], I found the spare room absolutely crammed with every sort of indigenous flower he had gone round and collected on the farm. He wanted me so much to take them to the show, and it was hard to explain that there was no class for indig. flowers, also that the entries had closed last Monday. But I did use some of them in inventing flowers for my miniature six containers, and that did get a first. We kept them for Sharpie to see, so Mbugwa wasn't entirely snubbed. Wasn't that sweet?

In November, Nellie sold the bulk of her remaining land to her neighbour Kathleen Seth-Smith. Besides the house, she kept back fifty-three acres, mainly to provide shambas *for her 'old retainers' whom she would not turn away. She was nearly seventy-five, not in the best of health, tired, and had accepted the fact that she would never to able to pass on the farm to me. Her first consideration was to see that her old retainers were provided for.*

20 November 1959 Yesterday I called together all the labour and went, map in hand, to show them where their *shambas* would be. Land to be cleared and tractor-ploughed for them. All the younger men are off; the only ones who want to stay and have *shambas* are Manvi, Kariuki, a new chap called Kachinka, the old one-eyed garden-boy Nganga and Karanja (herd).... We have settled that neither Karanja (cook) nor Mbugwa wish to retire; they will get a hundred shillings each per month plus meat and fat, but no *posho,*

---

* In September Sir Evelyn Baring, in an act of great gallantry, rescued an Asian girl from drowning in the surf at Malindi, very nearly perishing himself. He strained some muscles near his heart, and had to curtail his farewell programme, after seven years of governorship.

and can cultivate half an acre if they wish. . . . I am deeply sorry about the old cripple Kachuki who has the demon-working, old, old wife, as can't think what will happen to them, but stay they will not. . . . I am putting in pyrethrum seed-beds on the one irrigated acre I keep and hope to build up to five acres of pyrethrum, and have kept the bit with plums, figs, avocado pears, etc. on it. Veges must go. It is all my fault for wasting so much money, and there it is, the milk is certainly spilt, so no good grousing. My one idea now is to see that no money is wasted any more or spent on things that aren't really worth while.

19 December 1959   I duly went to N'bi for the Flower Show, a very good show indeed. . . . Returned via Kiambu where I stood myself a truly magnificent present of three pheasants and three W. African guineafowl from Mr Cade, who is a bird maniac and now has four hundred pheasants and innumerable other edible fowl. The pheasants have been very difficult but these are second-generation Kenya ones and he hopes have settled to a routine. He says there is a lot of money to be made in guineafowl. You aren't allowed to breed the local ones (game laws) but the hotels are mad to buy these at Sh 17/50; they come purple, speckled, or lavender and are very sweet.

27 December 1959   If only one could be left alone! I already avoid the PO till afternoon as I am tired of people saying either 'I hear you've sold to Kathleen, well done, I hope you stung her', or, 'How *could* you?' – what the hell has it to do with anyone? . . . The farm jumble took place as usual on Xmas Day and went off very well. I made my present to old Kariuki those riding breeches you sent; he was thrilled and is thinking of buying a horse.

'*I am living in horror of someone doing something about my seventy-fifth birthday tomorrow*', Nellie wrote. Someone did.

18 January 1960   I write completely overwhelmed, I really am. I took a lift early to Nakuru with Tom Petrie and on my return found on the table a letter from Hans with a cheque inside for Sh 4323/ 90 and a list of thirty-five names. It is quite stupendous and I don't know where to begin to thank you all. Tomorrow I am going to pop it into the PO savings and want it to sit there towards a new car, but as a token I want a wrist-watch to wear daily – a good working one and not all that *maridadi* but something that won't look too lumpish worn with a silk dress.... Hilda and John came over with a cactus and a pot of marmalade, Nils sent a freshly caught trout and Lilian some china not yet unpacked. I am bewildered....

Early in 1960 the Wind of Change, taking Kenya unawares, struck suddenly with gale force. That the country was set on a course towards majority government was generally accepted, but it was to be a balanced, orderly progress at a moderate speed, based on a multi-racial constitution and allowing time for Africans to gain political experience, and for a larger educated class to emerge. In October 1959 Iain Macleod had succeeded Alan Lennox-Boyd as Secretary of State for the Colonies in Harold Macmillan's Tory government, and in January 1960 delegates representing all the political parties in Kenya of both races were summoned to London to hear new British proposals for the country's future. It soon became apparent that a drastic change had taken place in British intentions. The aim was no longer to be a constitution that preserved a multi-racial balance; there was to be an absolute African majority based on one-man-one-vote with no strings, and a complete and early British withdrawal. In effect, HMG had decided to yield to pressures already being applied, which they knew would intensify, and to surrender the fortress before, instead of after, the siege.

Lancaster House, as the conference became known, signposted the early end of the road for white settlement. Among white farmers, the sense of shock was great. Public pledges, often made and recently repeated (Lennox-Boyd was the last to do so), had reassured the settlers that their place in Kenya's political and economic future was permanent and secure. The government-supported and financed post-war settlement scheme was still in operation – in fact it remained so until well after the Lancaster House Conference – encouraging new settlers to take up land and to help them to get established, on a guaranteed tenancy of forty-four years in the case of tenant farmers. So news of the British government's turnabout in policy was received by most Europeans with a deep sense of betrayal, by some with anger, and by all with sadness. Michael Blundell who, as leader of the multi-racial New Kenya Group, accepted the proposals as inevitable and came back resolved to make them work, was greeted at Nairobi Airport with a shower of thirty East African sixpences, if not quite silver then the nearest approach. The Federal Independence Party, led by Group Captain Briggs, refused to accept the terms but was fighting a battle already lost. African politicians, split into parties based on tribal loyalties, were naturally jubilant and became increasingly impatient to see uhuru finally achieved, and resentful of Europeans' continued presence on land they now regarded as their own.

6 February 1960   Everyone here is in the deepest gloom about the Conference although we don't know the details yet. It is the time factor that is so disturbing; how is the Euoprean farmer to make out economically when everything is muddle and inefficiency, as it is bound to be? Of course settlement is killed stone dead; a lot of people, those who can, will go: commercials etc. will stay on and no doubt Kenya will eventually flourish but we settlers have had it; feeling is very very high against Macleod and also Renison [the governor], who I suppose just rides to orders.

20 February 1960   I've had about thirty acres ploughed; it cost a hell of a lot and I wonder now whether I ought to have done it. Kathleen is in deep despair, Antony [her son] has written telling her not to spend one more penny, to clamp down on all fencing, etc., she is really looking ill and miserable and is frightfully upset.

26 February 1960   Yesterday Sylvia Pease rang up to ask where she could get a siren like I had in the Emergency. I said I'd sell her mine cheap. (I was never able to sell it.) So took it over and found her in no end of a flap, saying times far far worse than Mau Mau were ahead, and the settlers would all without doubt be got rid of by murder. I thought it quite important to calm her and did it so well that she ended up by thinking the siren wasn't necessary after all. Rotten salesmanship!

9 March 1960   The before-storm lull goes on. No one seems to be doing anything at the moment except shut down on development and get their money away. Mrs Earlam told me people have shut down in Nakuru even on having hair-do's! Sounds like sackcloth and ashes; anyway I am going to have an iron wave prior to going to judge the flower show at Eldoret.... The police inspectors in the Rift Valley are fifty below strength and they can't recruit a single man, so are promoting African corporals to be sub-inspectors. And so on.... African Elected Members are clamouring for Jomo to be the first prime minister.

15 March 1960   All well on my return except that my guineafowl have died – dehydration, I think. Eldoret area just as gloomy as here and a lot of talk about packing up among the younger and be-childed people.

In April I broke my journey from the Central African Federation, as it then was (now Zambia, Malawi and Zimbabwe)*, to spend one week only on the farm. Nellie gave one of her parties on the lawn, when we all sat at rickety little tables under a gnarled old olive tree, creepers smothering the little house, the garden bright with flowers that seemed always to be in bloom, sunbirds hovering with their quivering wings, tiny waxbills, that Nellie had christened animated plums, hopping about at our feet, the dachshunds stretched out in the sun; and troubles were set aside. I assured her that a home and welcome awaited her at Wood-folds, but she advanced many reasons against final retreat: mainly that, if she left, her old retainers would have no right to stay and nowhere to go, and she could not bring herself to let them down – a

* Zimbabwe was named Zimbabwe-Rhodesia in 1979.

feudal attitude, as she agreed, but she was made that way. What was left of the farm had now become virtually unsaleable, and her chances of getting compensation were nil. But she was still resolved to go her own way. To add to everyone's troubles, the climate again turned sour; periods of drought alternated with violent storms and floods.

22 May 1960 The drought has got simply terrific, grass all brown, people wilting and maize going at the rate of knots. Friday morning woke up to very low cloud, quite a fog, and bone dry like dry ice. Never seen it before. Then at 4 pm two thunderstorms met over this house. Torrents of rain and lots of hail which we could have done without. I was paying wages outside the kitchen door when a flash and a bang went off absolutely overhead and a horrid rending noise; don't know what was struck – something. Muchoka took to his hands and knees and fled round the corner – a new technique to avoid being struck by lightning, but anyway someone was as frightened as I was. We got 2.7 inches in about an hour – just a flash in the pan. No rain since....

29 May 1960 A strange and very disastrous affair assailed the capon industry. All rations, all routine, all everything has been the same for all pens for months. Shortly after dawn on Tuesday one pen of about 150 capons suddenly went berserk and cannibalistic and nothing would stop them tearing each others' entrails out before our eyes. They refused all food, we separated all we could and took every measure I could think of, but of course no room for solitary confinement at such short notice. They killed fifty-four of each other before it all calmed down that afternoon. It made me feel more sick than you can imagine.

13 June 1960 I have decided to say the school must go away. The teachers' houses want renewing and the school buildings are very dicky. I started the school thirty-two years ago as a tiny thing, when I had a thousand acres and quite a labour force. I have now fifty acres and there are a hundred and fifty-three children in the school of whom twenty come from this farm, three teachers, and everything expanding, and lots of other schools around. So they can pack up at the end of the year.... The Rose Show was a great success. In the *banda* there were 135 feet of banks of the most lovely blooms, it was a sight of sheer beauty. Over two thousand people came through the *banda*. EAWL ladies did the catering and sold over fifteen thousand lunches, taking £850 gross.

Kenya's progress towards uhuru was rapid but uncomfortable. Although victory had been conceded, the ambitious young African leader, Tom Mboya, appeared to many to be activated more by racial passion than by a desire to cooperate in the various measures that preceded full independence. Hard-core Mau Mau detainees were being released in large numbers, many of them 'extraordinary, emotional men with the eyes of fanatics and only one idea in their heads – the release of Kenyatta – wearing dirty, odoriferous monkey skins' in Michael Blundell's words. There was a resurgence of Mau Mau oathing and murdering under other names, such as the Land Freedom Army. To add to the general feeling of apprehension, the débâcle in the Congo led to a stream of all-but-destitute white refugees.

17 July 1960   Only a few are as yet emerging through Kenya – about four thousand will have come, and presumably gone, in due course. The rich buzz through in rich cars. I met a party picnicking just outside Nakuru in a lorry with household goods and several most charming dogs. People who are meeting refugee trains say that local Africans are as foul to local Europeans as to the refugees – 'Your turn next, off you go', sort of thing. ... The more one thinks about it the more unlikely does it seem that our settler sort will be able to make out here. I agree that other Europeans will doubtless come, and farms will be turned into companies and so on, but a quite different sort of country, that's all.

27 August 1960   The Hawes family came up after tea yesterday, principally to tell me that they had decided to go home for keeps. It is somehow quite a minor shock; brings home to one what it will mean when lots and lots of people do clear off. Margery loathes the cold and England generally but says that she is 'through with Africa'. There is a sort of hysteria, I think, going on about black faces. Bridget said it was getting her down at the British Council in Mombasa when papers arrived with 'Get out you British' scribbled all over them. Margery says she gets black looks in the street in Nakuru. I think this is rot as the only black face she need have any trans-actions with is her factotum, Kachunji, who she admits is sweet. I don't think you get exactly welcoming faces in say Oxford Street of an afternoon? However everyone must decide for himself....

A little light relief, or at any rate relief, was provided by an attempt by a former house-boy to kidnap the daughter of one of Nellie's old retainers. With the help of two of her staff and Michael, a Dobermann she had been given, Nellie pounced on the would-be kidnapper in the darkness, but he escaped into the bush. A police inspector came to investigate and departed again.

5 September 1960   Well, you would have thought that would have ended the evening, but at 2 am back came the Land-Rover with the inspector saying there was an emergency and he wanted to use my telephone. Of course I listened to every word. He first rang Jean Scott to ask about Tom Petrie, who had been badly slashed and gone to her to be tied up. She said his condition was deteriorating, which sounded horrid. The inspector then rang Nakuru police and told them to get a statement from Tom on his arrival at the hospital; the dogs were to come immediately but no one could say where the dogs were to start from. That *was* the end of the evening except that the dachshunds' tummies were upset by the excitement and they made messes all night.... Mbugwa told me with my early morning cuppa that Tom had been attacked in his house and got badly slashed but that he had killed a chap with his gun. I think this is all Mbugwa's imagination.... *Later*. Mbugwa wasn't romancing; Tom *did* slay his attacker who was one of Kathleen's pet Kipsigis – her No. 2 on the farm, in fact. It looks as if Tom was alone, just finishing his supper, when this chap and two others burst in and slashed him badly on the face and he may lose two fingers. Tom fired and the chaps went off, and this one was found stone dead in the chicken-run. Tom was alone until his brother came home sometime much later and took him to Jean Scott's. I found the policeman's torch yesterday behind my telephone, the glass all smeared with blood. 'Bwana Petrie's *damu* [blood]', said Mbugwa delightedly and ghoulishly.... Education man came yesterday. Frightful complications about the school as *no one* will have it on his land. I can't cut off the education, bang, of 156 future ministers? I will *not* spend money on the school nor let any African spend on it; no European will have one; impossible to have it in the township (far from the best solution) as there's no money and building standards are prohibitive. I shall say they can carry on here on the strict understanding that they are to go the moment they can, and absolutely no lien on this farm.

10 September 1960 Tom Petrie is getting on all right; he had three blood transfusions and won't be out of hospital just yet. It seems he had just collected a lot of cash from some stock sales and had it in the house. The Kipsigis went straight for that and got away with the cash-box.... Kathleen says the diochs [finches] have taken fifty per cent of the wheat on her land.... Had a most enjoyable morning being shown by Grace England how to make miniature cheddars with no apparatus at all; all tests done by sniffing and the feel of the curd.

25 September 1960 A few blows in the farm/garden line. Egerton College numbers are right down, even lower than in the Emergency, so the veg. cheque is sadly reduced, and I must say I thought that *was* a safe market. Then, price of barley has gone shooting up so that knocks out the capon trade. My lovely tomatoes I think have succumbed to wilt. They aren't for a serious market of course but I did like to see them so beautiful.... Have been busy turning surplus milk into miniature cheddars.

6 October 1960 I think most people feel at the bottom of their hearts that it will become in time impossible for the old school to carry on. Personally by the time the dogs are put down I really don't think there will be enough of me left to be worth passage money.... I think race relations are getting worse and worse except of course between us and the old chaps; the African politicians are absolutely out of touch with their own people.... The Stewarts had to have a sale this week, theirs are the best Ayrshires in the country and they averaged £21 for cows in calf and sold very, very few.... Did you realize that a lot of resettlement in Israel was based on what the Old Testament said about the right sorts of trees to grow, where the wells were, and they made entrancing little heaps of stone to catch the dew. I wish all the T. Mboyas had been under *Roman* colonialism; that would have taught them.

18 November 1960 My two acres of pyrethrum are hanging on by their eyelids but should be bursting with flowers normally, so far not a single picking, and of course no more planted.... Terrific hoo-ha about Gicheru's Naivasha speech in which he said the white man would after independence have to '*piga magoti*', which means go down on his knees, to the African. The press has said that he ought to explain himself, but he hasn't bothered; all pretty hopeless....

15 January 1961 Politics are still raging here. Michael Blundell, I hear, was very heckled at Njoro but apparently had all the answers. Mary Wright misbehaved herself I'm told – may not be true – and boxed a woman's ears because Michael kissed her, and then threw a jug of cold water over Michael at a club supper. Where does that get anyone?... Am having a wonderful fruit season at the moment, plums, figs and blackberries all together.

19 January 1961 Well here we are, age seventy-six and all. Ingrid and Nils came to lunch bringing a Swiss roll filled with lemon curd, delicious. About 12.30 came the Adamses, bringing two beautiful succulents and a gloxinia in a pot, and a cucumber; just after they went came Mary Wright with a bottle of champagne. We all had a glass of sherry; it was a bitterly cold grey sunless day and *siafu* about; should have meant rain but it turned out to be a shower that registered 0.01 inches.

28 January 1961 Leslie Brown's flamingo lecture was marvellous, at least the film was. It is terrifying to think how utterly purposeless all that flamingo life is; they are very good-tempered birds, never a cross word so far as one could see in all that dull life; very different from the dear little doves.... Please if you remember could you tell me the definition of the word 'gimmick', and also what is a disc jockey?

17 February 1961 I took Eve down to C-B [Cavendish-Bentinck]'s open-air African meeting. He spoke in a near-whisper to his interpreter so the Europeans had to take it in Swahili. An oration sans gestures, voice inflection etc. is quite different from the Tom Mboya style and I couldn't help wondering whether the Africans continued to think that age spells wisdom. They asked quite sensible questions about land and education. C-B has a charming baby hippo stuffed by the Coryndon Museum and given him for electioneering. A hippo is his symbol, a giraffe Michael's. What a world – voting for a hippo or a giraffe! This afternoon we went to the opening of the bird sanctuary at Lake Nakuru, which was a *very* high light for me.... Jean Anderson has got a most remarkable dog. For years some Germans with all the precision of their race have been working (N. Kinangop) on a New Dog. Scientific crossing of peke and dachs. Result, now apparently uniform, has an eighteen-months' waiting list. This one about the size of a large dachs, marvellously clean lines, smooth, light brown coat, and the chunky profile of Chinese sculpture, and a peke head in outline but slightly longer nose, tightly curled tail; East and West have met at last.... Oh dear, this drought *is* depressing; shrubs dying; birds have stripped all the brassicas; mouse-birds reduced the jacarandas to skeleton trees.... Dolly now talking of suicide and swimming out to sea.

25 February 1961   I feel very bitterly and deeply about being such an infinitely poor relation, crawling home and being a nuisance whereas I ought to be the counterpart of the terrifically rich eighteenth-century uncle coming home from the East Indies to spend millions on his family.... Drought absolutely raging – hotter than I've ever known; everything a smoke haze, though where the grass to burn is I don't know, as mostly everything is bare earth. Politics raging too, of course; the situation in S. Rhodesia looks awful and Congo too. It hardly bears thinking about, the near future I mean.

5 March 1961   The 'Security Section-Leader' for this district came up Wed. pm. We all pay Sh 10/- and some 'iron rations' are banked at Egerton, where we all assemble, and it seems abide, until 'flown out'. Of course this is not anticipated, but presumably might happen after independence if the army doesn't get paid and mutinies. Not a bad thing to have in mind as the Congo stories increase in horror....

20 March 1961   Saw the bank about future farm programme; they *insist* I put in every bit of pyrethrum I can this year and they will see things through till it is bearing. I am at a loss to understand why they are so keen to help people on – I suppose it is a nice change from the streams coming to get their money out of the country. Old Karanja (herd) says it is going to be a rotten year for rain, there are too many rainbows about. There was a beauty yesterday which filled him with gloom.

25 March 1961   The political situation gets worse and worse. Tom Mboya has repudiated Lancaster House completely and calls for full independence this year.... Time is up for Jomo to go to Maralal.* Do you remember our safari with Hugh Welby when we picked out the site for Maralal? And now it is in the headlines.

1 April 1961   John Graham's heifers got into my irrigated bit and ate off completely the last of my poor cabbages. Poor they were, but they were my last bit of rabbit food. Young ones are already beginning to die from lack of greenage and cats eat lettuce leaves, if they can get them. Two poor little duikers [small antelopes] went ahead of the car for half a mile the other day, so weak and slow I had to crawl, they were obviously trying to make for the bush near the river, poor little devils – not lack of water in their case just starvation.

23 April 1961   Maybe instead of hanging on I ought to pack up and come and turn knobs for you in the kitchen while I am still un-senile enough to do it. Pros and cons are: hanging on, one might get better compensation when the blow-up comes, certainly not otherwise, and a bit longer for the dogs to live. Would *they* mind either way? I just wonder whether I *could* have them put down now.

28 April 1961   Am very taken up with a new thought. There is a lot of loose talk going on about Portugal. I'm sure Lisbon, Cintra, Coimbra, etc., are too snobby and grand for words, and Oporto a

* Jomo Kenyatta was moved to Maralal from Lodwar, in the NFD, where he had been held in detention, in April, preparatory to his release, which took place on 14 August.

terrifically high standard of living. Daisy went once to a place they were trying to make into a second Riviera on the Atlantic coast where they got nothing but Altantic gales and rain, rain, just like Cornwall. But I have been studying the map and a very ancient encyclopedia. There is a place called Faro almost exactly half-way between Lisbon and Gib. It is on the Mediterranean shore, has a row of cuddly little islands in front of it, some mountains not far off and a mighty great river to the east (Spanish border). At least one can pronounce the name. The encyclopedia says the south of Portugal has a perfect climate, rich soil, abounds in luscious fruits and fish, grows maize and they plough with oxen. Now, why shouldn't there be some fisherman-style cottages capable of conversion to mod cons, etc?... Grateful as I am to you beyond belief for again saying I could have a perch, the thought of endlessly weeping grey skies, cold, dark, putting down dogs, gets one down. If we had a little rhino's nest [a pun: *faro* means 'rhino' in Swahili] Gervas might welcome it in the winter months with a luscious garden and mod cons. No quarantine for dogs in Portugal....

4 May 1961　Saw Hans and Viveka on Tuesday; they've had every single leaf of every crop and every single blade of grazing destroyed by army worm. The whole farm, they said, is a heaving, wriggling mass of black slime. This place is *supposed* to be too high but they have disposed of Michael Pease's farm and are now at Mary Wright's. Really the poor farmer has taken it in Kenya. We are dispirited too over gardens.

7 May 1961　I am sure you will have read in the home press about this ghastly murder at the Osbornes [close by] on Friday night. It looks horribly like a really true-to-type Mau Mau murder, as it wasn't for food or money. The only *non*-Mau Mau aspect is that they didn't rush upstairs and kill the two babies. I think the brave chap was the house-boy who ran two miles to fetch neighbours when he heard David's cries for help. *Later*. Just been summoned to a special meeting of the Njoro Settlers Assn. re the Osborne tragedy. I can't see what they can do, but shall go as I rather think I've got the wrong ammunition in my gun. As I couldn't find my ammunition I told the police I'd accidentally put it down the old *choo*, so got a permit for more. Now I've found the old stuff and it looks quite different from the new.

11 May 1961   Over two hundred people turned up for the emergency meeting about the Osborne affair; of course a lot of hot air was talked, but on balance I think it is better to be slightly hysterical if it means shaking the govt. people out of their complacency.... It was of course a ghastly murder, but I cannot think why David Osborne, who was always in a flap about security (he had his mill and also house burnt down before by Mau Mau) should have let himself go to sleep with an open door and no weapon, and his wife too. But there it is – this forest has got these dreadful people in it and we are all back practically to Emergency conditions, and it is a dreary, dreary thought. Everyone went to the funeral on Tuesday, the largest ever I should say in Nakuru.... Everyone says the 1952 pattern is emerging daily – it isn't really a life. I am sure that in the end farmers *must* go. I think and think of schemes; all of them bristle with drawbacks.

20 May 1961   I devoted most of yesterday afternoon to *The Mottled Lizard* and had a howl for about two hours; it is very, very sad throughout. I don't know whether the howl was due to all the packing up etc. being just round the corner now, or to the realization of how hideous and awful we've made this lovely farm between us – whites and blacks – and spoilt it for ever. It's so much worse since you saw it; John Adams's *watu* have ringed and killed all those lovely thorns, it's now all *shambas* and bare as a table. Just up the Graham road is this horrible new school with a hundred-foot iron roof, no trees, no proportions, no fence, no trellis, etc., and the stink on that road. I simply don't know where to walk.... No more rain....

1 June 1961   As you know, the Purvii decided to clear out leaving everything, that lovely little place just abandoned, animals put down etc. Donald's health has been rotten and on Friday when the pantechnicon came to take their heavy stuff to be shipped to the UK he had a bad heart attack; ambulance telephoned for at 10 am and came at 3.30 pm, luckily Donald still alive but one side paralysed and in great pain from heart. Poor Mabel is absolutely distraught.

The vet is coming on Thursday to put down the horses, Pluto [her Boxer dog] and the cat, and they were due to fly next week. It is all a tragedy.

11 November 1961 Went to Egerton on Thursday evening where they have lectures almost every week and invite people. It was a shock. I don't quite know why. I have been to such a lot of those 'evenings' – hall always packed with neighbours, a few cheerful students, lots of staff. This time there was only the vice-principal introducing the lecturer, locals only self and Adamses and Sullivans, the hall crammed with black students and I think only two white ones. I suppose the sense of shock came from missing all one's own sort. I suppose one had a sense subconsciously of belonging to a community and knowing everyone; now it was brought home so much that we are 'out'.

The climate did nothing to raise morale. After a devastating drought and attacks of army worm, things went to the other extreme. In this one year, the country experienced in the early half the driest period for forty years, and at the latter end the wettest since rainfall was recorded. Floods ruined crops, paralysed transport and killed thousands of cattle; whole districts were cut off and their inhabitants would have starved had it not been for air-drops by the RAF; a disaster relief fund to which HMG contributed £1,000,000 was raised to enable stricken farmers of both races to buy seed and start again.

18 November 1961 The floods get worse and worse. The administration has been supreme over famine relief and the railway has done marvels.... Everything is wet and sopping and the wheat all round a total write-off. A lot of wretched sheep are being pastured on a *vlei* up to their hocks in cold, grey mud. I gaze anxiously at the cobs of maize; so far they are all right but nothing ripening or growing.... The Kikuyu butcher at Njoro has a most alluring board stuck up with prices – it begins: 'No. 1 steak and ferret Sh 1/70' [ferret = fillet]. I ordered two pounds of ferret on Monday.... More rain and flood damage, perfectly grotesque; Mombasa is on food rations and so on.... I'm sorry Charles is off his feed as I think it's very bad for him. No underfed person is ever relaxed and happy;

conversely most slightly overfed people are. Some eminent physician said that he had never treated a case of a happy person having cancer. (I suppose you might say that once you'd got cancer you wouldn't be a happy person?) Anyway, nothing is worse for human relations than underfeeding, so tell him to face his food like a man.

25 November 1961   The rain goes on and on and on. Everything is so soggy it is one vast quagmire. I nearly sink squelching from house to garage. The damage to the community can hardly be esti-mated but must run into millions – feeding thousands for a year, getting land and buildings back into shape, bridges, etc. Thank good-ness for those 150 sappers who will re-build the bridges in no time, and how much nicer for them to show off their skills instead of sitting about in those awful barracks. . . . A woman and child tried to ford the Njoro river just up in the forest here, and were next seen in Nakuru Lake, poor things, quite drowned. . . . More rain, the Mom-basa line out of action again. A Dorobo has been discovered in the lake besides the woman and child.

3 December 1961   The deluge ended true to form – I got 6.5 inches in the last five days. (Meru has had 88 inches since 1 October.) Still it looks as if it's letting up. . . . Maudling [Macleod's successor as Secretary of State for the Colonies] seems to have done very well, poor man, but of course no one will listen to him. There was nearly a very ugly riot at Eldoret when he went there, entirely stopped by General Service Unit and only one chap (KANU) was killed, but when there are no GSO about what then?*

9 December 1961   Floods at last abating. My ram pump eventually surfaced, but it was tangled up with a tree and somewhat the worse for the encounter; however I got bits done in Nakuru and now it is working again ever so well; no excuse for not having a bath except that there is no *kuni*; but have found another dead thorn tree so it will be all right. . . . The fig trees which I am abandoning to Kath-leen on 31st are laden with fruit, ditto avocadoes; shall be so sad saying goodbye to them.

* GSO was a unit of the police responsible for dealing with civil disturbances. KANU, the Kenya African National Union, was the major nationalist party of which Jomo Kenyatta was the leader.

17 December 1961 Believe it or not, after three blessed fine days back came the torrents; I had 2.34 inches on Monday night and another 1 inch next day; N'bi 5 inches in one day. One more week and the maize should have been safe with its cobs pointing downwards; as it is most of them were still vertical and goodness knows what damage has been done. Tough to have had a beautiful crop almost wrecked by drought and the next possibly quite wrecked by wet?... Mervyn Hill is sunk in depression because the *Kenya Weekly News* is doomed to possible extinction because of adverts drying up.... Oh, the blessed sunlight; I hope the house will dry out; being all sodden timber and sodden earth it is very damp and cold.

24 December 1961 Had the farm 'do' on Sat. afternoon to clear the air a bit. Karanja as usual cooked for the multitude, the same meal for years and years so I suppose they like it – endless cups of tea, rock buns made with dripping and curry puffs.... Lots of daylight attacks going on these days on Europeans. I don't think the BBC mentions anything short of murder, but the last one was unpleasant. A farmer, wife and four children going back from Naivasha to his farm just off the main road; two miles from his house encountered boulders on the road, a masked gang coshed and slashed him, cut open his wife's head and knocked out one child; however they went off when they found the farmer hadn't got the payroll money they expected him to have. Another man was held up near Kitale but the gang was chased off by his wife with a *panga*. And so on. *Xmas*. Well, here we are, Xmas morning and all my thoughts with you. Lovely blue sky, white fluffy clouds, brilliant sunshine and lots of carols on the transistor. Party last night at Ingrid's went according to plan; a sad little party really with 'the last' hanging over all, and poor Hans feeling absolutely rotten.

6 January 1962 Ingrid has had the most awful thieving; lorries arrived one night and took the cobs off an acre of maize; three sheep stolen and endless ducklings, and petrol taken out of the car's tank though it was sitting just outside her bedroom window and the top of the tank wired on.... What is the end for us all? We know no more than two years ago at Lancaster House time. The gloom is very deep and real these days. But the country is so lovely! Looks as if the sword of Damocles is falling, falling.... I'm afraid at the moment I have no specific views on what to do next and cannot actually face up to putting down the dogs. Doubtless it will all come.... I began to make enquiries this week about smallholdings for old retainers.

13 February 1962 I must tell you about my trip to Lake Baringo, a highlight indeed. David Roberts went there first to shoot crocs for a living. The crocs paid, but not enough, and he started in a small way buying fish from the local fishermen, cleaning them and sending them to Nakuru with dry ice from Ravine, but that didn't work. Then he got the capital from somewhere and built a deep-freeze plant and she joined him with their four small children; they lived in tents for two years; now they have a grand concrete house which is the factory on the ground floor, and a very comfy house above it with plumbing etc. and spare rooms. The offal is all disposed of by the fishermen before they bring in their catch, so there is absolutely no smell and it's all spotlessly clean. But the Roberts' real life is with animals. As you arrive, you push your way through six eland, a young wildebeeste, several zebra, a young grantii and a small buck. They are the tamest animals I've ever seen, and never a cross word. An Alsatian and a ridgeback also about and masses of birds; even the crocs are amiable. They come and bask on the short grass round the house at 2 pm sharp every day; they do snatch up geese occasionally which get too close, and once caught a dog by the tail, but David rescued it. The Robertses are hoping to work up a bird trade; they don't really like it, but it *is* profitable and they must do it, the fish future being so uncertain. The birds go to zoos, mostly flamingoes, cormorants and pelicans. Both the Robertses know every single bird you can think of; they are such a nice couple. They took us in a motor-boat to a picnic on one of the islands, uninhabited, except for masses of herons nesting in the flat tops of the thorns; it was a heavenly trip.... The wildebeeste and zebra are constantly in the house. Sunday afternoon we came sadly home; it is a Kenya of fifty years ago (except for mod cons) and absolutely marvellous to live so utterly with the animals.

24 February 1962 Am bats on plain salads at the moment with excellent vinaigrette sauce made at table; trying different kinds of lettuce; cook all veges in the outside leaves of lettuce with no other water, discarding leaves when cooked; very good flavour results, and all vitamins.... The big olive trees are in flower; I wonder how long it takes for the fruit to mature? Shall I be here to garner it?

8 April 1962   One is seldom rewarded for do-gooding but on Thursday I went to the usual terribly boring Maendeleo prize-giving at Njoro and there met the DC Nakuru, who is a winner; he has excellent schemes for resettlement and listened most ardently to my old retainer worry, which he said was very much in his mind too, and between us we think we have had a brainwave. He says the Resettlement Board are buying up odd farms on compassionate grounds, and will use these for immediate relief for unemployment, and later draft these unemployed on to the main 'high density' settlement schemes. Now if we turn our old retainers into unemployed, they would have a priority as smallholders in their adjacent districts.... It is all very vague at present, but if one could see people like Karanja etc. fixed in a neighbourhood they like on five-acre holdings on high potential land, and only had to pay some small pension, it would be a great relief as all responsibility would cease....

15 April 1962   Oh dear, what do we do about everything? I have written to ask what is the extra premium on sabotage insurance as everyone seems to think that cover is necessary. The old home would certainly be a good subject for arson, in fact a well-directed kick might achieve general disintegration.

30 April 1962   Charles Goff proposed himself for the weekend, his news from the Kinangop is indeed depressing – a mass flight mostly to S. Africa. What really does shake me is that the old Mervyn Rays, who seemed so utterly built into the side of the mountain in their really lovely home, are off too. And masses more. Poor Charles is abandoning thousands of lovely roses quite unsaleable even at Sh 1/- a time, and the Sherwens leaving all their really superb apples, pears, daffodils, bluebells, etc. There's something much more personal in fruit and flowers than in wheat, veg. and pyrethrum, trees one has planted, so very painful to leave. Hans has abandoned the idea of leasing a farm in the UK, labour costs too high and with his dicky back he simply could not do the really heavy work, so he is out on a limb and very depressed.

At Nellie's urgent request, I had tried hard to get hold of some pairs of men's long woollen pants, formerly called combinations, for her old retainers. This proved difficult; shops no longer stocked such garments but an advertisement produced several replies. The head of a small firm in Suffolk wrote to offer several pairs free, and so did an old lady in Yorkshire who had some pairs that had belonged to her father laid by in lavender. So in due course a consignment of long pants arrived at Njoro and were distributed on the farm.

10 June 1962 The long pant situation is marvellous. I will of course acknowledge everything and write bogus letters in Swahili from recipients. I think everyone on the farm will be long-panted, and any extra will find very grateful homes from Salvation Army Europeans. I'll write Swahili letters for them too.... Poor Arnold Thornton shot himself on Thursday night, which was a ghastly thing. He had been warden at Egerton for ages, his contract was up and wasn't to be renewed, they were terribly worried about the future, their savings were bringing in nothing, and so on. A casualty of Lancaster House?... I had a delectable morning learning to make Pont L'Evêque cheese at Grace England's. An enamel bucket, ditto basin, some amerikani, a cake rack, an old tin tray, some hottish water, *voilà*.... Unwillingly, I am setting forth with the antique French card-table Billy Sewall gave me to deliver it to the transport people for shipment to the UK; how I hate its going. *'Partir c'est mourir un peu'*, especially with tables, it seems.... I've written to Charles to ask him to get some seeds of a climbing strawberry which is in the catalogue of a Paris seedsman. Besides being a lovely way to get the seed, I thought it would be good for Charles's French.

13 August 1962 Have taken a census of everyone living on the farm, oh dear: it works out at adult males fifteen, ditto females eighteen, male children twenty-nine, female ditto forty-three, total a hundred and five, isn't it awful? I hasten to add that very few of these are on the payroll. Old Nganga the gardener has a family of thirteen. No one seemed to know whether the last baby was a boy or a girl, so I put down hermaphrodite, which will give the census men something to chew on.

28 August 1962 Am playing with great delight and satisfaction (and practically no expense) with a new form of gardening. You line small holes with polythene, fill them with whatever form of soil is suitable for the crops, and await results. A tremendous water-saver, and one can make use of every bit of dud soil, plant under trees, and so on. So far everything I've tried has done marvellously – pansies three inches across – so am planning more holes to try things out.... Have gone very hot on sour milk and have it daily for breakfast with fruit – saves tea or coffee.... Edna [a neighbour] is furious about the man being sent to the moon. 'How ridiculous sending people to the moon – how are they going to get through heaven?' And she wasn't being funny.

The political situation continued on the boil as full independence grew nearer. Jomo Kenyatta had been released from detention in August 1961 to take his place as leader of KANU, and in April 1962 he joined the transitional government as Minister of State. In January and February 1962 a second conference had been held at Lancaster House to settle the final shape of the constitution. This time the main issue lay between the Kikuyu party KANU (Kenya African National Union) and the rest, mainly Kalenjin, Hamitic and Coastal tribes, headed by Ronald Ngala and somewhat loosely united in KADU (Kenya African Democratic Union). The former wanted a unitary form of constitution, the latter a federal one. The conference lasted for seven weeks and a federal constitution was agreed. Another general election was held in November.

4 November 1962 Voting went on apace, the Kikuyu scraped the bottom of the barrel. The DO had to intervene once when he saw a very very old Kikuyu woman obviously almost dying brought in extreme discomfort on a sort of stretcher, about to be carried into the polling booth in great pain. Perhaps *she* understood that voting paper?

11 November 1962 I'm sure everyone ought to start by being a healthy animal, and build up from there re intellectual prowess. Unless people eat, and eat the right sort of protective food, and take all exercise possible when developing, they only become the usual sort of nervy, ulcer-prone modern, and *joie de vivre* goes out for keeps.... Hans is off today week, after a job in a sort of export firm. Viveka going on farming till they see if he really can hold down the job. Charles and Kit Taylor off to Somerset for keeps in April, Donald trying to sell the farm to follow.... Flower Show was called a 'garden party' on the racecourse.... I won a cup for Veg. Display, being the only entry, had thirty different kind of veg. of indifferent quality but well set up. Goodness knows if it is any use going on with these shows; Kitale and Thomson's Falls say they've never had better shows than this year, but it all falls on the same tiny band of old showers, and to what end? And *such* an effort.

18 November 1962 Poor Hans is flying off tonight, he rang up Friday to say goodbye, said he had frightful cold feet and sounded very emotional.... My one thought and aim is to get rid of the overdraft; that comes second only to the settling of the old retainers. I am working all I can on that. Once the old retainer problem is settled I shall sit back and live as cheaply as possible and see. If it all proves impossible I shall try to sell to a Kalenjin African; they hate houses so could easily do with a converted store. I should hope that Mbugwa would stay on, as I could let him have quite a large *shamba* for himself and Njombo's widows. Anyway that is definitely my programme.... On Wed. Nils dashed in to say goodbye and he and Johnnie, two dachshunds and innumerable budgies and canaries (Johnnie's) went off next morning. They are bound in slow stages for Pretoria where they report to an association which welcomes them, pays them £30 for one month, and finds jobs etc.... Anyway there it is. They've gone. I went over to see Ingrid next day. Last weekend it was her birthday, she of course made a feast of it and next day collapsed with awful tummy upset as she always does when overdone. Her beloved little border terrier Lollipop had just been killed by *shenzi* dogs – she adored him; their best ram was stolen Tuesday night; the diochs are ravaging the wheat; the women won't turn out to pick pyrethrum, and so on. But *nothing* will make her listen to any other plan than to 'carry on and see'.... You will have seen that poor old Archie Ritchie has died. It seems a long time since I first met him, as a young man just on his way back from the Foreign Legion in Spain, with a hawk on his wrist. He was six years younger than I.

24 November 1962   I have got the most marvellous cauliflower now ready at four and a half months, grown in a polythene bag 12 inches across and 12 inches deep. Of course it is a sweat getting it started but a great solution re water and labour if it works. The curd weighed five and a half pounds, and was delicious, the wing-spread was four feet and the greenery (for rabbits and chickens) weighed eight pounds; bag intact and being cropped again; watering almost nil.

9 December 1962   On Friday I went to a War Memorial Hospital special meeting to help pass an almost unanimous vote in favour of the hospital becoming multi-racial. A lovely man with a moustachio bristling to heaven was the only one to oppose it. In the afternoon a really sad meeting – speech day at the Girls' High School. Out of the blue a week ago orders came to close that, and the Francis Scott School [the boys' equivalent] as from Friday. Of course it is the right thing to do, as numbers have fallen so tragically, but utterly the wrong way to do it; real hardship for parents faced with having to pay £60 a term for boarded children at Eldoret instead of day children in Nakuru, and the staff seemingly thrown out on their ears. The headmistress made such a pathetic speech and the girls themselves were utterly miserable.... I saw Billy Lambert and asked after his son who was a cloak-and-dagger chap at fifteen. He has got himself a commercial pilot's ticket and a tiny plane and flies up and down the coast, lands on solitary beaches in Somalia etc, all solo, and flies masses of prawns to Mombasa and makes a packet. A really adventurous lad, lucky to find something like that to do rather than in an office.

1963 — 5

6 January 1963 I continue to flap about the old retainer scheme as no word has come and I have failed to get hold of anyone; there is an African DO, also a chief at Njoro, both permanently invisible. It is getting very tricky as the wretched devils ought to be on the move to get new *shambas* dug.

14 January 1963 The situation is pretty tense over the Land Freedom Army 'confessionals'. Karanja seems very nervy. A confessional party at Ingrid's, headed by the DO, sat from 7.30 am one day to 1 am next morning, then all the next day and half the one after. Nearly everyone admitted membership.

Another gap occurred in the letters while I was in East Africa, once more gathering material for a book to be published as Forks *and* Hope. *I was not much on the farm but Nellie's old friend Daisy Balfour came on a visit, and we all had a short holiday in Uganda's national parks. When I returned to England in April, Nellie was still struggling with the old retainer problem and had reluctantly decided, as a measure of economy, to dismiss the cook Karanja and manage for herself, with some help from Mbugwa. The exodus of European farmers went on.*

12 May 1963 The Englands spent £6,000 on their place and are getting £2,500 for it and going. Rebecca spent more than that on her really excellent house at Gilgil and has sold for £1,600. Viveka is definitely going in October. It is horrid when people go for keeps.

16 May 1963 The cubby-hole I've turned into my kitchen is ready to move into any time by just carrying in the Afrigaz cooker, but difficult to finalize because Karanja is so very, very sad. I've told him to go off all next week to see if he can get a job or make any plans for one. I explained that I had no money at all for the moment to help him, but would try to help later on. He at once mentioned several friends who had been given lorries by their ex-employers.

20 May 1963 Well, the first elections are over and only one DO coshed on the head. I went down to Njoro on Sat. with a few chosen ones, others having gone at daybreak. About a thousand people there, representing about three thousand voters. Everything was very well done. I've never seen anyone better at his job than the little African in charge of my booth – so good-natured and unflustered – and a very tricky job checking up on everyone for hours on end. We all had to dip a forefinger into a bottle of indelible red ink; at the next election, another finger, and so on, so you can't vote twice, and we'll all have bloody finger tips for weeks. On the way some KANU youths made KANU noises at me, so I said 'Cock-a-doodle-do' back at them, which left them guessing. This was the Regional vote; Wed. and Thurs. is for the Senate, and next weekend the Lower House.

25 May 1963 I go down to register my final vote tomorrow, Sunday. Nothing could have been quieter than the voting, except at Isiolo, but of course if trouble is coming it will be after the voting. One well remembers the deadly quiet just before Mau Mau and what wonderful control they had. Voting still as popular as at the start. . . . Karanja (cook) is walking the countryside trying to find himself a niche. . . . I've invented an excellent gadget for heating up a single plate – I refuse to light the oven or grill for just one plate. I bought a 14-inch *sufuria* [saucepan] with a loose lid, dug out some scraps of wire from the store, and hied off to the *fundi* at the Njoro welding works; caused him to fashion a sort of cake stand with two tiers, to fit inside the *sufuria*. The bottom tier takes a dinner plate, the top one is a sort of hot plate, and a bit of rubber tubing off an old enema make a handle to lift the whole thing out with; it works like a charm, and one evening I even steamed asparagus while keeping the main dish warm. I've bought the kitchenette two little gifts, one a new grater as I found so much grated thumb in the cheese, the other a one-egg poacher. Meanwhile I send you a recipe for Tian.*

---

* A vegetable dish, presumably Chinese in origin, of which Nellie was particularly fond, comprising dried brown beans (soaked overnight), courgettes or squashes, spinach, garlic and herbs, assembled in a casserole and topped with breadcrumbs, grated cheese and minced anchovy fillets.

2 June 1963   Yesterday about 6.30 pm was returning from my dog walk when I saw two seedy-looking Africans hanging about; of course that is what one is on the lookout for, when not a soul is about on the farm (public holiday). Dogs of course charged, and great waving of sticks and *pangas*. I very nearly behaved in the old colonial style but didn't quite remove their stick and *panga* with my own hands. These two turned out to be Mr Hamisi and partner, now owners of the Fawcus farm, come to look at my house-cows which I advertised for sale. Mr Hamisi is a Muslim so justifiably agitated at Michael [the Dobermann]'s onslaught. I was asking £30 for Tinka-belle and £25 for Gilian but let them have the two for £50. I also threw in my very old, very small and not very efficient separator.... They are nice chaps; I said I would call on their four wives one day, but the dog problem they understood.... £400,000 for independence celebrations says Jomo, and over a quarter of a million for enlarging LegCo buildings – I suppose hot air does take up a lot of room.

10 June 1963   The Nakuru Show was quite fantastic, as if nothing was the matter anywhere at all. No European paid the slightest atten-tion to any African and vice versa – there may have been African high-ups there but if so indistinguishable from everyone else. Whites gay as larks – not once did I hear a murmur about its being the last show. The girls had the smartest of new dresses, the cattle parade I thought supreme, the arena nearly filled with every breed, all sleek and terribly expensive.

24 June 1963   The week has been fairly hectic with Muchoka departing. That was, and is, horrid. I miss him more than words can say, and think I always shall. The awful thing was that he hated going so much; a wonderful, loyal and trusted servant over the years; never his like again. How one loathes these changes.... Karanja is still off somewhere looking for a job. I should very much like to be a good cook but see little chance at present as the cooking has to be fitted in between other jobs and that is not the right approach to cookery.

14 July 1963   Betty Roche and I went to Lumbwa on Monday and bought a pedigree Saanen goatling billy. We are having a very modest goat enterprise between us, partly to be able to keep old Karanja (herd) on, partly to have some animals that you don't have to bring up to kill (though we may have a roast kid ever so often), and partly for fun. We don't mean to embark on a goat farm. Mike Barrett [the new principal] is mad about them at Egerton and has a flock of Saanen, Toggenburg and British Alpine. I have always adored goats.

18 July 1963   The N'bi Flower Show was very good, lovely stuff. To my huge embarrassment the RKHS sprang a presentation on me – a cheque for £70 and six silver spoons. Too overwhelming – cheque has gone into the stocking.

11 August 1963   Cookery is getting on, its graph definitely jumpy, but I did make, one evening, the best omelette I've *ever* eaten any-where. A Lyonnaise, my omelette book calls it. You chop a teaspoon very finely of mild onion, sauté it lightly in butter, let the butter go deep, dark brown, and throw it over the omelette just after 'folding out'. I'm sold on nut-brown butter....

24 August 1963   Ingrid arrived to tea in a fearful flap. A large car full of Nandi drove up to buy her farm, and while she was trying to find tea-cups and non-existent sugar for them, the telephone rang and that was the Central Land Board valuer saying he was coming next day to value the farm. She kept on bleating both to the Nandi and the valuer that the farm wasn't for sale, but he came sure enough and was quite beastly, she said. The valuation was £10 per acre, which would pay her debts and leave her with £2,000 – but where would she go?

1 September 1963   AGM of the Njoro Settlers Assn; main business was a resolution opening the Assn to all races. The resolution went through without a murmur.... Comings and goings and sales and leases. David Petrie's plot down the road is a hive of Kikuyu in-dustry, tree-felling and charcoal-burning, and sheep swarming among the stumps; a Kikuyu village has sprung up at Adamses' corner.... Kathleen Seth-Smith departs today.

15 September 1963   Karanja (cook) blew in for the weekend to visit his country estate and his two wives, he looks and seems very cheerful and happy. He has been selling charcoal, he says, in Nakuru. . . . Viveka's part-time manager had an armed raid on his own farm at Ol Kalau, summoned there to find sixty-seven sheep, dead or dying, strewn about. They just don't put these things in the papers any more. People really are abandoning their farms and just leaving that district

24 September 1963   Mbugwa went off at 10 am yesterday to see Jomo at Njoro; returned slightly inebriated and could only talk about the thousands of women he'd seen in beautiful clothes. I asked what had Jomo said. Mbugwa replied, 'Not a word, but he had twelve motor-cars with him mostly full of police.' Jomo also never uttered at Elburgon but let himself go at Nakuru in the evening, saying KANU was to be the only ruler of Kenya.

As indeed it became. On 1 June Jomo Kenyatta had been appointed the first prime minister, just over six months before uhuru was proclaimed on 12 December. It was at Nakuru that he made his famous 'Harambee' speech (harambee *meaning 'pull together') and called on everyone to let bygones be bygones and to work towards a prosperous and united future regardless of race.*

7 October 1963   Royal Show in N'bi was really a terrific success, a record crowd, fifty-seven thousand, through the turnstiles. A lot of padding with army panache which won't be there again. I thought underneath the holiday outing spirit the general European depression was deeper than ever.

13 October 1963   Except for being irritated by being told every five minutes by Jomo to keep calm, everything here seems apathetic, the real worry being the drought, and the maize not pollinating properly owing to hail. . . . Have actually learnt from Mbugwa how to produce the perfect poached egg. It is awful to use those little cups that produce an anaemic *bun*; Mbugwa pops in the egg just when the water in the skillet begins to simmer, mothers it around very, very gently with a perforated spoon, pops the cover of the skillet on and off,

off and on until a beautiful veil is established over the egg, and then ever so gently removes it. I've done it!

27 October 1963 Was amazed last night; they played the Kenya National Anthem for the first time on the wireless. I waited for something garish, blatant and cheap, but the most beautiful melody came over, restrained, sad, with the sadness and mystery of deep down Africa in it. And this only after one modest sherry!

9 December 1963 Went down to N'bi for RKHS council on Friday; long day in the horrid city which is worse than ever with 'Kenyatta Avenue' hitting you in the face,* flags of all nations bar Union Jack and so on; traffic awful. Had an entrancing session with the fish warden about domestic ponds; quite a possibility of getting a small pond here. There are nine-thousand in Nyanza, some smaller than my project, which give regularly two good fish meals to their owners. I asked him to fit me out with a pair of prawns from the Athi river which they tell me are delicious eating; he said, alas, he had tried hard to breed them himself elsewhere but they wouldn't.... Stood little Ingrid [old Ingrid's grand-daughter] and self a blow-out at the Lobster Pot and very nice too (except for the bill). She is thrilled and no wonder as she and David Matthews go in a little van on Thurs. to televise the whole Independence do, and they alone are responsible for it for the whole world.

Independence was declared on 12 December.

15 December 1963 Well, an end to this last history-making week; it couldn't have been quieter or duller here. The weather felt the same about it as I did – grey, almost weeping clouds all the time, right on one's head, and, for here, cold, cold. The farm people couldn't have been sweeter or better behaved. They all got Wed. and Thurs. off on full pay. Independence Day we started off Xmas-like on the lawn with jumble, and sweet-scrambles for the innumerable brats. Then I whacked out individual bags to each head of family containing meat, suet, bread, sugar, tea, according to size of family, also four gallons of milk, twenty-five bottles of beer, fifty oranges, and

---

* The name had been changed from Delamere Avenue, and the statue of Lord Delamere (by Kathleen Hilton Young) removed.

prizes for the sports. The afternoon was completely quiet – sleeping off beer I expect.... Some pretty good muddles it seems in Nairobi: Duke of Edinburgh was fifty minutes behind schedule for flag-raising; Mr Obote got stuck in his Rolls thirty yards from royal box and had to walk; the traditional dancers wouldn't stop and VIPs had to weave their way through howling mobs to get to their seats. And so on. Nearly three hundred stock thefts during the three days. On London news yesterday it said that Kenya was about to stop relaying BBC bulletins because BBC had lately referred to ex Mau Mau as gangsters instead of as freedom fighters. Was freedom ever mentioned at Lari, and when they slashed cattle, crucified dogs, cut the Rusk family into small bits, buried Gray Leakey alive, etc? And this embracing of the forest 'major generals' and taking them to GH garden party in 'uniform'? Well, enough of Independence – oh, one more thing – I had steeled myself to see the Kenya flag over the DO's office at Njoro instead of the Union Jack – there was no flag at all. I suppose it hadn't turned up, like the chief's uniform, or been pinched.... Viveka is really off on Saturday; the man who wanted to buy the farm could only get a loan for half the agreed price so the deal is off and it may take ages to find another buyer. But she must get Philippa to school and join Hans so there it is. Ingrid is very, very sad.... Am writing this on Sunday morning with a blazing fire, wearing an English undervest plus a sweater and sheepskin boots and my hands are blue with cold.

18 December 1963   As is my wont, I got two new *kanzus* yesterday as the present ones are in tatters. When I produced them, Mbugwa said no, they weren't wearing *kanzus* any more, only European-style trousers, etc. This was a bit of a shock, as though the custom now is pretty general, I didn't think these chaps would bother. I said all right, but silly of them as *kanzus* saved their own clothes; of course I wasn't going to supply clothes. Their faces fell a bit as I think they visualized smart steward suits at about Sh 100/- each; what a hope! I shall get them aprons in due course to cover some of the grubbiness of their own clothes; so standards fall.

29 December 1963   Yesterday I went to a party, really an interesting party. A son of an old, tough, illiterate peasant on Tom Petrie's farm

– one of the old sort – is off to the USA this week on a two-year scholarship teacher-training course, and threw a party for a hundred to celebrate at the school. I don't know which Europeans he asked but I was the only one there – John said he forgot. I was asked to tea at 2.30 so went at 3.30 when people were just dribbling in. The lad – our host – has no personality and, it would seem, few qualifications, but maybe will acquire both, and anyway is humble and tremendously thrilled, as are all the old folk. I think it is the feeling that there is now *opportunity* for the humblest which really thrills them. This scholarship was one of forty which were an *Uhuru* gift from the USA. The lad, Mr Duncan Njeroge, was educated first at my school and has been teaching at Naivasha. I was glad to get into conversation with Mbugwa, who has been sunk in glumness since the *kanzu* incident and is *so* boring when glum; however his charming smile came back at the party; he was sweet with the tots. The number of girls of about fourteen with babies was disgusting – all pupils at the school....

This school which Nellie had started produced some successful pupils. Some years later, old Ingrid (who remained on her farm Sergoita until 1975) encountered one of her former farm totos, *who had been a pupil at the school, in Nairobi. He had become a prosperous business man, and invited her to visit his family at Karen, a fashionable suburb of the capital. Ingrid explained that she had no transport. 'That's all right', he assured her. 'I'll send a car and driver for you. I've two cars so there's no problem.'*

4 January 1964   Only farm news is a complete strike of women, who demand a one hundred per cent increase in wages. I called them all together and explained that this would put all work out of court as no profit in veges could possibly be expected except from the status quo. They were adamant so the meeting broke up.... Mbugwa was hopelessly tight again last night. He said would I untie his apron as he was defeated by the knots at the back. I said certainly not and went off haughtily to bed leaving him pirouetting in the dining-room hunting for knots. It is too boring, this weekend tiddliness.

19 January 1964   Well, my birthday [seventy-nine] was full of incident. At 5.30 pm Gachinga rushed in and said people were burning down the beautiful signpost Kariuki and I had erected that morning on my boundary: '*Hapana ruhusa kwa wageni kuingia hapa*' ['Strangers not permitted here'] to replace the one destroyed at *Uhuru* time. So I dashed out to find a column of smoke and three of the most villainous-looking chaps who waved *rungus* at the dogs. I said 'If you hit that dog I'll kill you', so they didn't hit a dog, and I didn't kill them. We then parleyed, and they said they weren't going to stand for that sort of notice. I told them to clear off *my* farm and they sat down at my feet, so I walked back to the house to telephone the police. These men had threatened Gachinga and chased him about a hundred yards and also Mbugwa, who had had to run very swiftly, he said. After about two hours the police arrived, of course dark by then and the chaps had gone back to the forest. Tomorrow I will put up another bigger and better signpost.

Unrest was general at this time, strikes frequent and unheralded, and in January mutinies broke out simultaneously in the armies of Kenya, Uganda and Tanganyika, aiming at military coups. In the three capitals, the situation was tense. The three presidents – Kenyatta, Obote and Nyerere – asked for help from British troops which were promptly flown in, and the mutinies were quelled.

26 January 1964 We seem to have lived through a mutiny since I started this letter; can't say I noticed it much. Went to lunch at Adamses'; weather perfect, and the setting, the little red tables, and the shadows of the thorn trees, all so lovely. But a sad little party, somehow. Transistors busy; people who had been in Nakuru said it was a bit of a shambles with military and police cars, road-blocks galore, and rumours of looting in the Asian shops but nothing reported. One wonders how much *is* reported these days. And now five hundred soldiers under arrest, quite a hole made in the Kenya army. It seems that Jomo really has been the strong man, didn't disappear, and said that mutineers will be dealt with.

8 February 1964 Muchoka turned up to collect some stuff he had left behind; says all is well, he has four cows in calf and a bull, and hopes for another piece of land from Govt.... I went into Family Planning; Muchoka swore that none of his wives was pregnant but

263

it turns out that one went away from here in June in that condition, so has had a dear little one since she left. I ticked him off good and proper and he roared with laughter; he has three wives and fourteen little ones so far.... GH is now known as State House, much confusion it seems with Steak House, and furious telephonings about why hadn't the table for six been kept and could they do a bit better next time over the food.

Under Kenyatta's policy of 'Harambee', Europeans as such were not expelled or officially harassed, except in a few individual cases; on the contrary, in some directions their skills and capital were valued. But Africans needed their jobs and their land. So officers of the Colonial Service (who were given handsome golden handshakes) and most of the farmers (as distinct from ranchers and plantation owners) sooner or later had to go. Nellie was nearly eighty, rather deaf, walked stiffly from arthritis, and knew that her Kenya life was coming to an end. But, like others, she postponed the final decision almost from day to day. Meanwhile, there were still new 'projects', the garden and an interest in food.

10 April 1964   Don't be scared about my mushroom project. You see, mushrooms have a great gourmet appeal, and out here, out of season, one can only get dried ones from Hong Kong which aren't mushrooms but slabs of cotton wool marinated in vanilla. My present acreage measures 12 by 18 inches; if a success I may extend to a box three foot square. John McNab ruined one crop by liquidating red pepper mite which was really eating the 'plaster mould'; when the poor little mites were no more, the mould moved in to kill; but his next crop is coming along....

4 May 1964   Mbugwa came on duty Wed. pm in the state of wildest excitement – someone had had twins, a boy and a girl. Eventually I made out it was his beloved sheep, just as I was going to lecture him on Family Planning. He of course was sozzled, only *pombe* this time; still, it is maddening.

10 May 1964   Found an invite from Grahams to lunch as Edna had made a curry. And *what* a curry; she nursed it for three hours; its texture was simply wonderful, not dry and by no means sloppy, just a little sauce to scrape up; wonderful flavours; altogether a dream of a curry, the best I've ever had....

25 May 1964 Colin has had bad luck in that the high-up African who bought the farm next to his, a Permanent Secretary, never paid for various hirings of implements and contract work Colin did for him. Finally, after much unpleasantness the Perm. Sec. produced a cheque which bounced twice. Colin insisted on seeing him, whereupon he said 'The matter of my cheque bouncing is entirely between you and your bank.' Colin sold £6,000 of produce off the farm last year, but now is off to S. Africa.... Rose had a beautiful heifer heavy in calf slashed and murdered last Sunday. She says she doesn't know how she can carry on her milking, the milkers are permanently drunk and go on tugging away at the udders till 8 pm sometimes missing out teats altogether.

In June Nellie flew to England, mainly to settle future plans. Her friend Daisy Balfour, now over eighty, had with great generosity offered to buy her a small place in the Algarve in Portugal. The Dollards, friends of Daisy's who had left Kenya, had bought a plot of land in the Algarve for themselves and were looking round for something suitable for Nellie. She did not want a flat or villa on the coast, which was beginning to become fashionable, or in a town or village. She wanted to be in the genuine countryside, away from tourists and among Portuguese peasant farmers working the land, where the dogs would be happy and she could have a garden. And she wanted to live, if possible, in an existing Portuguese dwelling, however humble, that could be provided with 'mod cons', and not something modern and alien to the country. When she returned in August to Njoro she had accepted Daisy's offer, and later a quinta, or smallholding, was bought. It had a dilapidated dwelling on it and a small orange grove, some olive trees and almonds, and looked across gently rolling countryside, a little way inland from Lagos. Moreover the idea of settling in southern Portugal had also appealed to a Kenyan friend of Nellie's, Dorothy Powell, who shared many of the same interests, such as gardening, birds and other animals, and country life generally. Nellie returned to Njoro to find further deterioration in the situation as she saw it, and with her mind made up to leave.

6 August 1964   It is obvious that there has been a big change in unsettledness and run-down-ness since June. Strikes everywhere go on and on. Old Will Evans, it seems, who was stricken to the core about the behaviour of his labour and the rudeness of Trades Union officials, said to his wife 'this will kill me' at close of day, and died in his sleep – well out of it all. Young Cloete killed himself a short while ago from despair, and a man at Kiambu shot his wife and then bungled his own head wound. And so on.... Kate and Anne Petrie were returning to Thomson's Falls last week, stuck near three lorries also stuck; not only did the lorry drivers refuse to help but kept yelling 'Get off the road, you bloody bitches.' Then six chaps from a nearby farm appeared and couldn't have been more helpful, but were set upon and driven off by the lorry-drivers.... Howse and McGeorge are packing up at the end of the year....

22 August 1964   Have started on the last tidy; there is a pile of stuff waiting for dry weather to burn; there are a mass of problems.... What to do with lots of dear photographs you used to send, the Woodfolds book you gave me, Jos's medals, the 'Goya', a charming edition of Trollope which I've read and re-read, blankets, kitchen equipment, silver. Sales out here will be a farce once the landslide of departures really gets under way. My target is to have everything disposed of somehow with only things like files and diaries to be burnt the day before I leave – for keeps. Life has become completely pointless here. I was mad about the seeds I bought from Roberts and now I couldn't care less whether I sow them or not.

27 August 1964   Heard from Rose – stock thieving now beyond anything, a lorry comes every night and takes a full load of her heifers away. I don't see how she can stick it out – says it is just like Mau Mau, only more so. She found one beautiful in-calf Hereford cross heifer lying with both legs hamstrung. That is pure Kikuyu work, not done for meat.

25 September 1964   Dorothy and I are really working at the Portuguese language; it is all quite straightforward as to grammar, etc. and of course idiomatic as you get on, *but* the *pronunciation!* ... Have found a delicious form of food: I make a huge pot of lentil soup (very proteinous); this is dull in itself so I add a bit of light curry sauce which makes all the difference, then to make a complete meal add a hard-boiled egg or some flaked fish or any old thing.

2 October 1964   After a lot of thought, I have decided to apply to be bought out on compassionate grounds. A great many old and ill farmers have been bought out, as a rule on generous terms. There is now no more money available for this, but it is said that there will be, one day.... I am taking every possible step to find somewhere for my old people to go, so far without success.

12 October 1964   Rose came to stay a night; she has had at least £500-worth of good cows stolen in lorries. The police found twenty-five gallons of Nubian gin in her kitchen made by her cook; he only got fined Sh 40/-. He said he only did it to pay school fees; doesn't drink himself, unlike Mbugwa, who was quite quite awful this weekend, could hardly stand all Sat. evening and spoilt everything.

29 October 1964   Yesterday a very small car crammed with very large Kikuyu turned up and said would I sell them the farm? I said maybe; got Karanja to take them round the boundaries. They came back and asked my price; I said, 'Five thousand shillings.' One said, 'Surely that is wrong?' I said, 'Yes, indeed, I meant fifty thousand, thank you for correcting me.' We talked a bit and they went away. Three of them returned this morning and said yes, they wanted to buy. I said all right, but I won't do a thing till the cash is actually in the bank, and you can't get occupation till the crops are off, say end Jan. or early Feb. I don't think for a moment they have the cash or will be able to get a loan. The poor old retainers are shocked and miserable, but it may be just as well as they have now had some sort of warning.... An odd occurrence Sunday afternoon. I had just settled down to an afternoon at Portuguese with the gramophone and Linguaphone records when, after five minutes, the gramophone packed up. So went out on to the lawn to see if my beautiful brood of chicks wanted more skim – found them plastered with *siafu*. Another ten minutes and they'd have had it. Such a do getting the devils off them, they were dug in all round their little toenails and everywhere. By the time I'd got them off, the poor little chicks and my hands were covered with blood and some of them were very shocked. I dossed them down in an empty rabbit-hutch and proceeded to try to catch mother hen, who was distraught between mother love and *siafu*. The lawn was alive with *siafu*, little hillocks of them everywhere eating everything alive – used pints of pyr. and paraffin. However, chicks survived and yesterday, when I tried the gramophone again, it was in perfect order, so it was a psychic message from mother hen. Did you ever?

5 November 1964 I saw in *The Times* that dear Herbert Meade died last week; he was very old and ill, but it is all sad-making, dear Herbert.... The govt. is making a drive to get all Indian traders out, now they've deported a Patel at twenty-four hours' notice. A wretched little trader in Sabukia had petrol poured over him and was set alight, so the govt. has revoked all Indian trading licences in the district on grounds of security.

22 November 1964 I really tried to get on with things re old retainers in Nakuru and went to see one Binnie who is involved in a settlement scheme at Ol Kalau. Finally he said he would find out if anything could be done on the lines of their making themselves into a co-op and so eligible for a loan, and my giving them this land and nothing else. As far as I can see, even if I sold, it would only be for about what I should have to give them in cash as *baksheesh*, so they might as well have the land as anyone else, and they wouldn't be allowed to have it unless they became a co-op. Of course they couldn't run a co-op, poor old things, but one would just have to forget about them, having left them settled on the land.

6 December 1964 I held a *baraza* with the old retainers this morning and said 'Your Government is going to buy up all European land, not all at once but over the next few years, and many Europeans including myself think it is a mistake to wait so long to go. So before selling this farm – and you know people have come to ask me to sell it to them – I offer it to you all, if you make yourselves into a co-op. My price for the farm and everything on it, house, stores, plantations etc. etc., is £1,000, and I think if you put put down £500 in cash – and cash I must have – the Govt. may lend you the other

£500. Or they may not. So go away and think about it, and two or three of you come back on Tuesday morning to go and see Mr Mwangi in Nakuru (new partner of the solicitor Forbes) and tell me if you want to buy the farm or not.' There was a murmur of 'We want to buy', but goodness knows. The Land Bank may say it is too small a unit for eight or nine families. They know I have asked £2,500 from the Africans who came, so must think mine a generous offer. I suggested they should bring in Karanja (cook) to be one of the syndicate; he is much the most intelligent. Ingrid's old retainers say they are going to buy her farm for £7,000 plus loans. Sven Munk has sold his farm to Africans; God knows where they get the money. . . . There is a horrid gang going round Gilgil; they murdered the beer hall manager and stripped Nell Cole's church.

13 December 1964   On Tuesday I took Mbugwa, Karanja (cook) and Kariuki to see Mr Mwangi of Barber and Bellhouse, a charming man who said he'd read all your books and is a great admirer. I told him the scheme, and left them with him. He wrote me a chit afterwards. He recommends a partnership, not a co-op, which is too complicated and lengthy; it seems they can be given a loan of up to ninety per cent. They are desperately anxious to get the land, and indeed it is their only chance of getting anything anywhere, and of course they want to catch the March rains. . . . Mr Mwangi has given them a fortnight to raise the cash, and then they are to see him again.

18 December 1964   The old-time wobblers seem to think they've got the £500 cash for the farm. The oldest, smelliest and most battered of them all, old Wamwea to whom I gave sanctuary when the Purvii went, asked for a lift to enquire into his financial position at the post office; said he had so much money in the bank that they had to send to N'bi for it. I said good, good. . . .

13 January 1965   I gave over the farm to the eight old chaps on Tuesday and now have two cripples only on the payroll. Nothing can be finalized till after the Land Bank meeting but I thought they might as well have what vegetables etc. there are. I've never seen people *appear* to be less interested and more reluctant. Karanja (cook)'s gangling son, who has failed in all exams always, appeared in a dinner-jacket suit and trilby hat and leant up against a post; I saw him the other day gaze a long time at the compost pits, in the end he stroked one bin and then went home. The schoolmaster partner who swore on the application form that he would keep all the accounts is without a clue as to what a cash-book is. I sometimes wonder whether they aren't regretting their action and will run out on the deal. However, provisionally Dorothy and I plan to fly to Lisbon on or about 1 July, collect a car and some camp equipment we are ordering from the UK to meet us there, and proceed to the plot, to camp there and see what can be done about everything.

20 January 1965   I have worked out the best of systems of cooking for one, especially when the one wishes to take off a few pounds and stay there. Twice a week, say, make a large *pot au feu* with two pounds of topside and two pounds of soup meat and usual veg. Cook for at least five hours at 250. That night have a hot cut off the meat and as many of the veg. as required; thereafter for days and days have a nice bowl of bouillon, possibly with an egg poached in the bouillon and grated cheese scattered over – the most complete protein meal. Every evening, a platter of the cold meat thinly sliced, salad, and horseradish sauce. Perfect; as stocks get low so you replenish them; if people turn up for meals, there is always something.... My bird-table is a fair sight these days, hardly hopping-room, some are getting very tame indeed, especially waxbills. Others include several sorts of weavers, bishop birds, sparrows – whom I prefer to call finches – starlings, Cape thrush, bulbuls, sometimes mouse-birds. My trouble is that I feel I am laying on a Caliban act, as when I go, no one will feed my birdies and now they just stuff their little crops till they can hardly hop and never forage for themselves. So is it right or wrong? Am having great fun reading Aldous in Portuguese. The book is called 'Goodness and Genius', or is that too free a translation?

27 January 1965   My old retainers have made themselves into a partnership of eight called 'Mataguri Farm' (*mataguri* means they have been here a long time). I took three of them to see Mr Mwangi; with them in notes they had £590; this represents nearly sixty per cent of the purchase price and they have applied for a loan from the Land Bank for the balance.

8 February 1965   Today I hand over the farm, or rather partnership registered as Mataguri Farm, and there is a lot to see to. I keep on the two aged cripples who aren't in the partnership to do garden round the house etc. till I go. Otherwise the *watu* will be wageless, which I think they will find a shock. Mbugwa stays on to be paid according to the amount of time he appears for work.

13 February 1965   I disagree entirely with your attitude to Winston's funeral, in fact sternly disapprove of the suggestion that 'the old man's wake' was overplayed. For a few hours millions of people were gouged out of their filthy little runnels of cynicism, sneering and money-grubbing, and actually worshipped and did homage to greatness. It all gave England a spiritual boost, goodness knows how much needed, so I am sorry you wrote as you did.

6 March 1965   The old 'European Store' at Njoro is now no more; all pulled down and turned into a petrol station. Old Rambhai [the owner] is off to India at the end of the month; how he will be missed by all. Poor old chap; his wife died not long ago from cancer of the brain and he has looked so broken ever since. No more Cockie jokes. Do you remember one in the Hawking days, 'Do you keep dripping?' 'Yes, I do.' 'Then what are you going to do about it?' ...

11 March 1965   Got rid of my gun to a German firm to sell on commission – poor price but *such* a relief to be rid of it after twelve years or so. I may be murdered but can't be fined £250 for losing it. ... We plan to fly to Lisbon about 2 July, changing at Rome. All sea passages are booked for over a year and there are long waiting lists.

16 March 1965   Karanja is getting on with all the many applications for loans, permits and the like. I think, with my help, he has landed a very good contract with Egerton for veg. supplies as from October which ought to help the partnership to survive. I had a Japanese family to lunch yesterday, brought by Betty Roche. There are ten Japanese families in Nakuru now, the staff of a small technical training college to teach six different crafts, to enable Africans to set up as village craftsmen (metal sheeting, carpentry, building, etc.) on their own. Personally I don't think they'll ever get the markets, but who knows? This family consisted of a beautifully-English-speaking man full of charm and his attractive but not-a-word-of-English wife who is a professional doll-maker, a girl of ten and a boy of five. They overlapped with Dolly who was staying here, she annexed the man on arrival in a spate of talk; I saw him looking slightly startled at her saying that when she was in Tokyo in 1938 she was the only European in Japan.

23 March 1965 We are ordering camp equipment from Scotland to meet us at Lisbon and are going to camp on the plot and see if anything can be made of the shack.... Lilian Graham has fallen on her feet; she is to become châtelaine of Haile Selassie's guest house, and leaves for Ethiopia next week. She will hardly be able to make sweeping curtseys with those poor arthritic feet, nor rise hurriedly – it takes her five minutes to get out of a chair – to greet the Lion of Judah, but the lists to Fortnum's will be impeccable.... I thought I'd been stricken with a horrid flu virus that is going about, but Jean Scott found a septic wound in leg giving the trouble. She pumped every sort of dope into me and sent me to bed where I still (semi) am; it is these drugs that knock you endways, not the disease. Mbugwa is an excellent attendant; he was terribly tight most of last week but has been faultless over the weekend, bringing me tea and telling anyone on the telephone or arriving that I was asleep. I think myself that my aged heart has about had this altitude, but hasn't got to have it for long.... Poor old poodle, I made an appointment with the vet but he suddenly got so gay and happy that I cancelled it: however he must go to sleep ere long, he is fifteen. Michael is the real tragedy, as Dobermanns will *not* take up with new owners, so he must go to sleep, so active and fit and bursting with life.

2 April 1965 Karanja asked if they could cut down my beloved arched thorn tree which frames the Lake from my bedroom window, the most beautiful and beloved of all the thorn trees; I blew up and said not a single tree was to go while I was still here – just can't take it, even if it means being feudal to the last.

Nine years later, I briefly revisited the farm. Karanja was there, still exuding charm and gaiety but short on teeth; Mbugwa's grin was as wide as ever; old Karanja (herd) hobbled forth, the same battered old hat worn at the same jaunty angle. Their welcome was enthusiastic. Yes, they said, the farm prospered despite droughts, erratic markets, the usual hazards. Karanja's three wives had presented him with many children, and grand-children were coming along – at the last count nineteen. Every tree had gone: the beloved thorn tree and its fellows, even the gnarled old olive just outside the door, an ancient tree whose trunk Nellie had encircled with a bench where one sat for coffee and to watch the birds. The land was shadeless, everything was shamba; all trace of the garden had vanished and the little house, stripped of its creepers, stood nakedly among the cultivation, its plaster peeling, rust eating at its tin roof. No one slept in it, Karanja said, but he used it as an office, and sometimes for a meal served at the table by one of his wives. The forest across the river with its bearded cedars, giant podocarpus and grey-green olives, its glades and silences where bushbuck and waterbuck, buffalo and giant forest pig, had picked their way, and skin-clad Dorobo with their bows and arrows had trod without the crackle of a twig – the forest had been replaced by regimented blocks of alien cypress with shambas in between. Trees gone, people multiplied; Nellie's former school now mustered between four and five hundred pupils. Women still wielded hoes or plucked pyrethrum in the sunshine, small children herded goats, the round huts with their open-hearth fire had not changed.

12 April 1965   Our idea, utterly fluid, is to see what we can do with and to the Portuguese shack, *shenzi*-wise. We are absolutely determined *not* to have a modern bungalow type at vast expense. We should be all right camping for three months and may well have made a winter place of the shack by then.

19 April 1965   Have definitely had my last party, and Lilian will be the last house guest as am demolishing things from now on. The party consisted of entire Lindstrom family – only seven these days,

used to be twelve – the Adamses, Betty Roche, Lilian, Dick Prettejohn, Donald Graham and a rich friend of his, Andrew Wemyss.
My chaps' purchase has now been approved by the Land Bank with
a loan of £245 over and above the balance of purchase price....
Lilian goes tomorrow to the Ethiopian job; a niece of Haile Selassie
called Princess Aida wants to recondition and work up the old palace
at Axum which was the palace of the Queen of Sheba. Lilian is to
have the job of getting it going as a small but very VIP hotel. It is
enterprising of her to take it on at her age. She is doubtful if she
can do it owing to being more and more cripply from arthritis and
knees; but she'll have a try.*... Have sold the Peugeot to an African
in Nakuru for £75, delivery 8 June.

2 May 1965 A month of demolition ahead, and packing. The
Nakuru auctioneer said he would try to sell the good stuff at a sale
– Chippendale tables, dining-room table and chairs, etc. The ordinary rough stuff just wouldn't pay the cost of a lorry and he recommended selling them to the local *watu* for a few shillings each....
The vultures began this morning, headed of course by Mbugwa....
A woman at Londiani is taking most of my roses and Betty Roche
the hibiscuses Sally gave me. Mortlock brought along a N'bi man
who was looking for a Zanzibar chest for a rich American; he removed mine and paid £65 which I think is a good price. [It was not.]

8 May 1965 Had a horrid nightmare last night: was about to organize the putting down of Mbugwa instead of Michael and he looked
so reproachful.

23 May 1965 Viveka leaves the farm for good next Sat., she gets
terrible fits of depression, poor thing. Her cattle auction is advertised
for 28th; the *watu* who bought the farm have taken over.... I've
borrowed Diana Powell Cotton's Land-Rover to go birding next
Sunday with Rose along the new road by Lake Nakuru, it is so
lovely; a vital day for packing so I thought I'd go birding instead.
Have a farewell lunch today at the Stewarts; Adamses yesterday;
how I hate it all. The *watu* are cutting down trees all over the

* At the age of eighty-three, Lilian Graham died in Ethiopia less than six months
after she took on the job.

place.... You may leave Woodfolds one day, and beware of *taka taka* [rubbish] is all I can say.

1 June 1965   I finally left the old home, which is ankle-deep in *taka taka*, yesterday afternoon; did jobs in Nakuru, checked up on lorry bringing my 'good' furniture to be auctioned. Sat. night a most gruelling experience, as I *had* to go to Njoro Settlers' Assn. meeting where they made me a presentation, too exhausting but *so* sweet of them, a cheque for £75. Oh dear. Sunday a lovely morning: collected Rose and spent till early afternoon at the lake. Flamingoes in millions, masses of other birds and wonderful lights – just like living in an aviary, and not a sound apart from bird noises – and no quarrelling or fighting!

As a last farewell to Africa, Nellie and Dorothy, with two or three friends and escorted by Donald Graham (Lilian's son), went for three days to the Mara game park.

6 June 1965   Keekoret Lodge is marvellously done, every luxury. We took our own food. Seeing all the beloved animals at first worked the wrong way with me, i.e. made me wonder more than ever why I was going away at all; why not a cottage at the coast or at Kaimosi (wonderful birds there) and a trip to the game parks ever so often? Foolish of course to think thus. The Mara country was as lovely as ever. The first morning we took our early morning cuppas in hand and watched elephants in the bush a hundred yards away from our beds. All day we plunged over plains in the two Land-Rovers and during the two days we saw all the 'big four' and fourteen other kinds of game, plus many more birds. Saw a herd of buffalo three thousand strong, and drove through another herd of about a thousand to get to the dear lions, a party of twelve who could hardly be kept awake. Back on Friday afternoon to the farm to collect Holly and Rosie [the surviving dachshunds], and thence to Ingrid's. Viveka is here; grim to think of Ingrid here alone when Viveka and I are gone.... Mbugwa very sulky as Mary Wright has removed the panelling from the sitting-room walls. So goodbye to the old home,

1 July 1965   Write this from Muthaiga, everything going according to plan, fly late tomorrow evening. Little dogs have departed with

Grahams for Sabukia to await my sending for them from the Portuguese plot when things are sorted out. A thousand bloody good-byes. Australian wine for lunch, Eden Vale, very good. I will write earliest from Portugal.

So over fifty years of Africa came to an end. All the worldly goods that Nellie retained were packed into three wooden trunks, to follow by sea. The two dachshunds would follow too, by air. Nearly all the £1,000 that had been paid for the house, farm and all its equipment had gone partly in settling debts and partly in farewell presents to old retainers and others. She had very few clothes; a watch and wedding ring were all her jewellery, and the contents of the three boxes all she had to show, materially speaking, for one half a century of considerable effort. She believed herself to be a failure, as indeed she was in purely material terms. There are, however, other criteria. If Belloc is right, that there is nothing worth the wear of winning but laughter and the love of friends, Nellie would have quitted Kenya as a rich woman. So, at the age of eighty, rather deaf and rather lame, she set forth with zest and some excitement to make a new life in a foreign land.

PART III

Letters from the Algarve
1965 – 77

1965-71

Nellie and Dorothy were met in Lisbon by old Kenya friends, Eric and Myrtle Dutton, who had retired from the Colonial Service to Monte Estoril. After a few days spent in settling business matters, they entrained for Lagos in the Algarve, where they had another helpful contact in Judy Dollard and her husband, known as Poona. Nellie had by now consulted a better atlas, or looked more carefully, and discovered the Algarve to be on the shores of the Atlantic and not of the Mediterranean. The quinta, about three miles from Lagos, was now her property, and they went at once to inspect it. Nellie was always inclined to build castles in the air, and this castle turned out to be more like a shanty.

12 July 1965   We all went out to see the orange grove. It *is* in a mess, and a large peasant family are living in the shack – pig at one end, mule at the other, no windows and so on. But something *might* be made of it. It is jammed up near other shacks, no particular view, but it *is* in a country setting.... Living really is cheap if one goes to the market; anything Portuguese is *really* cheap and there are delicious melons, figs, peaches, plums and of course fish.

22 July 1965   Today we snapped up two rooms and a sitting-room in a small primitive fishing village about six miles west of here – the old women really do grill sardines off the boats in the streets – till mid-September, and then have taken a tiny house in the same village, Burgau, with lovely views over the sea. Have just had a lovely lunch of fresh mackerel, whole fish (one shilling), sugar melon (sixpence) and glass of white wine (sixpence).

Once settled in at Burgau, the two dachshunds, Holly and Rosie, were sent for and were met at Lisbon airport, Dorothy having by this time bought a small car. Burgau was an attractive little village with narrow cobbled streets, and a sandy beach where the fishermen hauled their

boats, each gaily painted, decorated on the bows with the 'Algarve eye',
and as a rule equipped with a curly-tailed dog. As time went on Nellie
discovered that 'there is quite a winter after all' with heavy rain, Atlan-
tic gales and unforeseen cold; the little house had electricity but of
an erratic nature, and minor electric shocks were a common hazard.

16 October 1965 Yesterday there was about 100 mph gale and
torrents of rain which upset the Atlantic quite a lot as seen from
this window. All fishing-boats tucked away and no fish in the market
except small grey mullet. They live in drains, don't they, and the
Algarve has no drains; what a puzzle.

Meanwhile a builder had been found to do up the shack. This was a
long shed made of mud bricks, whitewashed, and shared, like an Irish
bothy, between the family and their livestock. So a lot had to be done.
Nellie wanted to use only local materials; luckily there were good
Algarve tiles, attractive and cheap, for roof and floors. Two bathrooms
and two lavatories were installed, with water from a borehole equipped
with an electric pump. The track leading to the quinta was narrow,
twisting and unsurfaced, with a sharp hairpin bend which made it
almost impossible for lorries, so materials reached the site in a mule-
cart. Life at Burgau was by no means luxurious.

24 October 1965 The soddenness of everything is most thorough,
these houses have no heating of any kind, and the damp is very chilly.
A fuse has blown on one circuit and we have no light till the landlord
does something, and no fridge and a fish in jeopardy. *Most* luckily
we had enough empty gin bottles to stick candles into. I had bought
that morning two beautiful mackerel in the market and they turned
out to be very pregnant ladies, so I fried some roe by the light of
one candle and very good it was. . . . Dorothy is having a grand time
birding, she is a *real* bird-watcher, and is cultivating a little owl
which stays up till 11 am, she is getting very close to it. The downs
all along the cliffs are now swarming with v. small migrants, nearly
all of which she has identified – wheatears, redstarts, tits, all sorts.

31 October 1965 The whole quinta has been shamefully neglected,
the irrigation ditches blocked up, oranges want a terrific lot of over-

hauling and I shouldn't think the crop can be worth much. But we are eating our own tangerines and they are very good.... The little dogs love their walks but are getting v. fat and won't take to fish jelly which I've made them.... This last week has been *quite* lovely, deep blue skies and sun all day, though of course it goes away about 6 pm.

19 November 1965 Tuesday was a very bright spot, the best day we've had yet in Portugal. Joan and Randolph Cary, who is *the* bird expert of the Algarve, collected us, and off we went into heavenly country, wild as you like and not a soul for miles. All arid, wide-open spaces, and on the coast north of Cape St Vincent wonderful views of rocky coasts and beaches. In the spring it is all wildflowers they said. Lots of birdies, and Dorothy held her own remarkably well. Picnic lunch and back as it was getting dark.

27 November 1965 Have sold the orange crop for £31 5s 0d – a rotten price but so are the oranges. I gave the Carys lunch in Lagos; four people, pre-lunch drinks, excellent soup, red *vin de carafe*, grilled chicken, a pear each, bread, coffee and a tip – total £1 17s 6d. I have eaten there well for 4s.

4 December 1965 The countryside looks like spring as there is oxalis everywhere with sheets of butter-yellow flowers, and plough-ing going on madly between the fig trees, turning up deep red earth to match the cows, who pull one-handled orchard ploughs, driven by a man followed by an old girl sowing beans from a held-up skirt – really a very charming scene, and they work like blazes even on Sundays and plough a very good furrow.... Have made contact with a very popular and seemingly efficient bootlegger who lives in Porti-mão. I wrote him a discreet letter and he turned up at this front door – no mean feat – on a motor bike with a five-litre flagon of gin on the flapper seat, and this brings gin down to 9s a bottle instead of 11s 6d.

Then came a cold, wet winter spent in a rented house on the outskirts of Lagos into which Nellie and Dorothy moved from Burgau. It was more spacious but more bleak and windy, and was next to a motel.

281

Things did not go according to plan. Dorothy, like Nellie, had come straight from Kenya without a break after years of considerable strain. Her health deteriorated. In January she went to England for treatment, and did not return until the end of June. So Nellie spent the winter alone, and had to cope single-handed with the builders and with quinta affairs. The language was difficult; Algarvian speech is almost a patois, and her deafness was a handicap. She found an excellent teacher, however, in Senhora Trigoza, the well-read, educated wife of a retired civil servant, and walked three times a week to her lessons, a welcome break in more wintry weather than had been foreseen.

23 January 1966 It has been a world of continuous sea-mist or drizzle now for days, everything soaking to the core. I suppose the sun *will* appear one day. It's out of the question to get to the quinta as the last half-mile is impassable, with ruts and thick yellow mud. Dorothy's mother had just sent her Malcolm MacDonald's book so I am reading it. Marvellous photographs. It is turning the knife in the wound with a vengeance. Another knife-turning touch is these letters I enclose which came for my birthday.

Dear Mrs Grant, I am very very much happy because of remembering when you were born on 18 January. I got your postcard and of Huxleys. Also ourselves we are suffering too much because since you left this place rain has not yet fallen only sun. When you left this place we bought six cows which are known as Jersey. I remain yours faithfully Mbugwa Njombo.

Dear Mrs Grant, We are very happy for remembrance of born on 18 January until this new year we have. Here in our Farm we are still going on but we have got too much sun that our crops are drying up. So we are praying God to help us in this year and also you too. I remain, yours faithfully, Karanja Kineko.

28 January 1966 The very few people here I know are being more than kind. They seem to think, alas, that it is awful for anyone to spend five minutes alone, and do, it seems, want me to *spend the day* with them. The mere idea of course fills me with horror, but I do appreciate their kindness.

In March, Gervas and I spent a fortnight with Nellie and saw the quinta for the first time. We watched the arrival, by mule-cart, of a handsome

282

crescent-shaped slab of marble, locally quarried and fashioned, which
was to divide the 'kitchen nook' from the sitting end of her living-room.
She had taken on a man called Manuel to restore the irrigation, start
to make a garden, build a seed-house, put up walls and so on. When
she moved in, his wife Perpetua became her part-maid, part-gardener,
companion (insofar as they could understand each other) and prop and
stay for the next eleven years – in a sense, another Mbugwa. All the
furniture was locally made, the floors covered with rugs which Nellie
worked in cross-stitched squares which she sewed together. Above each
of the doors leading to the five rooms, all in a row, she had a tile inserted
bearing the image of the previous occupants – a pig, a sheep, a cow,
a mule and a turkey. When all was ready, the builder, Senhor Teixeiro,
invited her to a festa.

6 April 1966 The custom is for the client to give a feast to the
workers on completion of the building, but Snr Teixeiro and his
merry men put it in reverse and *they* gave the feast, which couldn't
have been sweeter. The *festa* consisted of nineteen people in the sitting-room, fourteen men and five women, *marvellous* feast and
arrangements, long trestle table, beautiful flowers. They'd brought
a cooker with gas and masses of food. Mr. T. was host (and had
Holly on his knee during the meal). I sat next to the little ironmonger-
interpreter in Lagos. Manuel was also present, looking like a seedy
duke I once knew (slightly). First course a marvellous chicken broth
with rice so large and fluffy I thought it must be tapioca. Second
course the bits and pieces extracted from the broth, third course
excellent chickens piled up with potato straws, fourth course
oranges. Red wine flowed. Songs were sung, food piled up on plates.
About 4 pm I thought they'd be happier without me so left – Senhora
Trigoza assures me that this was correct. Everything was so clean
and tidy, and so wise, in that they had no inhibitions about gnawing
chicken bones, as we have (so stupid), but all gnawed together, with
piles of little paper napkins by each plate. I wish I could cook rice
like that.

By the end of April the quinta was ready for Nellie to move in, a move
complicated by the arrival, after a flurry of contradictory telegrams,
of her old friend/enemy Dolly, who demanded to be taken on outings

283

and social calls. She was very deaf and would not use a hearing aid and Nellie, in the midst of trying to pack, unpack and move, found her a trying guest.

1 May 1966 After lunch I said: 'I'm going next door for half an hour's snooze.' I didn't really want a snooze but wanted to get away from Dolly till the shops reopened. The moment I'd shut the door she burst into loud song and never stopped for one moment till the half hour was up. I joined her in the sitting-room and thanked her for the concert which hadn't gone well, I said, with the snooze. 'Oh I am sorry', said Dolly, and thereupon sank in to a deep sleep in her chair, snoring loudly until I woke her up and returned her to her *pensão.*

At last the move was accomplished, and Nellie was excited by the sight of an azure-winged magpie, a bird peculiar to the Algarve, and to parts of Spain and Japan, 'flying out of my loquat tree and across my quinta!' Manuel dug up old, diseased orange trees while Nellie sprayed the healthy ones, and planted shrubs; things were on the move again. She started to interest herself in the possible cultivation of proteas for the European flower trade.

8 May 1966 Joan Cary confirms all the dope Betty Roche has sent from the Cape about the markets – unlimited – for proteas, and that we couldn't be better placed here. One can expect no return for three years, but that is shorter than oranges. They are extremely tricky to get going but pest-free when established. Betty has supplied a wonderful contact in Cape Town. So no harm in having a crack.... Went on a lovely picnic with Carys, Monchique valleys again. Saw a whole flock of azure-winged magpies – how lovely they are – also a golden oriole; nightingales were singing all day and wild rhododendrons out. Dolly, thank God, went on Wed. She ended up by writing me long letters saying how selfish, insensitive and generally cruel I was to her. Finally she wrote, 'Our paths will never cross again.' Not if I see her first.

Nellie had called her new home Quinta dos Passarinhos, the quinta of small birds, and tried to raise five azure-winged magpie fledglings brought from a nest in a cork tree, but they died. Not all birds turned out to be as sweet as they looked.

3 June 1966 A small boy brought in a seemingly tame little bee-eater. It was a dull, non-cooperative little bird, and very cross. It also died. To console me, Manuel brought me a little brown owl, which he swears won't die, and he catches snails galore to feed it. . . . He has fashioned a much-needed seed-shade shed, buying no new materials except one kilo of nails. With the blazing sun and biting wind nothing *could* grow without protection.

9 July 1966 What would we give (if we had it!) for a bushel of John Innes No. 2?! There isn't a square foot of turf in the Algarve, so no loam; we depend on Manuel's thieving from under the carob tree so unfortunately situated on the next quinta.

14 August 1966 Blazing hot here, I think hotter than Mombasa. Am struggling with protection experiments from wind and sun on small seedlings, mostly lettuces, and Manuel is thoroughly interested now. But the struggle against insect life is more than difficult and Dorothy has many tragedies with her flower seedlings.

13 September 1966 I am toying with the idea of buying a second-hand donkey cart, just the thing for the winter when this road is so awful, and Perpetua could drive home in it every night, and return it in the morning plus whatever it had done in the night for the compost pit. I should like a pregnant donkey mare, and very gay harness with little bells. And maybe I could also ride it and take the little dogs for miles over the hills.

22 October 1966 I've sold the orange crop for £43 15s, a rotten price but £12 10s more than last year. They are nearly all rotten trees; Manuel is at work uprooting (very unwillingly) about twenty which we are replacing with peaches, plums, pears, figs, a mulberry, a lemon and a grapefruit. Have planted four vines round the patio: two black and two Muscat, one early and one late of each.

4 November 1966 Bitterly cold weather up to 11 am and after that brilliant sun from mid-day and very dry. If I had teeth to chatter,

chatter they would. I pile on garments and use the heaters no end. But hands like beetroots practically all day....

2 January 1967 The Mahers brought an entomologist friend to tea. He is very frail, and looks himself like a very fragile insect. When the others went off up in the hills, he and I looked for ladybirds and beetles – found none, but I was able to show him the very spot where a praying mantis ate her husband before Dorothy's eyes, and then wished I hadn't, as it might give Mrs Entomologist ideas.

7 January 1967 The almond blossom is beginning earlier than ever known. This there is a background of clear azure skies and it is indeed out of this world. *But the cold*, oh dear! Today all the fields going into Lagos were white. Still blazing hot at mid-day, and little dogs pant sitting outside.

Early in the year, Dorothy had to return to Kenya to cope with the affairs of an ageing mother, and Nellie was again left on her own. Owing to the poverty and alkalinity of the soil, the many insect pests, the winds and the combination of blazing hot days and chilly nights, establishing a garden was much more difficult than she had anticipated. She persevered, and started up again with poultry and rabbits to provide manure and food. Self-sufficiency was her aim. The garden was soon yielding a wide variety of vegetables and herbs grown under irrigation among orange, almond and loquat trees. Manuel and Perpetua were hard workers, but did not take kindly to new ideas.

6 June 1967 I get into bad trouble with Perpetua by my gardening methods such as 'stopping' melons and thinning plums. The Kikuyu are much better gardeners, but we struggle on. The older one gets, the more compulsive it becomes to grow something, I find, but sometimes seeds seem as obstinate as humans.... I walked to Sargacal [the nearest little hamlet] to buy a bite for the bunnies, and most luckily found some straw being dealt with on a quinta, so was able to buy all the winter feed for the donkey, a great relief. Melons are in, hurrah, hurrah!

17 July 1967 I've never known such cross rabbits as I've got. They charge on sight, especially the buck. I daren't open his hutch unless armed with a stick. So different from the elephants, rhino, buffalo and lion I've hobnobbed with. And the cock attacks the dachshunds and encourages the hens to do likewise. Territorial instincts and aggression rife around here.

3 August 1967 The competitive spirit still flickers within me at times, and I'm now having a competition with myself over fourteen different recipes for tomato soup. It may go on for some time. At the top at the moment, in this blazing weather, is: juice of one orange, ditto lemon, four pounds rough chopped tomatoes all moulied (uncooked), diluted with white wine, masses of herbs, and croûtons, which I find essential for texture with all cold soups. Serve this ice-cold. I paint the lily when I do croûtons, and fry them in garlic butter; and last night I put diced ham in as well, using a slice cut so thick it makes perfect squares.... That damned hen got through an incredibly small hole in the plant-house yesterday and completely destroyed a sprouting avocado which I had tended for a year, and just potted up, and other things.

2 September 1967 Suddenly at 8 pm arrived the Harmans with a three-months-old, coal black, adorable dachs called Benjamin, very pedigree and miniature. They showered gifts on me: two charming antique-looking little lanterns from Spain for my outside lights, which I've always wanted, and with which I am delighted; a pound of real English bacon, a *great* treat; a small bag of Acta-bacta;* a bottle of good French wine; a tea-cloth depicting one red and one black dachshund; some worm powders; and a nice Spanish plate.

20 September 1967 My poor bunnies have got myxomatosis; apparently there are frequent outbreaks in the Algarve. Next door people have lost all theirs – twenty. One doe, mother of six, seems to be getting better, but mother of the other family, four, has it terribly badly, one eye almost inside out.

Nellie's interest in cookery continued, in fact increased. She took up the study of nutrition, and believed that her arthritis could be treated

---

* The brand name of a mixture, composed mainly of gypsum, dug into clay soils to improve their texture by reducing viscosity.

by diet. Minerals were to be shunned, especially salt – 'killer number one'. Meat she would cook for 'carnivore' guests, but not for herself, and friends who came to stay were treated to vegetarian dishes which they found delicious.

18 November 1967 No more cooked lunches – cheese, apples and a few nuts, and raisins soaked in a little red wine for a drink. Am going to refuse any lunch invitations from Tuesday.... We've had some delicious meals. One, raw chopped cabbage with tinned tuna fish on top and mayonnaise. Tuna fish of course really forbidden but we let ourselves go for once. Then one of plain boiled haricot beans with parsley butter – delicious. We've managed to keep ourselves in mushrooms from the hills. I think yogurt with chopped raw onion, herbs and grated cheese the perfect meal. And I've found a wonderful supper-dish, made fresh every evening. One tablespoon freshly ground wheat, one small carton yogurt, if wanted sweet with mashed bananas, dates and raisins, if wanted savoury with grated cheese, ditto onion, chives and other herbs.

In order to improve her command of the language, she was translating an English novel into Portuguese.

2 December 1967 I know it sounds silly, but I have a feeling it would be fun to 'get inside' the Portuguese language, and seem to have a flair for it in a somewhat flairless world. Senhora Trigoza told me that she was so impressed by a bit I had done of *The Prime of Miss Jean Brodie* that she read it to her daughter (intelligentsia type) who exclaimed: 'That isn't a translation, it's a bit of Portuguese writing, in spite of umpteen grammatical mistakes.' What sort of carrot is there to hold out for the donkey (i.e. financial reward – *very* little expected)?

Sadly, this project was ended by Senhora Trigoza's illness and death. Nellie could by then read and write 'proper' Portuguese without difficulty, but this was a different matter from the spoken word of the Algarve.

Life had now settled into a fairly regular routine. At about 6 am Nellie got herself her pot of tea and let out the dogs, who had a good

288

bark. At 7 came the BBC World News, with poor reception and, as a rule, very dull bulletins, even the daily disaster being presented in the form of a statistic, so many people drowned, burned, blown up, shot or rendered homeless. The first sound one heard, after the morning bark, was the rumble of the mule-carts' wooden wheels on the rough track behind the house, as quinta-owners started off in the dark to market in Lagos. There was a pungent early-morning smell compounded of orange blossom in its season, of moist earth when rain had fallen, of aromatic cistus from the hills. At 8.30 Perpetua arrived sitting sideways on the donkey. The donkey was tethered under a shelter with plenty of fodder and settled down to her function of producing manure.

Perpetua swept and tidied before proceeding, armed with a heavy hoe, to the terraced garden. Below the garden were the orange trees and, when the sun had risen, one could pick up ripe, sun-warmed oranges from the ground for one's breakfast. These oranges had the best flavour of any I have tasted anywhere. Manuel, who arrived on his motor bike, would haul the hose-pipe about to start the day's irrigation along little channels that criss-crossed the quinta between the fruit trees. Nellie or Perpetua fed the rabbits and let out the hens. If she had guests coming or staying, Nellie would prepare the day's food in the kitchen area with its calor gas stove. She loved gadgets, and there was a fine muddle of pans and tools of the trade, of spices and sauces and herbs from which her tasty dishes were concocted. No bird or beast has ever displayed a stronger territorial attitude than did Nellie towards her kitchen. Offers of help were firmly refused, and anyone who tried to encroach would be driven off quite ferociously. As time went on, she grew slower and more muddly, but her culinary standards remained high. When on her own there was little cooking; she wanted only salads and cheese. From the kitchen she moved out to the garden and spent most of the morning there, mainly in the polythene seed-house among her seedlings and plants. Despite the many difficulties, she managed to create a most attractive little flower garden round a small goldfish pool with water-lilies.

A pre-lunch aperitif and her simple one-course meal was followed by a session with the Daily Telegraph *crossword; her generous cousin Sally sent her the newspaper which arrived erratically, but the crosswords were always done in order. There were letters, needlework – she was never without a piece of work in her hands – and different ploys until, after a cup of tea, came a walk with the dogs, not very fast or far these days, but Holly and Rosie exercised themselves by chasing mice and birds. Manuel and Perpetua went at 5 pm and then, unless someone looked in for drinks, she was alone to stitch, read, get herself a bite of supper and then an early bed.*

Sometimes there would be visits to Lagos in the morning and a prowl round the noisy, crowded, none-too-clean market where fish beached that morning was on sale, together with a great array of fruit and vegetables. Later, supermarkets appeared, though not very super in size – mini-supermarkets, if there could be such things. There were a couple of bakeries where loaves came warm from ovens still wood-fired, and a spicy, aromatic smell of burning shrub roots was wafted into the street. The streets of Lagos were narrow, cobbled, full of bicycles and hand-carts as well as cars and lorries, and Nellie's skill in negotiating sharp corners, steep hills and one-way streets was remarkable. No lorry could daunt her. On the open road, one felt less secure. Conditioned by years of driving on African tracks where one stayed firmly in the middle of the of the road for fear of sliding into a gulley or morass, she drove almost as firmly in the middle of the tarmac, veering sometimes slightly to the left, which made for irritation among Portuguese drivers and for anxiety among her passengers.

Cold was her enemy: the Algarve was much colder than she had expected. It turned out that her quinta was in a frost-pocket, and temperatures well below freezing point were registered for a week or more at a time. The house was damp and inadequately heated, her circulation was by no means good and she suffered severely from chilblains. Gas heaters and electric fires helped to keep the cold at bay except when there were power cuts or gas cylinders ran out. But she battled on, and there was always tomorrow. She continued with a diet low in minerals, fats and sugar, high on vegetable protein and vitamins.

16 January 1968   Nutrition going strong: I am taking my big aluminium kettle to the junk-shop and have got a copper tin-lined one, and in my bedroom have a single-plate electric device which boils an earthenware casserole up almost as quickly as an electric kettle. Have actually heard of a *genuine* case of aluminium poisoning through utensils – all such should be jettisoned.... Must go and grind some wheat for lunch – heavy job, one tablespoon.

29 March 1968   Have been struggling to get seeds in and seedlings out, but the garden is a sore disappointment and I must scrap all my original plans and think something out for another day. Bougainvillaeas all dead bar one. Pouring rain and near-London fog all day.

22 December 1968   Yesterday I managed to get a vase of arums, a sweet vase of roses, and one of the delightful little dark blue wild irises. The arums and roses were from the garden here, irises from that land where we used to collect mould. It's like a bluebell wood now, all irises and grey rocks.

31 December 1968   Poor Perpetua was shattered by her grandson, born three weeks ago, suddenly dying of pneumonia on the 27th, and their other daughter's wedding had been fixed for yesterday, 30th. I drove the bride, Manuel and two others from near their house in Alimento to the church, and took the bride and groom, Manuel, a bridesmaid and another back to the reception. Poor Perpetua, clad in black from top to toe, had prepared a grand feast, and there were lots of fizzy drinks. I stayed for a bit, and ate too much marzipan, but refused the liqueur, which was arbutus tree brandy, very potent. The bridegroom is a lorry driver, and was somewhat nervous at being lady-driven back from the church. The bride is *so* pretty, and was charming in white satin, lace veil, wreath, etc.

1969 opened with an assessment of the economic position which did not bring encouragement.

24 January 1969   It is a sad fact but true, that Manuel and Perpetua's wage bill is beyond my economy. I really have tried my damnedest to make Manuel at least partly economic, but one *cannot* make anything pay in a peasant economy once you start to pay wages. Several people, including myself, have had a crack at garlic this year – result complete slump, and have sold my lovely garlic crop for the cost of *two days' wages* for Manuel! Others have had it worse. The trouble is that Manuel will keep on trying, but I get very little benefit from him for my enjoyment, i.e. the flowers and hobby part.

22 February 1969   Mabel arrived in true BEA style, i.e. they left Heathrow shortly after they were due to arrive at Faro. Taxi arrived with a jaded, frozen Mabel about 10 pm. *All* the hot water heaters have packed up. There have been two public holidays and the only man who can fix them announced, when I went to see him yesterday, that he was going to Lisbon to watch football. So God knows. We exist on a large saucepan on the gas and two electric kettles and Mabel must be very uncomfortable, poor thing. Neither Manuel nor Perpetua came Monday (weather) or Tuesday (carnival), and today being the foulest we've yet had I don't expect them. It just never stops raining and is really depressing.

Mabel's visit was followed by another from Dolly, plus an earthquake.

2 March 1969   Well, well, have we had a week of it, in our humble home. I don't know which is the most exhausting, Dolly or an earthquake, and a combination of the two is quite a thing. Dolly's visit, of course, lasts longer than the quake's, and that goes, too, for the noises they both make (earthquake noise was really horrible, a sort of half crackle half rumble) but, for actual frighteningness, the earthquake wins. In Lagos, a woman was killed, and many many poor peasants all around in the village are homeless. The vast hotels and skyscrapers seem to be all right. No cracks visible in this abode. Every day in Lagos some dear little pink, green or blue house or houses is/are demolished through earthquake damage, to be replaced by horrible cement ones.

After Mabel and Dolly, both in their late seventies, came her grandson Charles and his bride, Frederica. As a wedding-present she had given them nearly all her silver, together with Jos's gold half-hunter watch, which had survived fifty-three years of hazard in Africa. So it was ironical that the whole lot should have been stolen from Charles and Frederica's London flat a few months after their return from the Algarve.

15 March 1969   Poor Charles sounds deeply sad about the burglary, and I don't wonder. One wishes he could have been wearing Jos's gold watch. Perhaps it will be lucky – it spent a year once at Thika in the thatch of a hut, after it had been stolen; then plague broke out, all the huts had to be burnt – and there was the watch.

Racking her brains to think of some way by which the quinta could produce an income, Nellie hit on the idea of growing strawberries for hotels. The response of the proprietor of the nearest one was encouraging: he agreed to take all that she could grow. After much correspondence and trouble over import licences, plants of nine different varieties arrived from Hampshire and were planted out to see which did best and how they adapted to the Algarve. This entailed a struggle with Manuel, who had his own ideas, which did not include strawberries but were centred on broad beans and maize.

10 October 1969 Manuel had planted maize all over the place between oranges etc., and he and Perpetua suddenly started to harvest it madly. On Tuesday, with the donkey's help, they carried all the cobs in with their husks and deposited them in front of the house. On Wednesday they built themselves an igloo with a stepladder and some matting, and de-husked madly hour after hour, chatting ceaselessly. By Thursday mid-day the de-husking was done and a chap deposited a huge mule-cart load of farm manure as a straight exchange for the husks. Later along came another chap and bought the cobs for six hundred escudos. Everything was off the place by 5 pm yesterday and last night down came the rain!

2 November 1969 My latest ploy is trying to get my knee muscles into shape. I've got ridiculously weak-kneed lately. I'm following a technique prescribed for a woman here who went home in the summer for treatment. You lie flat on your back on the bed, with legs hanging over the end of the bed, tie weights on your ankles and lift legs one by one to level of rest of body. Keep absolutely rigid and locked, count ten, lower slowly, rest a little and do it again. Repeat up to thirty times for each leg. You should work up to an eight-pound weight for each leg, beginning with two pounds, but so far I can only do one pound on the right leg. It's an awful sweat, but worth it if it makes me able to cope with those beastly stairs in Lagos market.

19 January 1970   Could hardly have had a quieter birthday [her eighty-fifth] as didn't see, or converse with, a human soul. Telephone quite dead, and Manuel and Perpetua 'off'. The little dogs were my good companions, ditto bantams, bunnies less so. The quinta is absolutely waterlogged. I have various veg. coming on in boxes, mostly with plastic clothes over, or in the plastic house, and this entails a twice-daily murder-hunt for snails, which love any form of shelter.

A form of life which proliferated on the quinta was the snails. They needed no coaxing to thrive. Why, Nellie wondered, did they not appear on the menus of local hotels, as in France? Were they the right kind? She turned from hunting snails among the vegetables to hunting snail-books by correspondence, in the shops. One, called A Young Specialist Looks at Molluscs, *she found to be a useful introduction, but the most thorough studies were published in France. After further correspondence, the last word on the subject arrived.*

14 July 1970   The snail book has come and is enchanting, and I've borrowed a French dictionary. Did you know that snails sing sad songs to themselves while munching the herbage (and my seedlings)? They do, and their last song is heard when they are dropped into boiling water to be eaten. They should be eaten during their last moment of anguish, says the book. Thank God I don't eat snails.

26 July 1970   Am picking strawberries quite heavily twice a week, Red Gauntlets and Hummies mainly, excellent flavour but they have gone down in size. I hope it is the habit of strawberries to have a flush, a pause, and then another flush, but there is no one to ask in the Algarve about their habits here.

1 August 1970   My thoughts are puzzling over strawberries, and how to bend them to my will. I always knew that this year must be a year for learning about them, but it isn't so easy to learn. Now they are packing up after only one month, and I must try out all sorts of different amounts of irrigation, de-runnering, etc., to persuade them to have a new flowering. It means a blood row with Manuel every time I decide on any plan which entails the loss of a single fruiting plant.... Mary says there are twenty-two *real* millionaires in Luz, which was just a tiny fishing village five years ago. She says life there is one long party, mostly evening ones, which are fashion parades, and the chief talking point seems to be how does so-and-so keep up those flaps over her bosoms.... Figs are in full blast, yum yum.

19 September 1970   No news here at all except that I've fed some snails to the little dogs. They were a bit cagey, but I think will take to them. Perpetua winkles out the snails like lightning with a needle. I read that they count as *viande maigre* in France, and Lent consumption is tremendous, also that in the war the troops supplemented their meat ration largely with nice fat snails.... My harvest of maize cobs, superb onions and almonds is gathered round the kitchen door; I do wish there was a painter to come and paint it.

17 October 1970   Joan is said to have the best cook in the Algarve – she plans the meal so well, and all is so beautifully served. What to do when *they* come *here*? I think the only answer really would be a hunk of cold meat (which one can't get as a rule), beetroot salad with pickles, stewed tinned fruit with custard, and beer. I remember Evelyn Waugh giving me lunch at the Ritz one day and the sophisticated *plat du jour* was Irish stew, and very good too. But my fresh strawberries seem to go well. I took some Red Gauntlets to the Vickers' guests, great experts and commercial growers in Inverness, and they said I couldn't do better – excellent appearance and flavour.... All Luz I'm told shivering with excitement as Mary Quant has taken a cottage there for two weeks.

In October 1970 Woodfolds was sold, and early in 1971 we moved into a cottage close by. In April Gervas, whose health had been failing for some time, died within a few days of his seventy-seventh birthday. Soon afterwards I paid a visit to the quinta and found Nellie well, although impeded in her movements by weak knees. Despite the many difficulties with pests, winds and climate, the garden was full of colour and produce. Vines had grown up over a trellis which gave shelter for outdoor drinks and after-lunch coffee beside the little goldfish pool. Pelargoniums, oleanders and other plants in large pots stood around on low brick walls, and a vivid purple bougainvillea spread out its branches just beside the door. The outside walls of the long, low house, white-washed every summer by Perpetua, shone fresh and bright in the sun; the inside was brightened by vases of flowers, by Redouté rose prints and a set of Audubon birds. The little 'neo-Goya' painting Jos had bought in Madrid hung on a wall. The fruit trees Nellie had planted and grafted were beginning to yield; her strawberries were delicious; and when the almond crop came off, Perpetua would sit for hours, in her black skirt and old straw hat, cracking the nuts with a hammer. Strings of garlic hung behind the kitchen door.

The setting of her quinta was a gently rolling countryside where irrigated orange groves, vineyards, fig trees that spread their drooping branches like weeping willows, and small fields of maize, broad beans and other crops, were interspersed with patches of bush-clad grazing for the red cows that pulled the ploughs, and for the tall, long-legged sheep. Mule-carts creaked along the bridle paths loaded with fodder for the cows or produce for the market, and carried big clay jars, shaped like the amphorae of antiquity, to the nearest spring to draw water. Wild flowers were everywhere, according to the season: miniature irises and gladioli, cistus, sheets of mesembryanthemum. Hens and turkeys pecked around the primitive little homesteads, each of which had its pig, and its guard-dogs which rushed out barking fiercely but never attacked. The scene had scarcely changed for centuries, save for poles carrying power lines, little engines that chugged away to work irrigation pumps, and an occasional motor bike that bumped and twisted up the stony lanes.

But life was not without frustrations for those dependent on machinery. Often electricity failed, geysers refused duty, the telephone went dead, the pump broke down, the electric kettle fused. Other troubles loomed ahead. Inflation had set in, wages were rising, Manuel and Perpetua were costing more.

11 June 1971 Have been stripping strawberries, buckets of them for the compost all ruined by rain. A lovely flowering now in progress. There is a horrid glut of strawberries on the market, some huge company near Albufeira seems to have come into action. At the moment, I cannot think of any way to cope with the millstone of wages, but maybe a door will open.

A door did, though not to the prospect Nellie would have chosen. Manuel, tempted by the high wages offered by construction companies putting up new blocks of flats and hotels, walked off one day without giving notice and did not come back. This solved the wages problem, but Nellie and Perpetua, who stayed on, could not run the quinta on their own. The rabbits and bantams had to go, and Nellie agreed to lease about three-quarters of her land to her next-door neighbour, the Lagos harbour-master, for the almost peppercorn rent of £22 10s a year.

11 September 1971 It has been a joy gardening without Manuel. Perpetua does every job I show her in about five minutes and asks for more, instead of having about three days' argument and opposition. She has obviously had a years-long frustration about irrigation, and loves paddling about in the mud.... Was much interested in an article in the *Listener* proving that to prevent being overweight, and control cholesterol, we should all have eight meals a day. Horrid thought, but isn't it intriguing?

1972 – 7

As in Kenya, so in the Algarve: visitors came. Fewer now, they were all the more welcome, especially old Kenya friends such as Ingrid and several of her family, Rose, and Cockie, whose daily shopping expeditions to Lagos were always full of incident. A coming-out party at the start and a passing-out party at the end provided occasions for Nellie to invite the circle of friends that had gathered about her in the western Algarve, where she was becoming something of a legend. As time went on, she grew more and more reliant on the luncheons to which she was invited, and the small luncheon parties she gave in return. For these she took a great deal of trouble, and did all her own cooking and marketing. In her small black Renault, two corpulent dachshunds curled up in the back, with her shock of white hair and scarlet anorak, she became a well-known figure in Lagos, waved on by friendly policemen, her groceries carried out to the car by the mini-supermarket girls. She now walked slowly, and with a stick.

In summer, a picnic in the surrounding countryside was what she most enjoyed. Close at hand were the mimosa forest, a big reservoir cupped in hills smothered in sweet-smelling cistus, and the 'nightingale valley' (she had several bird-expert friends). Farther afield lay the Monchique hills which (when not swathed in fog) had Kenya-like views, and the windswept peninsula with its underground caverns and creeping spray-drenched plants at Sagres, where Henry the Navigator had planned his great voyages. But in winter there was darkness, cold, damp and isolation to contend with, and sometimes only the dogs for company for days at a time. Inevitably, old friends were, as she put it, dropping off the perch. Dolly Miles died at the end of 1971. (The promised legacy arrived, and was partly invested in a new cooker.) Daisy's health was failing and she could no longer correspond. 'I think, after pondering muchly', Nellie wrote, 'that those old ladies who are waiting to die are best off when, like Daisy, they live in a sort of haze, and don't worry, and sleep a lot. Happier than the ones who have mental clarity and arthritic knees.'

298

In June she came to England for the christening of her first great-grandchild, who was called Josceline after Jos. Age had not blunted her appetite for learning new skills. This time it was lettering. Her handwriting was remarkably firm and clear, but she wanted to acquire 'the fine Italian hand', which she would put to practical use by making posters and signs for the Algarve church fêtes. A Wiltshire neighbour of ours, Simon Verity, in the front rank of letterers, came over to conduct the lessons, mainly on the floor. Inks of various colours were added to her luggage on her return. Quill pens were also needed. She had spotted a flock of geese in a field beside the road to Malmesbury, and called on their owner, who was rather startled by being asked if she had any goose-wing feathers to spare. It appeared that wing feathers were at their best just before the moult, in July, so Nellie left an order for some which were duly sent. She returned to a sad homecoming: Holly, aged fifteen, had died.

Among the litter, which was deep and varied, in Nellie's 'office' was a rack of folders marked 'Projects'. A new folder was now added, labelled 'Dried Flowers'.

2 November 1972   You see, trying my hand at dried flowers *might* lead to an interesting occupation when I'm even more decrepit than I am now. I don't mean *pressed* flowers, which have to be assembled in flat collages which I'm no good at, whereas little individual arrangements for gifts might even be saleable. I'd be most grateful if you could get hold of a book, *The Art of Preserving and Arranging Dried Flowers*, by Nina de Yarborough. Peruse said book and find out what chemicals are required, especially the silica gel....

The hunt was up for silica gel. I sent her a small tin from a firm in Essex, but Nellie had bigger ideas.

24 November 1972   The local chemists here have never heard of it, but I've written to the Commercial Attaché at our Embassy in Lisbon to ask if there are manufacturing chemists in Portugal or a govt. lab which might supply. I said I wanted the silica gel for important research work on the Preservation of Portuguese Wild Flowers.... Yesterday the harbour-master and wife and I fixed the lease with the Portimão lawyer, who was quite excellent – dictated the whole thing then and there to a typing clerk and in a quarter of an hour we each had a copy to sign – wonderful efficiency.... My reading eyes have been a bore lately, always dimmed by tears. Seems to me a pinch of silica gel in each should do the trick and it would be quite a change to have pink eyes changing to a ruddy purple?

2 December 1972　There are plenty of flowers to practise on – I've got bombax, hibiscus, chrysanths, veronica, all incarcerated in a pound of borax for three weeks to try. I think one could work up something by hiring out small arrangements (in chopped bottles) to holiday flat takers, and also do a hire business with restaurants and hotels, changing the arrangements every so often. Just a thought. If it goes ahead, this quinta might become a mini flower farm.

Packets of silica gel converged on Nellie from all sides. It is in the form of crystals, into which the flowers are packed. The crystals draw out the moisture and turn blue; you then dry the crystals in an oven and they are ready to use again. You do not therefore need much silica gel, as it lasts almost indefinitely. But, on my next visit, I found an enormous drum, I think fifty kilos, in one of the two spare bedrooms, enough I should say to have dried all the wild flowers in Portugal. Nellie looked defensive, and remarked rather gruffly: 'It's much cheaper bought in bulk.'

8 December 1972　No Perpetua today; it is the Feast of the Immaculate Conception of the Virgin Mary, and so a public holiday. I do find this puzzling. If conceived on 8 December was Our Lord born 25 December the same year or the next? It is pelting and blowing a gale, have got the Dimplex on and it stays on till – March?

13 December 1972　Today I had a 'working lunch' here with Alwyn Kincaid [a neighbour] re dried flowers. He is definitely keen to work up something, and agrees with me – let's try local materials till we really know our job. We packed some Cécile Brunner rosebuds into the silica gel. What is hanging us up now is a reel of florists' gutta percha.... I've arranged the smaller spare room as a Heath Robinson workshop with two tables made of bricks and ex-strawberry packing-cases as tops. I'm not going to spend any money except on essential materials until I see how it goes.

25 December 1972   I had my mini-party last night, unrelieved geriatry. The Carys gave me a pressure-cooker, marvellous gift, the Harmans two delicious Rock Hens and lovely flowers, and Vickers a Dimplex radiator which is really a supreme present. I have two now which practically amounts to central heating. I had done two pickled ducks which were all right.... If not too heavy, could you possibly bring when you come a pound of stub wire? I note that you say you have only one pair of hands, but would point out that many a load has been carried on *head* or on *back* in many parts of the world.

1973 opened with much activity on the Dried Flower project, partnered by her friend the Master of Kincaid, who was a keen gardener and cook, and also turned old bottles into flower jars.

14 January 1973   Alwyn turned up yesterday bearing a handful of 'failed' flowers. They had, it seemed, been dried to perfection in silica gel but went limp again almost at once owing to re-absorption of atmospheric moisture (there's plenty of that). We have to learn.

30 March 1973   Sad news of the week is that Rosie died on Monday. No tragedy, her old heart packed up. I took her to the vet, who gave her an injection of digitalis; she was more or less in a coma and died about 8 pm. One thing is quite, quite definite, no more heart-tearing to bits, no more dogs of my own. Sukey [a visitor] came on Monday according to plan, that is quite different. I stood myself a gift this week, a large fish-kettle, so now must find a large fish to go into it, to spice or pickle.

7 April 1973   Kincaid has made a good job of drying two small daisies, but my daffodils, of which I had great hopes, have turned out – literally – a flop. Trumpets all limp.

Alas, limp trumpets were followed by other setbacks and the Dried Flower project gradually, like the flowers, faded away, leaving only

the drum of silica gel to mark its passage. Nellie was drawing in her
horns a bit but not altogether; there were still seedlings and snail-hunts
in the garden, picnics in the countryside, sauces and soufflés in the
kitchen, the social life which she enjoyed more than she would admit.

14 June 1973 On Monday I went to such a grand lunch party at
the Proparts. Others were Lord and Lady Haddington, cronies of
theirs, Lord and Lady Wemyss (all four earls and countesses) and
a very nice man, Sir Ronald Campbell. I liked talking to him – at
least I *think* it was him, it may have been Lord Wemyss. They all
live hugga mugga in East Lothian in stately homes. Lots of the Who
Married Who game. I didn't make a grand, or even little, slam, but
took quite a lot of tricks. One was: my godmother Evelyn de Vesci
was Sir Ronald's great-aunt.

29 September 1973 Monday to Friday was the visit of Pat [Nellie's
nephew] and Monique with Mary, really very pleasurable. They were
very thoughtful, and anxious not to give trouble, all very small
eaters. Mary is a real charmer.... How nice the young are when
you meet them, how foul they seem when you don't. Pat is of course
very perturbed at her not hunting young men and getting engaged
to Prince Charles. In spite of my failure to produce any blue blood
for them – simply had no time to soak any of my neighbours in silica
gel – I think they liked their Algarve visit.

18 January 1974 Have you read *The Chariots of the Gods*? Am
really convinced the author is right, though he is terribly sloppy,
that some extra-terrestrial culture *did* have spaceships, and *did* call
on the Earth, but obviously someone turned the wrong knob and
finished everything off. I think we are heading exactly the same way
with all our technology, population explosion, etc. etc. But to lesser
things.... My chief activity has been the first move in the Feather
Industry. The Harmans have delivered their first crop of Rock Hens
and I have treated their really good downy feathers for cushions. Perpetua is stitching bags in the 'quill-proof cambric' I bought in Reading
and finds de-quilling the feathers a delectable occupation. She is very
interested in the new 'skill', never practised, as yet, she says, around
the quintas.... I think I am on to a New Dish. I bought a bottle

302

of Beech Nut Baby Food, called Hake with Rice, and used it as flavouring for an ordinary basic soufflé, with herbs. It was *delicious*, tasting exactly like smoked haddock. *Later.* I gave the Harmans a most successful soufflé made from Beech Nut Baby Food – Rich Dinner Strained Turkey this time. Pat has very nobly sprayed my vines.

26 January 1974 Friday morning here *was* a do, the annual rabies inoculation at Sargacal. I felt I must have the poor waif dog done who insists on living here with me. Hundreds of dogs, huge and tiny, a good many fighters, and very few had ever been on a lead. Perpetua coped wonderfully with 'Doggie', who was a bit wild. It was horribly nostalgic as I went so many times with Holly and Rosie.

13 July 1974 I am still sold on yogurt and Professor Yudkin and am deeply shocked to hear you make strawberry *jam*. Very lethal – perhaps for the church fête? Not for my descendants I *hope*. Why not just plain frozen fruit (no sugar) in foil bags? Political blow-up here all very depressing. *Quo vadis?* Shall be so bitterly disappointed if this place turns out to be valueless for Charles.

20 July 1974 You are quite right, I love meeting the postman, or seeing him arrive. Sometimes in this baking weather he has a drink of water and short chat with Perpetua if around. I wish people wrote more and telephoned less.

3 August 1974 You mention a book about the Master of the Horse. Uncle (Hugh Lupus) Westminster was this for years to Queen Vic. and wrangled a great deal with her as she would insist on the bearing reins never being relaxed when waiting about. They were pretty cruel things but necessary for control when moving in traffic. Uncle W. couldn't bear her cruelty to horses. I don't suppose 'Master' has a lot of horses to master, but Uncle W. had a lot. . . . The dear Vickers made Sukey give me a present for having her to stay during their Scottish jaunt. It is the nicest outfit for making your own yogurt. I never feed guests now on anything sweet except yogurt and fresh fruit topped up with a bit of cream. I am entirely a Yudkin addict myself – but cream is allowed. . . . Must be 100°F in the shade now.

23 August 1974 Fancy tots' school fees beginning [her great-grand-children had started going to nursery school] *and* at what cost! Some sixty-four years ago I took you to some very glamorous Montessori classes at Pamela Glenconner's (Asquiths and all that) and am sure the fees weren't high. I remember the first class well. All the tots were put to sorting out different shades of skeins of silk. This was meant to occupy the whole session, two hours. You did it in about ten minutes and were the hell of a nuisance to Asquiths, other sprigs of the aristocracy and a bevy of nannies, and me, for the rest of the morning. Hope Montessori's have evolved better methods since.

30 August 1974 Great event is that I and my snifters have parted company. I did love them so, but the gin jumped from sixty to a hundred and one escudos overnight, which is too much. Have taken to the cheapest *vin ordinaire*, but I do lace the white one (which is like the bottom of a bird-cage in the mouth) with a sweetish and very slightly more expensive brand. Prices all round still soaring. . . . Yes, I do know what Chthonic means – to do with the underworld – Greek, pre-Christian, pronounced Thonic, so why that ch? Silly.

Nellie had a month in England in October, and returned with an extra-ordinary collection of objects, mostly low in value but large in bulk, and all packed into a plastic object like a smaller version of the barrage balloons that floated over London in the war. This burst as it was being loaded into the car to go to Heathrow and frantic last-minute thrustings into dilapidated suitcases took place. She had more company this winter; an attractive (and much younger) cousin, who lived a roving life in a small van, stayed with her for a couple of months.

30 November 1974 Marye really is the most good-natured soul, always ready to take on any job, and skips about looking for them. All the elderly gentlemen (haven't seen any young ones yet) fall flat before her, licking their lips while listening to her merry prattle. She does prattle quite a lot, but I remove my deaf aid. . . . The 'elevated strawberries' are looking very happy and cosy in their pots.

12 December 1974 Doggie is living far too much in Ritz style; 'peasant' bread has gone from three and a half to nine and a half escudos per loaf, so it is far cheaper to buy wholemeal flour at the local mill and make him his own bread, which I do.... There are now four dogs staying, or semi-resident.

In January 1975 Nellie reached her ninetieth birthday and resisted all attempts to celebrate the occasion, or have it celebrated for her, so it was studiously ignored by her friends. Despite all her resolutions, she had become very fond of the quinta dog, Doggie, and was much saddened by his end – 'He escaped to go out and die under the stars.'

1 February 1975   Now, another project, which I know you'll disapprove of *at first*, but take it slow, you cannot fail to see its good points. After going into the subject *in great detail*, I want to hire a caravan for June, to try it out. Now, if it proved practicable in June, I could buy a really grand caravan and live in it altogether, in your field? It could be tucked away more or less out of sight of the sitting-room windows? We could ask each other to meals, what fun.

9 May 1975   Have been experimenting with dried pawpaw leaves I got Dorothy Powell to send me. In Kenya they were our only tenderizer in pre-fridge days; we used to wrap bits of old ox or sheep in them overnight with excellent results – always understood that if you left the meal long enough, it disappeared. I got two lots of identical old cow and am doing a pawpaw dish today and a non-pawpaw one tomorrow. If it works, I shall try to grow pawpaws for their leaves only – they would never fruit here.

11 May 1975   The second part of my pawpaw leaf experiment took place at lunch today, and was most interesting. It was the counterpart of yesterday's old cow which I marinated with the dried leaves, but was straight out of the fridge and treated plain. It was as tough as old cow always is, whereas the marinated slices were ever so tender. So dried pawpaw leaves *do* produce papain, and *do* tenderize old cows. This means, if it goes on being effective (the true scientist would say more than one experiment advisable?) we can all have tender meat on our tables, obtainable in Lagos, instead of depending on the far-off butchery in Faro. But we must grow our own pawpaw trees. Am about to sow some seed to see.

18 May 1975 The Vickers dropped me back here and foolishly I hurried off to show Phyl a certain strawberry just outside the house, and my left (weak) knee let me down so I tripped over the step up. *Not* a fall, a trip, I just sank to my knees, but with bad luck hit the right, good, knee rather a bang on the bone, so it is now very stiff and sore and will take a few days to be less maddening. Getting around with a stick takes a bit of time, and there is so much to do.

When Nellie came to England for a month in June, a hired caravan had been installed. She was delighted with it, but, in the event, only slept in it for a night or two. After a busy month, she returned to the quinta with equipment for a new project – smoking fish.

4 July 1975 I did so hate going away.... I had the front row of three seats in the aircraft to myself. At least, to start with there was a woman in the window seat but I parked my tasty cheese next to her and she soon left.... Found the house spotless, Perpetua had cleaned it from head to foot and whitewashed the outside.

18 July 1975 My fish-smoking life is developing well, but no smoked fish so far. Went early to market, not a fish in the place. Then to the baker's, same with bread. No meat till the end of the week. Milk powder disappeared. Went to supermarket, no tinned tuna or sardines, tonic water, etc. So bravely, like Marie Antoinette, made do with a packet of rusks. Shopping is *hell*. A new thing about the naked tourists is that they nearly all scratch, due to harvest bugs which flourish. In this heat, nothing to be done but sweat and scratch.

2 August 1975 Fish smoking. Progress has been made in that Perpetua and I tried out my Flower Pot Smoker, and it makes a very good draught. Now I have to get the right sort of sawdust, to be had from a carpenter in Lagos. Meanwhile have asked a Norwegian couple to drinks to try out the Smoker. Three fish cosily freezing here all ready.

8 August 1975 Great news re fish smoking. Shortly we are having a mock-up with Perpetua and my Heath Robinson smoker, and the Norwegian couple, with Dollards, are coming to see if it works.... *Later.* Smoke party went quite merrily; used big flower-pot, but found the heat too great. The Norwegian is coming next week to adjust its draught, and lend me his small portable outfit, last word from Norway, also his book, indispensable to a smoke fan. It tells you how to make smokers out of wheelbarrows, and/or cardboard boxes. There is a lot to smoke cookery, and other things can be done besides fish, e.g. chicken livers, lamb, summer sausage, octopus, bear, corned buffalo, frogs etc. etc.

15 September 1975 Had marvellous luck on Friday, looked in at the market and found it flooded with a fish called *sarga*, which is a half-grown mackerel and said to be the best of all for smoking, and tastes like salmon. So bought a kilo for ten escudos, then picked up half a kilo of chicken livers and on Saturday I smoked three eggs, the *sarga*, chicken livers and some cheese. Political crisis said to be over on radio this am. For how long?

These were years of political upheaval in Portugal, culminating in a coup which left a revolutionary government more or less in control. Many of the supporters of the former régime were jailed without trial, property was confiscated, and among foreign residents there was apprehension and alarm. Some fled. The stirring events which took place in Lisbon and Oporto were, however, but palely reflected in the Algarve. Its peasant inhabitants were not good revolutionary material and Communism, which certainly existed – all the white Algarvian walls came out in a rash of red hammers and sickles – was of a relatively low-pressure kind, although several hotels were taken over by their work-forces.

Among the Portuguese, certainly, there were arrests, intimidation and disappearances, but foreigners were left alone. Nellie showed no signs of panic; political upsets to her were nothing new, and Perpetua, she rightly considered, was no downtrodden proletarian worker freed at last to mete out rough justice to her capitalist employer. Both Nellie and Perpetua ignored the revolution, but could not ignore the steep rise in prices that resulted and the disappearance of many commodities from market and shops. Later in the year the collapse of Portuguese rule in Angola resulted in an influx of refugees.

13 November 1975 Four hundred Angolan refugees have arrived in Lagos. No wonder we have no milk. Appeals going forth for warm garments, blankets, knitted things, etc.

18 December 1975 Just a week to the annual schemozzle called Xmas. It is colder here than it has ever been since my day, freezing in the daytime between pelting showers. Nothing attempting to grow or burgeon and I don't blame them.... On Boxing Day am laying on a 'wine and cheese' here to repay a bit of hospitality; only twelve in all, can't be bothered with more, mulled cheap red wine only and God knows what eats. Eggs have jumped from sixteen to thirty-three escudos a dozen.

8 January 1976 On Sunday the Vickers and the De Knoops lunched here, full of a wonderful sermon from the Chaplain, Edwards, about alcoholism. He said he had buried more people who died from alcoholism in the Algarve than anywhere else in his life. And Geoff Batchelor said he had never attended so many death-beds from alcoholism as in the Algarve. And I've been here for ten years and never come across a real alcoholic. All very odd to me.

19 January 1976 My shameful birthday passed off quietly, high spot was a glass of sherry before lunch (the Chenerys gave me a cherished bottle for Xmas). Have put it away against Jos's birthday, 15 February, I think.

4 February 1976 Re future plans, I think and think, and come to no conclusion. This cold patch has confirmed my conviction that I just could not take the UK climate. If you feel the cold beyond a certain point you just curl up and feel rotten, and of course I should get asthma. One would not like to be alone here all winter. The solution would be a p.g., English or Portuguese, but where to find a bearable one? Angus says I could only bear with a deaf mute who could answer the telephone, and he is right.

8 February 1976   My chief worry is my *hatred* of cold. I really had no idea, till this last spell, how rotten the cold can make one feel, when one can't totter fast enough to warm up and the cold gets right inside one.

11 May 1976   Since my poor Doggie died in Jan. '74 other quinta dogs have appeared. Doggie, from being a miserable, terrified nonentity, developed the best canine qualities under sympathetic treatment – courage, loyalty, affection, sense of duty – and he exercised himself, galloped after the car as far as the tarmac road, but was always there to greet me when I got home. Since then there has been only one 'steady', a beige curly-coated about sixteen inches high, with pale eyes. I call him 'Curly'; he is the most withdrawn dog I've ever met. Perfect table manners, good tempered, doesn't snarl or bite or bark, terrified of Perpetua for no reason. Curly didn't turn up on the day after I got back, but his wife came on Sunday and doubtless told him I was back. The wife is hopelessly nervous, a tall thin yellow bitch but attractive eyes set in black rings like spectacles. I have hopes of a son of theirs, curly-coated and the same eyes.... Why is my cooking so bad? I don't know....

24 May 1976   Have had such a battle with Perpetua over fashioning a wigwam for my very special climbing French beans. She has always staked beans *after* planting out or sowing, and *would* not stake first and then plant out (from pots). However in the end she got quite interested, and I've now left her to do another wigwam all on her own. I have given her the first lesson in shopping for me. Every entry into a shop is a high adventure, entailing lengthy and emotional reports on all that went on. She was a great help in that she coped with awkward places, e.g. steps with no banisters, like at the flour mill, while I sat comfortably in the car.... Such a lovely dish today of 'Cambridge Favourite' strawberries; they are really red and large now. Oh, the globe artichokes, must freeze more bottoms. Oh, these veges; plus enough lettuces and globe artichokes to stock a boarding-house – we have run into a glut of peas, carrots galore, and the new crop of onions being thinned....

1 June 1976   I wonder if young Jos ever found a bird's nest this spring? Too young, I imagine, to prowl on his own, but could be

309

shown? There is such a great biological inheritance, it seems sad not to benefit from it. I remember a walk at Woodfolds in 1949 with Julian and Juliette [Huxley]. We went in the car to some lane; Julian knew it all. He pointed out a speck in the sky and knew what bird it was, and what it was up to – told us what was going on in every hedgerow. For myself I regret deeply not being a naturalist. Could have been – there was a sweet old retired Canon Smith who lived in Shaftesbury, and was laid on by my mum to teach me botany, *circa* 1900. He was full of lore, but alas no inspired teacher, and never embarked on field work. The consequence was I developed a fierce hatred for systematic botany. There were sort of extra-mural exams in those days, one called Cambridge Preliminary. Under the aegis of Canon Smith I took it. Alas, my papers came back b.f. – bad failure. Oh dear, the sweet old man was so sad! I suppose if you are an animal lover you aren't a formal botanist. All the nature study I ever had was lovely days with brother Gillie and Lot Pitman the keeper. I don't think you ever forget the smell of damp woods, and gamekeepers' lore.... Yesterday I smoked the six excellent mackerel Perpetua caught in the market; I started boning them at 8 am and finished the smoking at 4 pm as dried them in the sun, and it needed time and watching.

29 July 1976   I'm very thrilled with the Soil Association booklet re weeds. I've put Ernest Chenery in strict orders to get me seed-heads of all Algarvian weeds, especially rue and all the mints. Every door now has its bunch of rosemary attached to the curtain rod, and there are *no immigrant flies*. A few residents still left but very soporific and liquidatable.

Nellie was lent a book by a former member of the Colonial Service called The Flagwaggers, *and sent her comments.*

27 December 1976   I do think those erstwhile colonial civil servants were mostly wonderful chaps, especially when young; the older ones were apt to get over-blinkered perhaps? I remember a party of us were camping above Naivasha once, after walking from Nyeri, and a PC who was nearby sent a chit across to us beginning 'I am Naivasha.' We nearly replied 'We are USA, Japan and Russia' but

didn't, contented ourselves by addressing our reply 'N. Traill Esq'
(for Traill was his name).... Am thrilled with the book about Polish
Jews. Have always wanted to know much more about Jews. Is there,
by chance, any paperback by any one of these brilliant young bio-
graphers on Jewish history brought up to date – decaying faiths
always interesting?... Such gloomy weather, visibility so poor can
hardly see to read even with all lights on, and the power is despicable,
all flickery and ever so weak. Oh it is so cold, so cold.

1 January 1977 Twice now Phyl has given me a good old Xmas
stocking (*such* fun to undo) so I copied the idea and made up one
for old Geoff, now a forlorn widower. There were two patés, one
pair of socks, one box of matches, one cake of soap, one small cheese,
one small home-made cake, soup packets, orange, banana, etc. Phyl
put in mine things so hard to get like gelatine, brown rice, matches,
plus a bottle of booze. The weather has been quite foul, rain, rain,
rain and no visibility, lights on all day.

*Amid the cold and damp and dark an exciting new interest had come
into Nellie's life. A talented painter in Praia da Luz, Valerie Ryshworth-Hill, had been making glove puppets to entertain the children
in an orphanage in Lagos. A demonstration of her puppets set a spark
to Nellie's imagination, which flared up in the old enthusiastic way.
Puppets might, she thought, amuse her great-grandchildren, 'the tots',
and spark off their imaginations too, acting as an antidote to the dreary
materialism that all too often, she thought, stifled the creative impulse
of the growing young. Besides, puppets were fun.*

2 April 1977 I had Zenia Rudd Clarke to lunch yesterday as I
wanted clippings off her toy poodle in case one can make puppet
wigs therefrom. That clever Valerie Ryshworth-Hill can't keep away
from making heads [for puppets], and does them excellently in a trice.
I want to go into the wig question with her, but the telephone is
dead. I had a thought of trying to puppetize the Mad Hatter's tea
party, and borrowed *Alice in Wonderland* and am going rather
wearily through it. I fear Alice is finished as regards the modern
child. You could make a story, I think, out of Alice being read aloud
to a bunch of modern children who would react by saying

reflectively, 'I wonder what drug she was on?' But I still think puppetry *might* stimulate the tots' imaginations, and I'm all for having
a go. The Silver Thimble [a needlework shop in Bath] recommends
a book, *Making Home Puppets*, but I don't want to buy it without
seeing it first, and anyway my puppet project may be blown to bits
by this beastly arthritis in my thumb joints, it makes one so slow
and clumsy. We shall see.

*Sometime during the previous summer, Nellie had dropped a pair of
garden secateurs on to a leg; the scratch turned to a sore and the sore
to an ulcer, which caused pain and trouble. For several years a retired
London consultant surgeon living nearby, Geoff Batchelor, had kept
an eye on Nellie's health. Often of an evening he would walk over to
her quinta, a couple of miles or so, for a chat and a glass of beer, and
if any medical advice was needed he generously provided it without
fee, as he did for many other British people living in this part of the
Algarve. He treated her leg, but at the age of ninety-two ulcers do
not clear up easily, and Nellie, like many another, dreaded the idea
of hospitals.*

*In April, yielding to persuasion, she came to England for treatment,
and seized the opportunity to pursue her puppetry. She made contact
with an expert puppeteer, in fact one of a whole family of puppeteers,
who made everything themselves and travelled round to give perform-
ances. Mrs Fletcher came over from Maidenhead with a boxful of puppets and their appurtenances to show Nellie, who was Cockie's guest
at the time. I found her sitting on the sofa surrounded by puppets and
their gear, her blue eyes shining with excitement like a child's, waving
her arms about – she gesticulated a great deal – and exclaiming, 'It's
a new world! A new world!' She was totally hooked, and this time her
battered suitcase, on her return, was full of the wherewithal for making papier-mâché masks, wool for wigs, plasticine and glue, and a book
of instructions.*

*She should not have gone back at all. The ulcer had only partially
healed. But she was confident that the healing process would continue,
and meanwhile had promised a couple living in Rhodesia, and thinking
of retiring to the Algarve, a 'perch' on her quinta as paying guests
while they looked around. She did not want to let them down, so back
she went to her quinta for the last time.*

312

7 July 1977 I much admire the photo of Jos on a pony, but the people who run the riding place will never produce any young Lester Piggotts if they only supply heavy-shouldered fat mounts. They should have rather scruffy, thin and highly bred ponies like the Welsh, so that the young can develop riding muscles.... The Ryshworth-Hills come tomorrow to begin in earnest 'deep' puppetry, most exciting.... Perpetua is still in an odd mood. I think she is 'in shock' from having seen a small car sliced in two and won't go out in small cars any more, only in buses. So our shopping expeditions have ground to a halt, very sad, as they were getting on so well. But if she won't, she won't, and when an Algarvian doesn't want a thing to happen, it doesn't.

9 July 1977 Leg is getting on fine, but arthritic knee's the devil. I do *badly* need four packets of plasticine, any colour, to continue puppet masks. Each mask takes two or three days to dry out.... I hope you can read this, I can't. Now, on another subject. If I depart this life, don't worry. No case of suicide, haven't the guts, but five chums went out pouf, like that, so why, in the words of the old song, oh why, shouldn't it be poor little me. I would really sooner get it all over and done with, a horrid time for you clearing up I know but that has to be anyway, so *don't* grieve unduly, see? Church fête this morning. Am not there. Poor Phyl the queen-pin.

Perpetua's refusal to travel in a small car put an end to expeditions to Lagos. Nellie's friends did her shopping, and took it in turns to bring her cooked lunches and eat them with her, so she had company every day and a good meal. But she was still alone at nights. One evening in July, her knees collapsed when she tried to get out of her chair, and she spent the night on the cold tile floor. 'Not very nice', she wrote, 'but quite all right, and no harm done at all.' She continued to pursue puppetry.

30 July 1977 Could you make enquiries about a book, *The History of Puppetry*, by Guiseau? Don't buy it on my account, I just want to know more about it.... Am so cripply Perpetua has to lift me from my chair and bed. I think that should get better as the ulcer, the last, is obviously on the point of drying up. Perpetua is being marvellous. She is coming on Sundays, and every day at 8.30 am and helps me to dress, goes at 7.30 pm after putting me to bed. I don't feel up to staying with you or Cockie or anyone, it sounds ungrateful but is really kind to others. Did you have a nice birthday?

It was clear by now that Nellie was coming to the end of the road. She had agreed to put the quinta on the market and come to England for good in the autumn, but this programme was being outstripped by events, and in August I flew out to pack up everything and bring her home. I found that her ulcer, contrary to all that she had written, had got very much worse, and plainly had a septic infection. A week had been allowed to organize matters at both ends. Apart from clothes to go with her, all her possessions were stowed away in the three big wooden chests she had brought from Kenya, and which had gone out there with her in 1912. 'Do you mean to go on with puppetry in England?' I asked. 'Of course.' So the half-finished masks and wigs went into the suitcases. Looking round, I made some trite remark about the sadness of taking down pictures, packing ornaments, stripping the house. 'Yes,' she said, 'the end of a chapter.' But it was the end of the book.

The night before we were due to fly to England, she collapsed into a kind of coma. Next day, instead of driving to Faro airport, an ambulance took us to the British Hospital in Lisbon, where she died peacefully thirty-six hours later, on 21 August. She was buried in the Cemetery of St George's, where for nearly three centuries many British residents in Portugal have been laid to rest under the shady ilex trees.

Naturally I received many letters, and the one I think she would have most enjoyed ended, 'Dear, dear Nellie, I am sure she won't want to Rest in Peace; she will invent a new way of stringing harps.'

Swahili Glossary

askari	an African policeman or private soldier
banda	shed, temporary dwelling
baraza	meeting, open-air gathering
bibi	married woman
boma	enclosure for livestock, also fort
choo	latrine
debbi	four-gallon petrol or paraffin tin with many further uses
dudu	insect
duka	small shop
fitina	quarrel or feud, generally complicated
jembe	pick-axe
kanzu	ankle-length robe for men, the usual coastal attire
kerai	bowl or basin, used as a measure for grain
kikapu	woven basket of traditional shape with handles
kongoni	hartebeeste
kuku	chicken
kuni	firewood
liwali	judge, used of Arab leader in the coastal province
maridadi	smart, decorative, colourful
mira'a	chewing-twig
moran	young men of the warrior age-group
m'zee	elder (noun), old (adjective)
neapara	headman, overseer
ndege	bird
ngoma	African dance
njama	tribal attendant on a chief
panga	tool for slashing bush etc., machete
pombe	home-brewed beer
posho	maize meal
rungu	wooden club

salamia	to greet
shamba	smallholding, farm
shauri	business, arrangement, discussion, agreement
siafu	savage, biting ants that proceed in columns
shenzi	crude, rough, inferior
shika	to seize
suferia	saucepan, cooking pot
taka-taka	rubbish
thahu	a form of tabu among the Kikuyu
toto	child
uhuru	freedom
vlei	impervious pan that holds water in the rains (Afrikaans)
watu	men, often used on farms of the labour force
wazungu	white people

Index